I dedicate this book to Angel Delgadillo, an angel for Historic Route 66 and an inspiration for me.

A special thanks to my husband Kyle, my children, Bud Lage and my Roadie Buddy Jeanette Lage. Without Kyle I couldn't have made the Route 66 trips happen, without Bud I wouldn't be able to keep my focus on my focus nor have a roadie buddy (his wife) for many days and nights, and finally without Jeanette, I wouldn't have had so much fun on the Mother Road, corn field turn arounds, circling the round about multiple times and many Katheryn Hepburn sandwiches. Love you all.

The Perfect Escape An Adventure on Missouri Route 66

Copyright ©2019 Cheryl Church

Art Credits: Cheryl Church

All rights reserved. No part of this book may be used or reproduced by any means, graphic, electronic, or mechanical, including photocopying, recording, taping or by an information storage retrieval system without the written permission of the author except in the case of brief quotations embodied in critical articles and reviews.

ISBN-9781979443166

Other Publishing:

The Perfect Escape "The Whimsical and Odd World of Cheryl Church"

The Perfect Escape "An Adventure on Route 66"

The Perfect Escape " Visionary & Fantasy"

The Perfect Escape "An Adventure on Kansas Route 66"

The Perfect Escape
An Adventure on Arizona
Route 66

Second Edition

By Cheryl Church

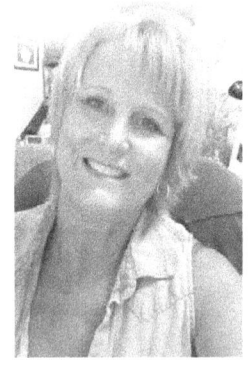

Note from the Author:

Compared to our modern times, the Mother Road's past, though often difficult at times, still seems to be the simpler life. It is my hope that through my artwork you will recognize the significance of the road, how powerful it is to our country and our history. Within the book are montages of iconic landmarks and must see places along the route. I have included vintage cars, signs, buildings, puzzles, maps, plethora of information, places where you can glue down your own photos or get stamps from the many iconic stops along the Arizona Route 66 Highway.

Many landmarks along the route have changed or even may be gone, with only the memories left behind and maybe a foundation. I enjoy researching the history on these places as well as drawing images that relate. When I started the Route 66 coloring book series, I had not planned to add so much writing I had just wanted to title pages with interesting facts but as I traveled the road and researched locations the book grew. I felt that there were such fascinating stories of our wild west past that I had to share my findings.

This book is not a historical document, but it is my discoveries as I have researched the road for the past years. All the stories that I have written about throughout this unique travel-coloring book were gathered from researching the World Wide Web, or as my husband says, "the internets", visiting with Tourism Bureau's and people that I have met through my adventures on Route 66. I sincerely hope that you enjoy the plethora of information as well as the coloring experience. If you have never traveled Route 66, I would highly recommend it. Each experience I have had has been worth the adventure.

Route 66 has proven to be the lifeline of America, the vein that the blood runs through freely.

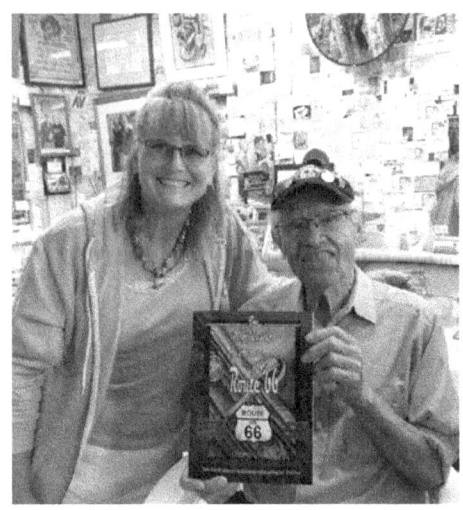

    This book could not have happened if I had not met Angel Delgadillo, the man who never gave up on his town or Route 66. He did not know the word "no" and completely understood the meaning of our constitutional wording, "We the People". His blessings and inspirational (pep talk) speech to Jeanette and I upon our visit to Seligman brought tears to our eyes and smiles within our hearts. Many times I have felt that what I was doing was wasting my time, Angel assured me that it was worth my time for many to enjoy.

    I had prayed many a times on how I could use my art for good. Because of Angel's precious words, my traveling partner Jeanette Lage and the support from family, friends and the people I have met along the way of my journey on Route 66 who have shared their stories, I was able to complete this book.

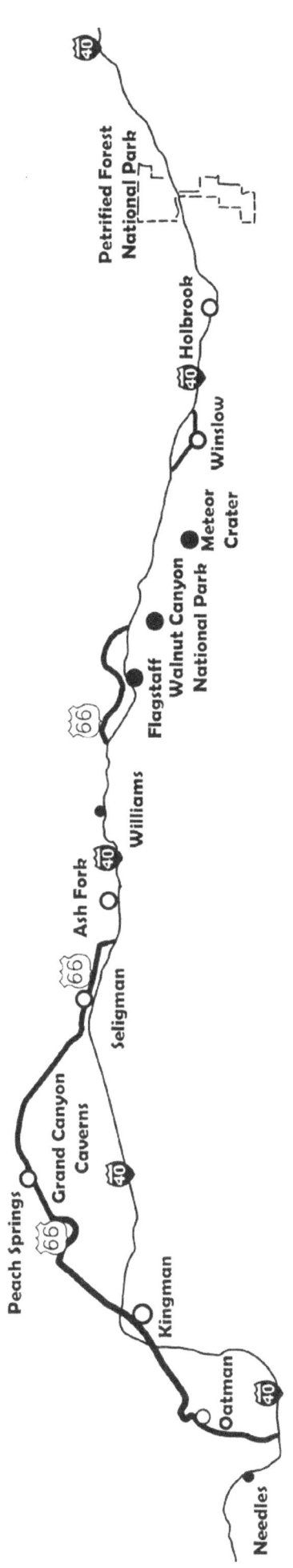

Front cover
"1954 BelAir"

Thank you Howard Algers for the use of your car for the Arizona Route 66 book

Water color on Arches

21" x 13"

Matted and framed

Original artwork available for purchase

Limited edition prints available

website www.cherylchurch.com

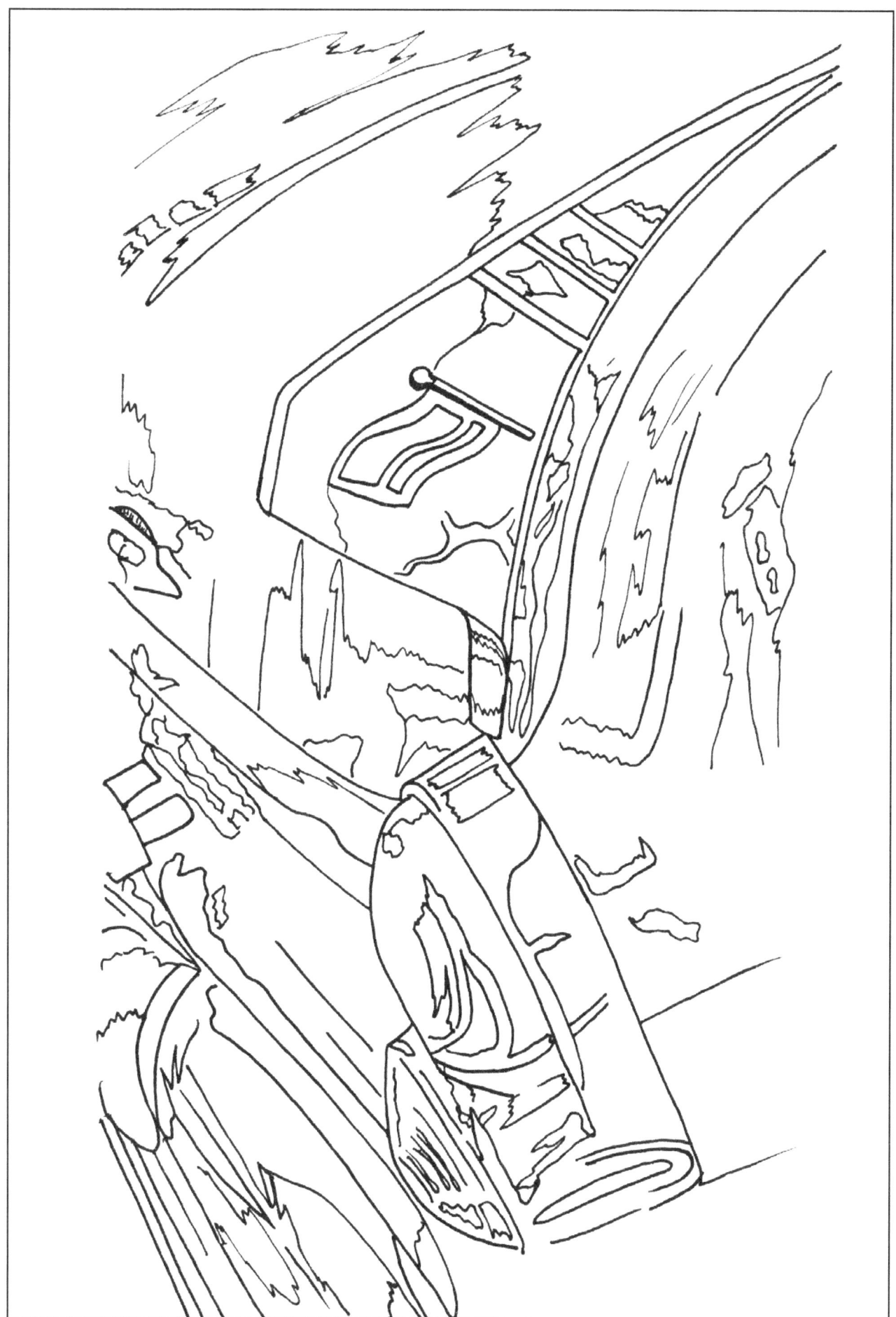

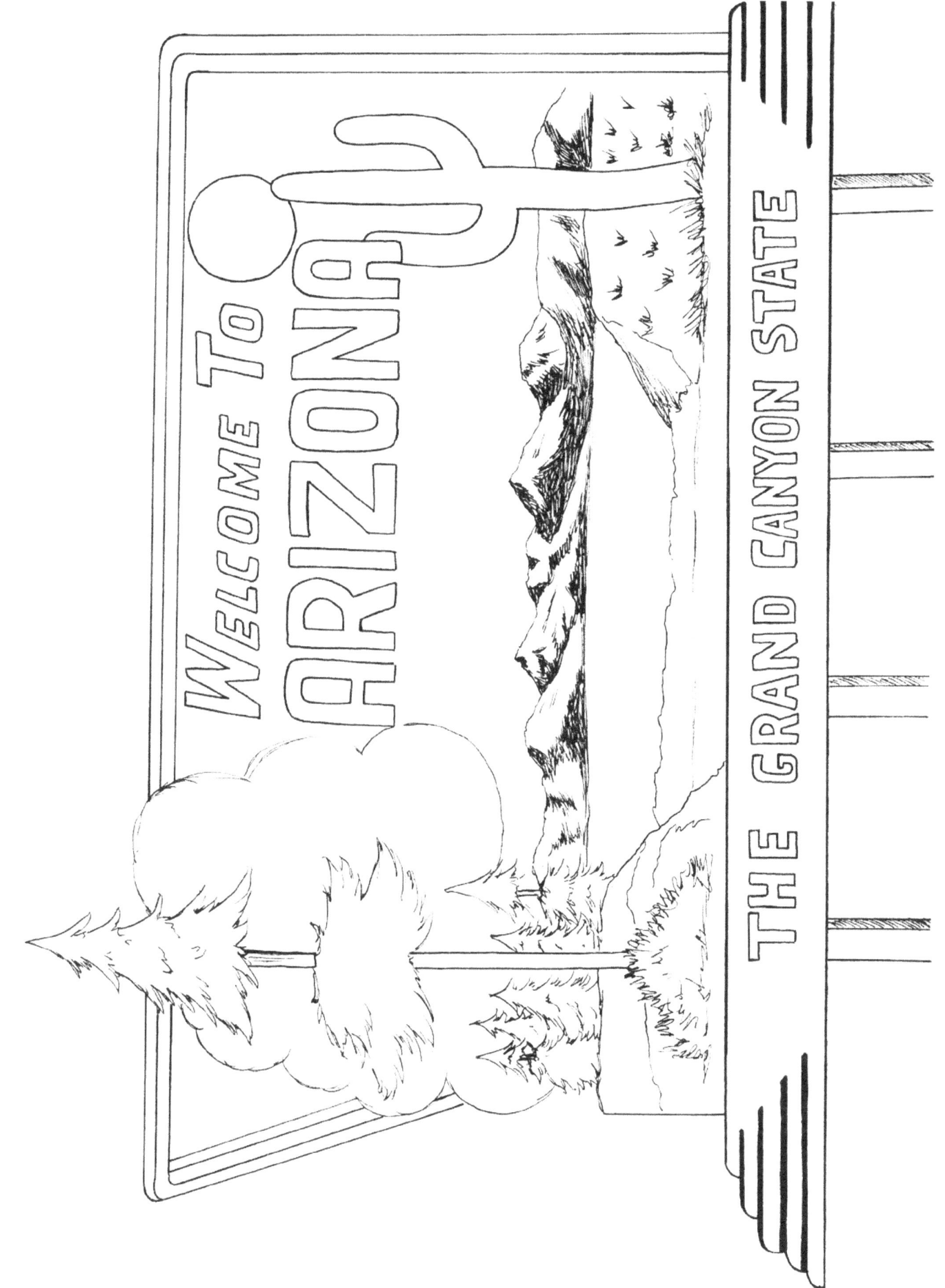

Route 66
The Golden Road

Route 66 held a special place in Americans' hearts from the beginning. The great road carried us through a new era of a nation on the move. The thousands of stories of hope, heartbreak, love, hate, starting over and dreams of new beginnings linger in the air to this day. They are stories of the past that makeup our great nation, a nation that has been through hard times, war and rebirth. Route 66 was one of the original highways within the U.S. Highway system. Throughout the years, the route acquired many names such as: Will Rogers Highway, the Main Street of America, and the Mother Road.

Route 66 is the most celebrated and famous two-lane road, which fed our culture's love affair with the automobile.

During the 20's the federal highway officials were faced with the growth of automobile ownerships. They needed a better road system that was not disjointed, which caused confusion as Americans began traveling across the country.

The decision to accept "66" as the favored route's designated title was made in Springfield, MO on April 30, 1926, which gave Springfield the right to claim the distinction of "the birthplace of Route 66."

After all the red tape, the road became reality on November 11, 1926. Road signs were erected the following year.

The twentieth century version of the Oregon Trail began, laying its path along old trails from the early explorers and the wagon trains, wending its way westward. Across eight states, 51 counties and three time zones, Route 66 proved to be one of the most memorable, written about and historical roads ever created. The Golden Road provided inspiration for many artists and writers, including John Steinbeck, author of "The Grapes of Wrath", who gave Route 66 its best-known name, "The Mother Road."

Once you drive part of it - you'll want to drive all of it!

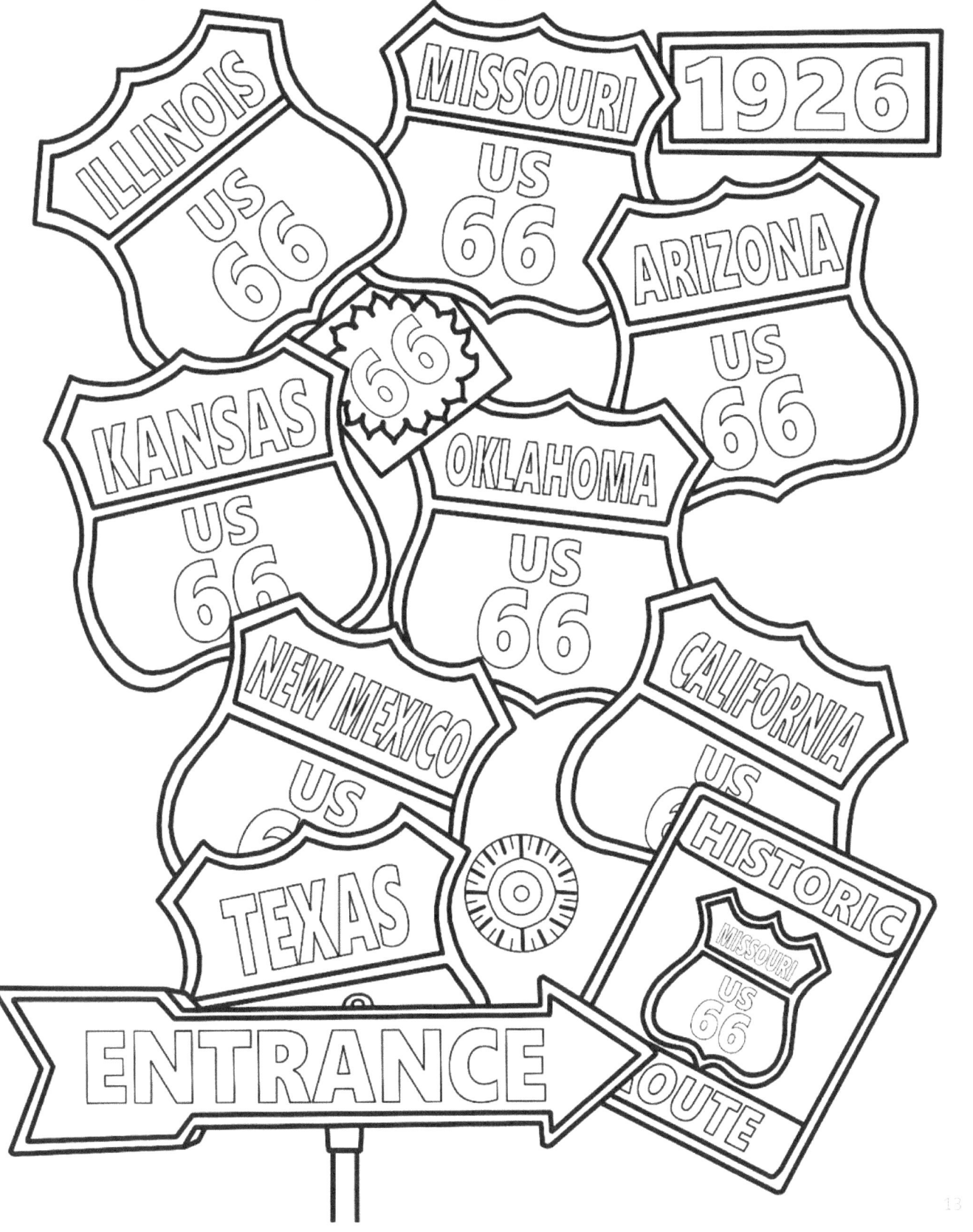

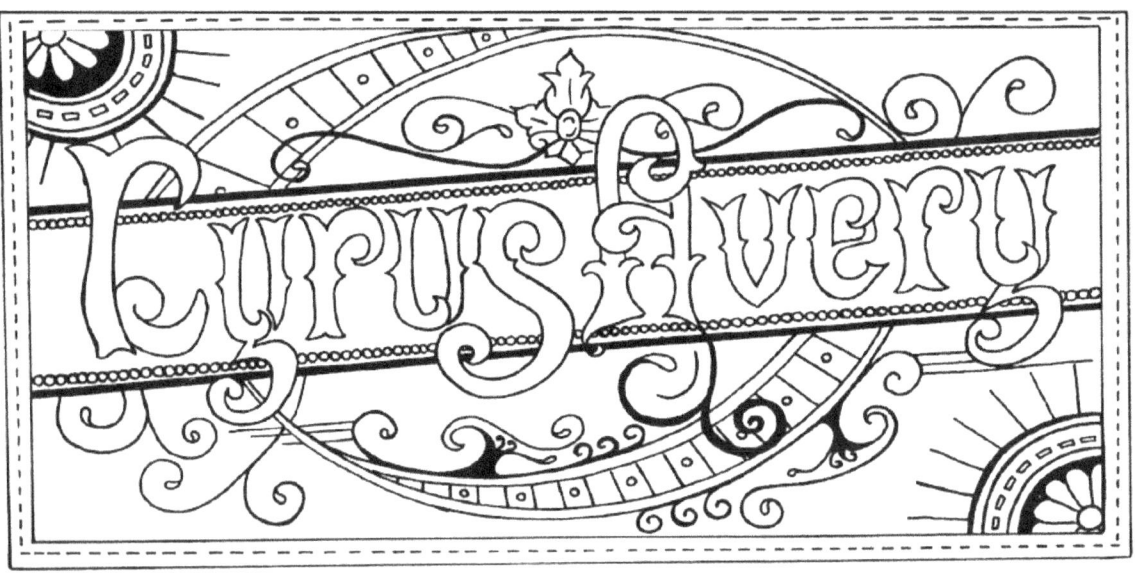

The known Father of Route 66 was an Oklahoma businessman by the name of Cyrus Avery (1871-1963). Cyrus and his family journeyed west from Pennsylvania by covered wagon to Missouri and later settled in Oklahoma. He made a living in farming, real estate, and oil, among other ventures. Cyrus was a big part of the Good Roads Movement, advocating for the highway, developing a national system of numbered highways as well as pushing for the road to pass through Oklahoma. To boost tourism on the roadway, he titled the road "Main Street of America." Cyrus also pushed to get the entire highway paved, which was completed by the late 1930's.

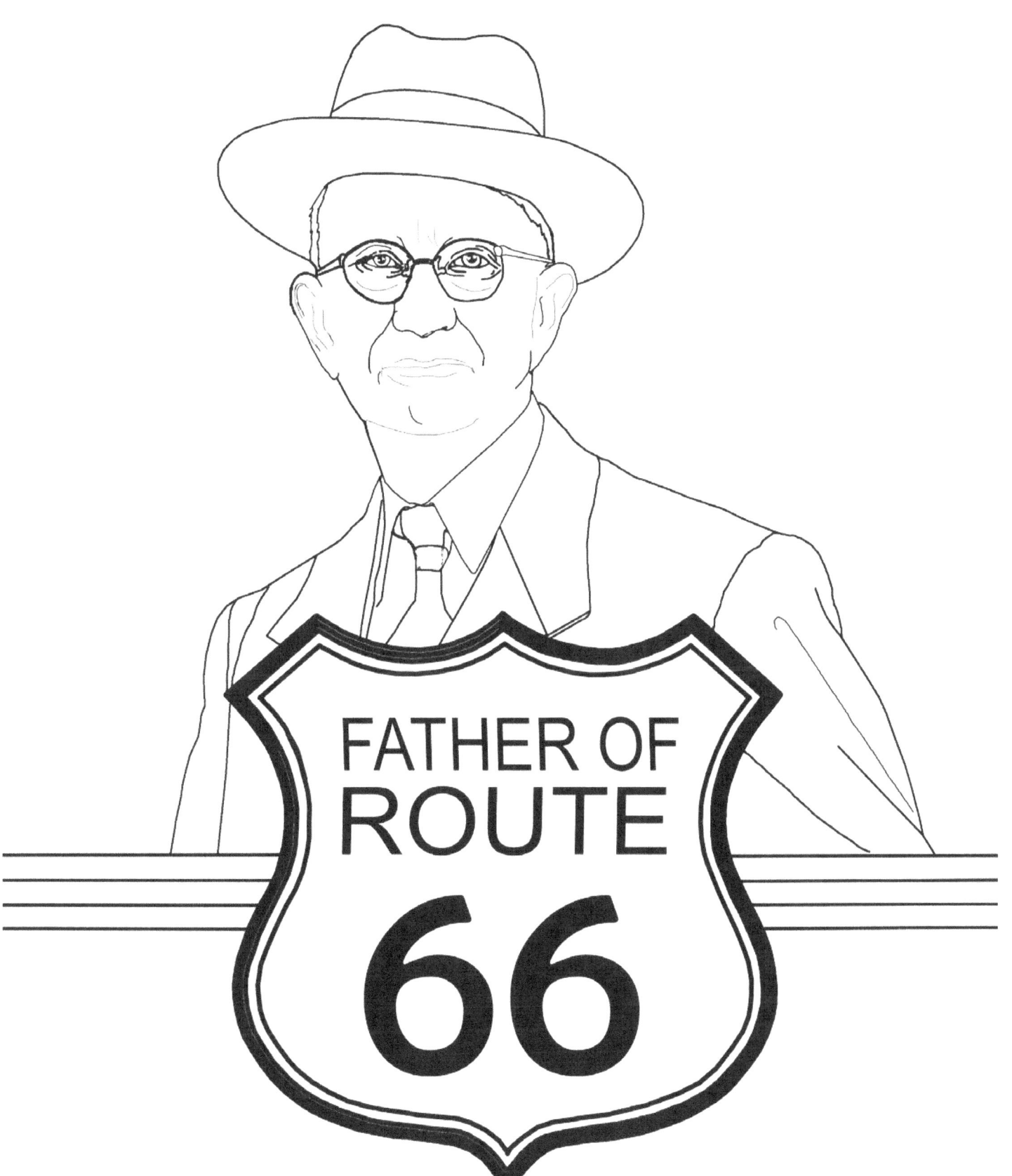

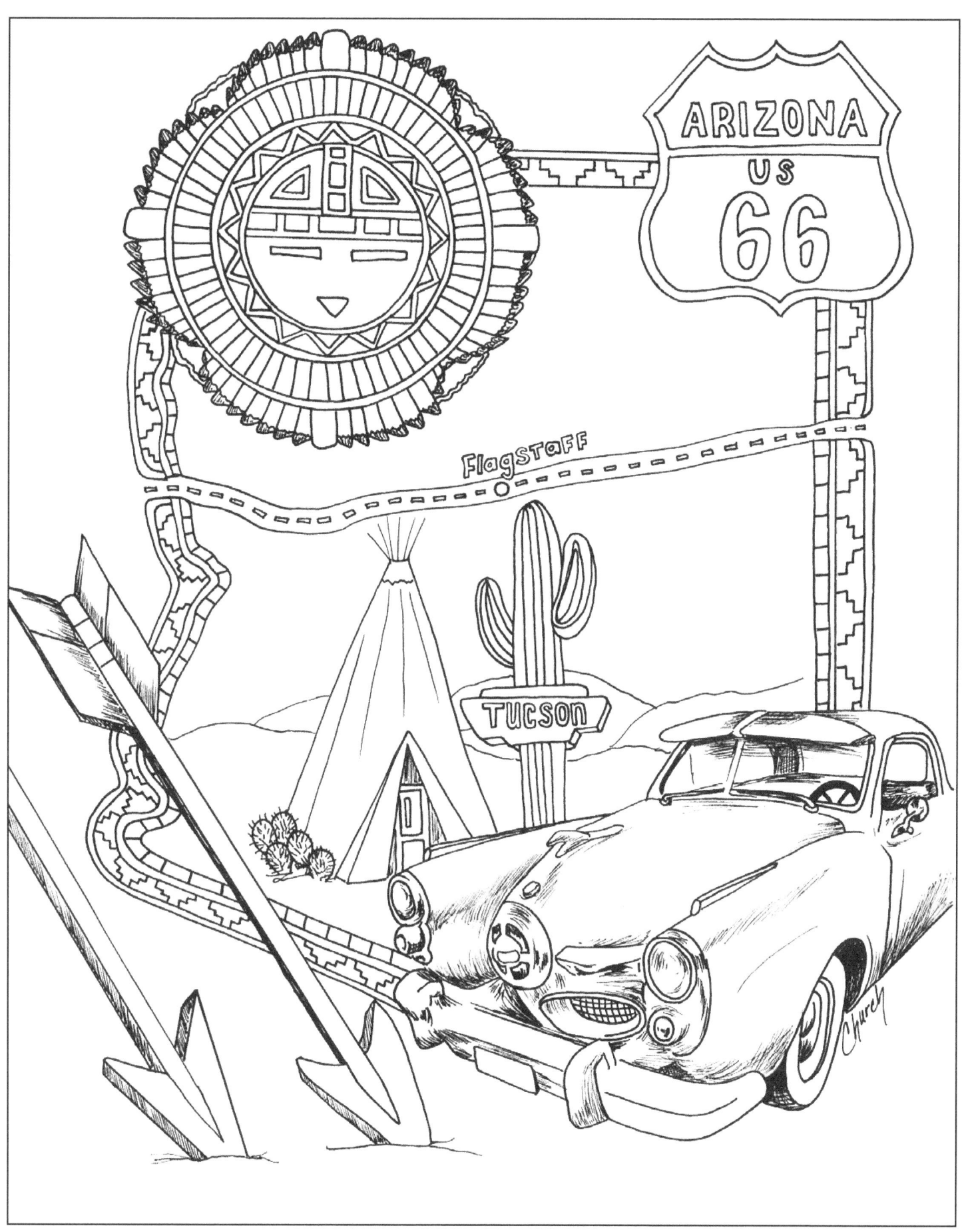

Arizona

"The Grand Canyon State"
State motto is – "Ditat Deus" meaning God Enriches

It took 22 years for Arizona to get admitted into statehood on February 14, 1912, entitling Arizona with the nickname the Valentine State.   Joining the Union as the 48th state and the 6th largest, the Valentine State closed the gap between New Mexico and California.

Arizona's beauty and mild winters make it especially popular for tourists, not to mention it does have one of the seven natural wonders of the world in its back yard, the Grand Canyon. The beautifully carved Grand Canyon is 277 miles long, 18 miles wide, and 1 mile deep. There are more than just canyons and tall cactus to see in Arizona; the brilliantly colored rocks and clay in the Painted

Desert, the million year old fossilized trees in the Petrified Forest, and ancient Indian ruins that have been designated national monuments are just a few of the must see places. Of course, there was also the big shoot out at the O.K. Corral in Tombstone, with the Earp brothers and Doc Holliday.

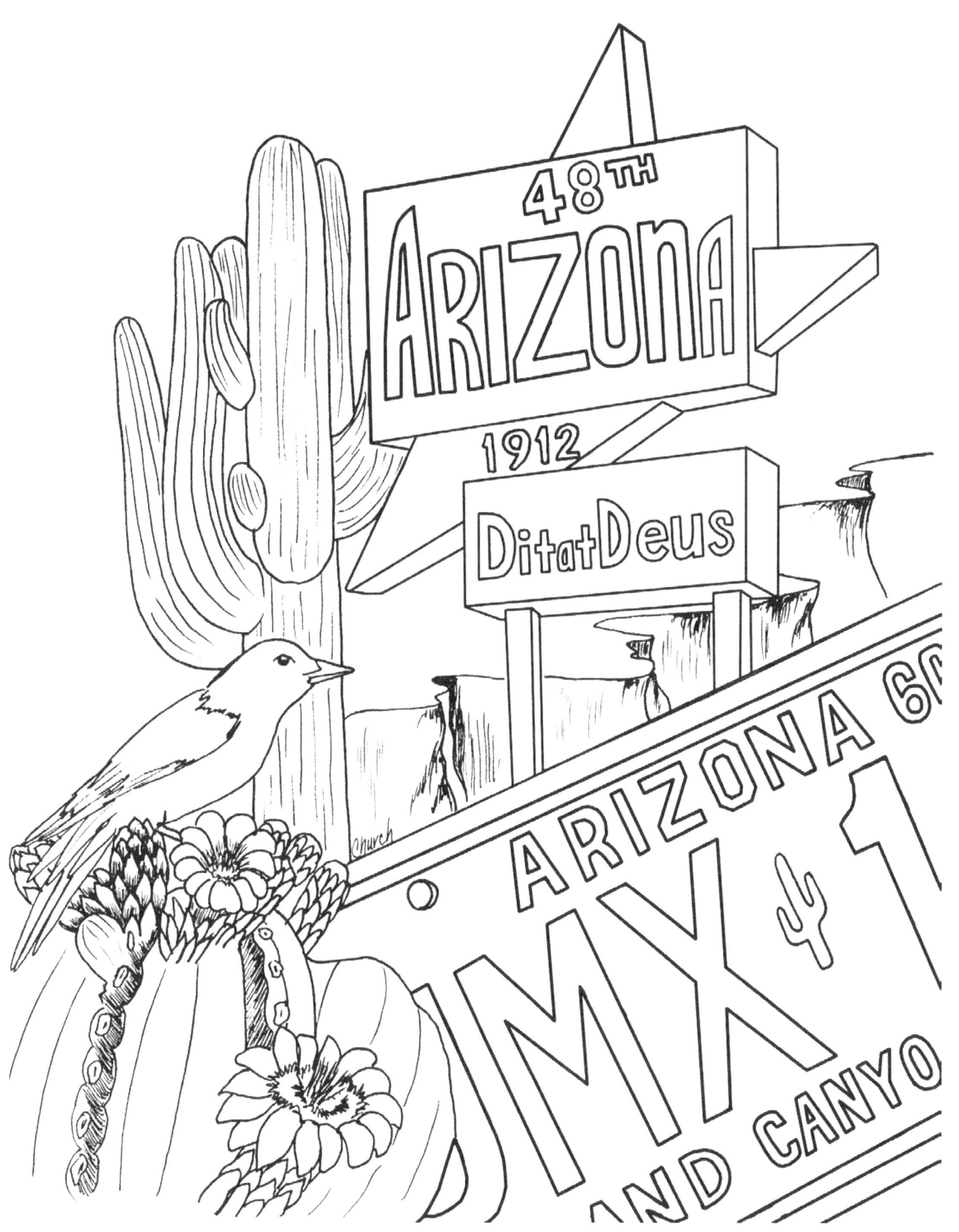

The towns and cities
of
Arizona Route 66

The historical Route 66 traveled through many small towns and cities supporting a lot of families through the many 'Mom and Pop' operations. Some of the towns are gone now, some are flourishing and some are barely hanging on.

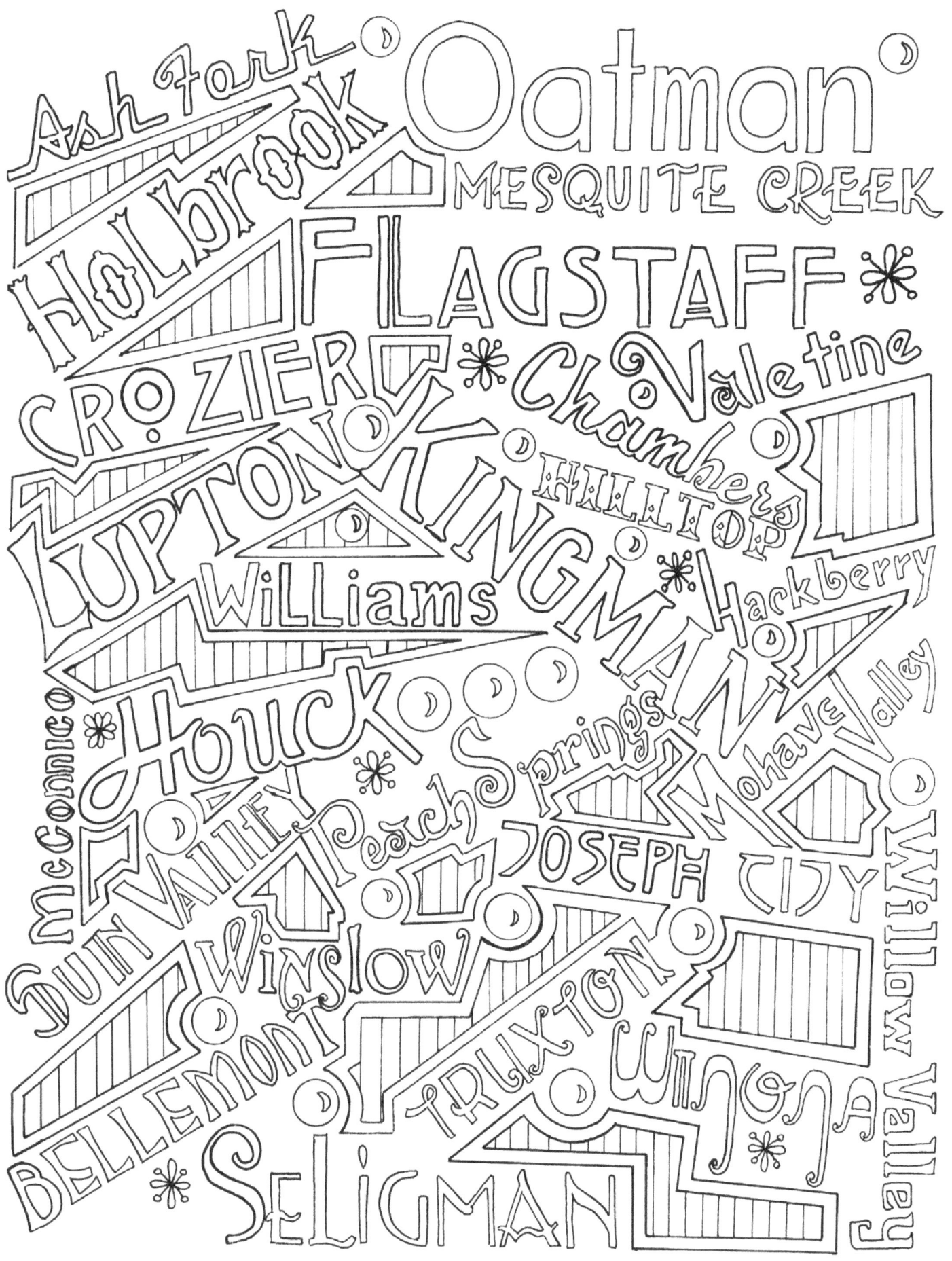

The Hottest and the Coldest

Arizona has the greatest percentage of its acreage designated as Indian tribal land in the United States. One of the oldest, continuously inhabited settlements in the United States belong to the Indian Hopi village, Oraibi, which has been in existence dating back to 1150 AD.

Arizona is the only state that can yield both the highest and lowest temperatures in the country within the same day. This type of environment makes it ideal for the state bird, Cactus Wren, which relies on the plentiful Saguaro cactus blossoms for nourishment. The beautiful blossoms spreading throughout the land became the state flower in 1931; nineteen years after Arizona became a state.

Most of the states in the U.S. recognize Daylight Savings Time, however, Arizona is one of the two states that do not.

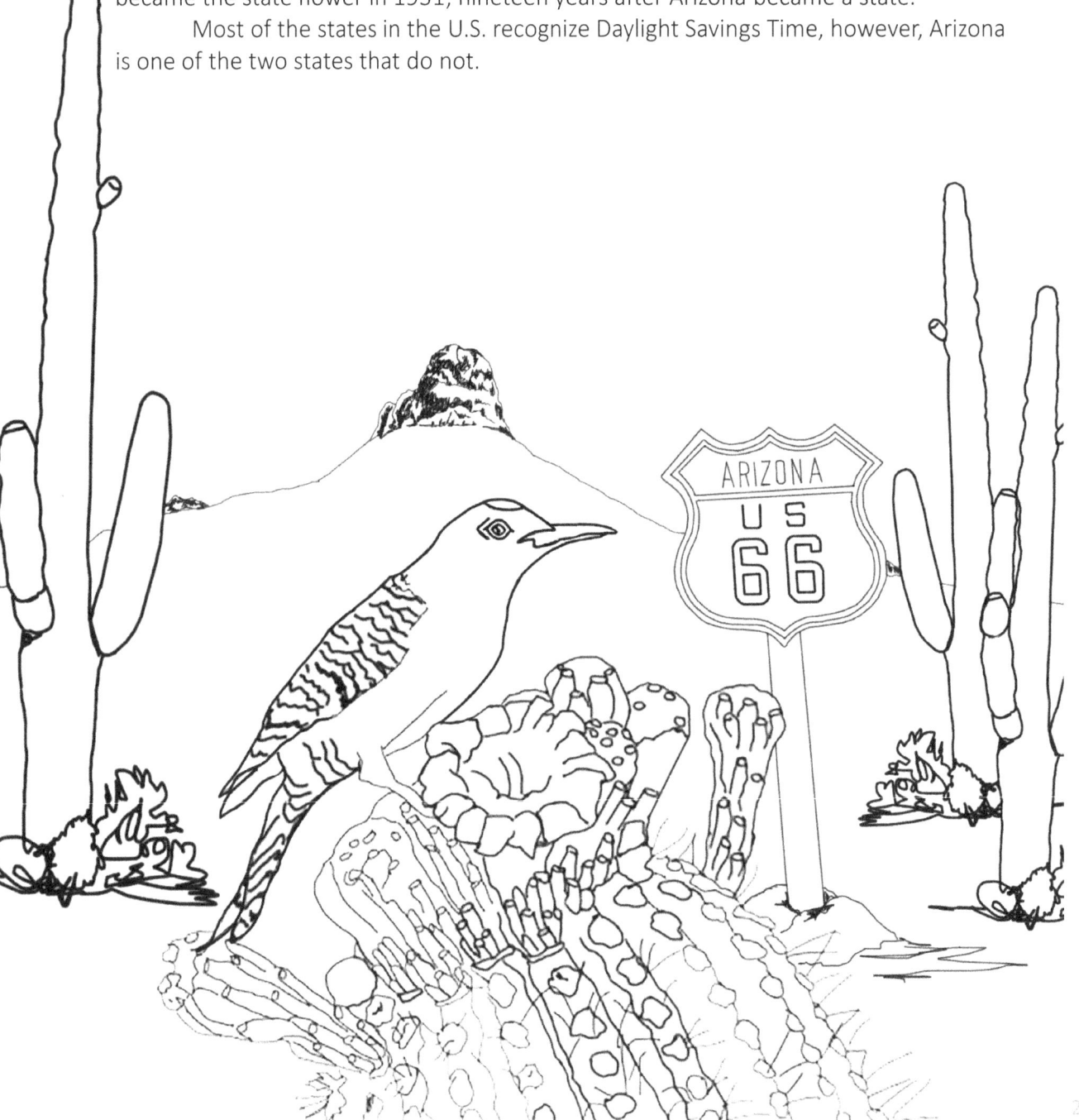

State Line Attraction Exit 359

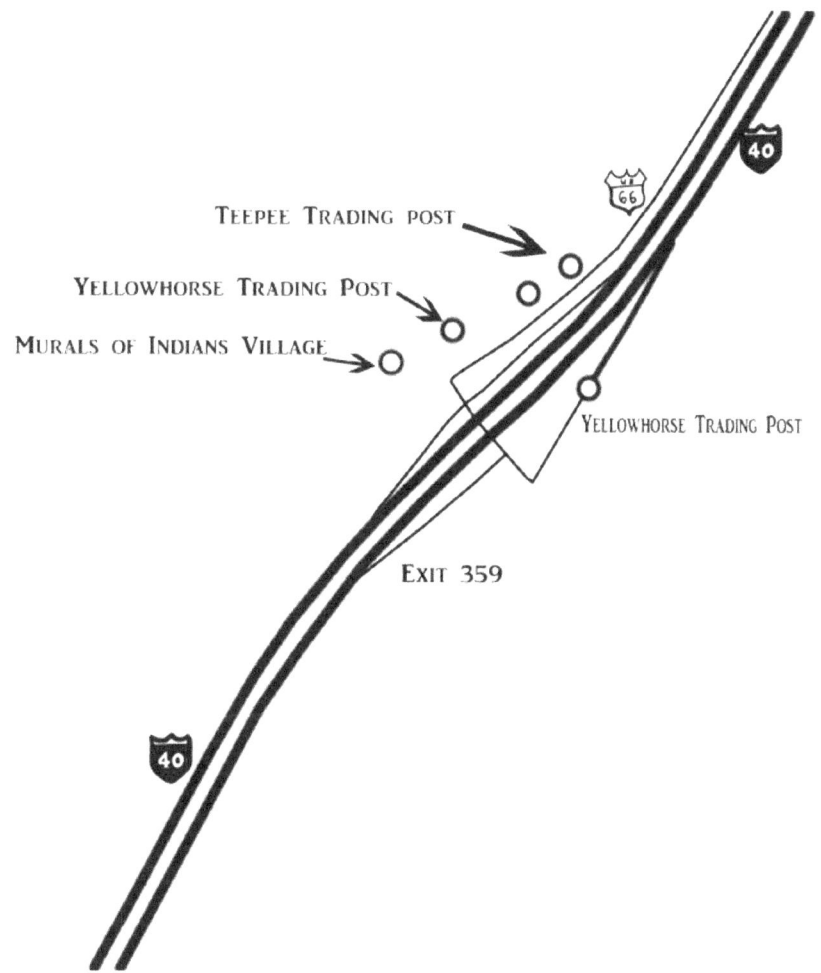

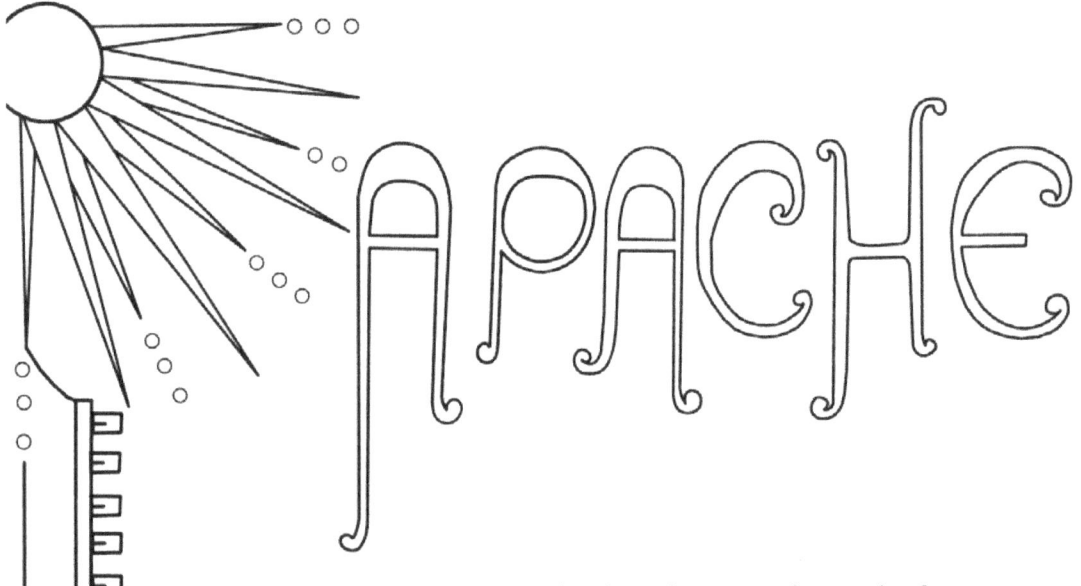

Apache county was developed in 1879, being the first county of Arizona holding the Fort Apache Indian Reservation. At the time of origination the Apache County territory covered over 21,177 square miles. The county has the most land designated as Indian reservation in the United States. Reservations within Apache County are Navajo Nation, Ft. Apache Indian Reservation and the Zuni Indian Reservation

Apache County

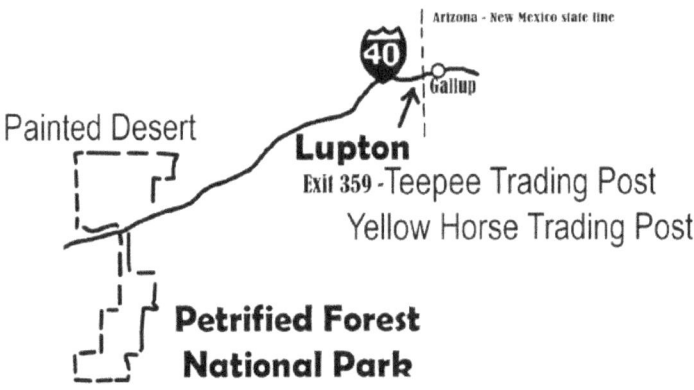

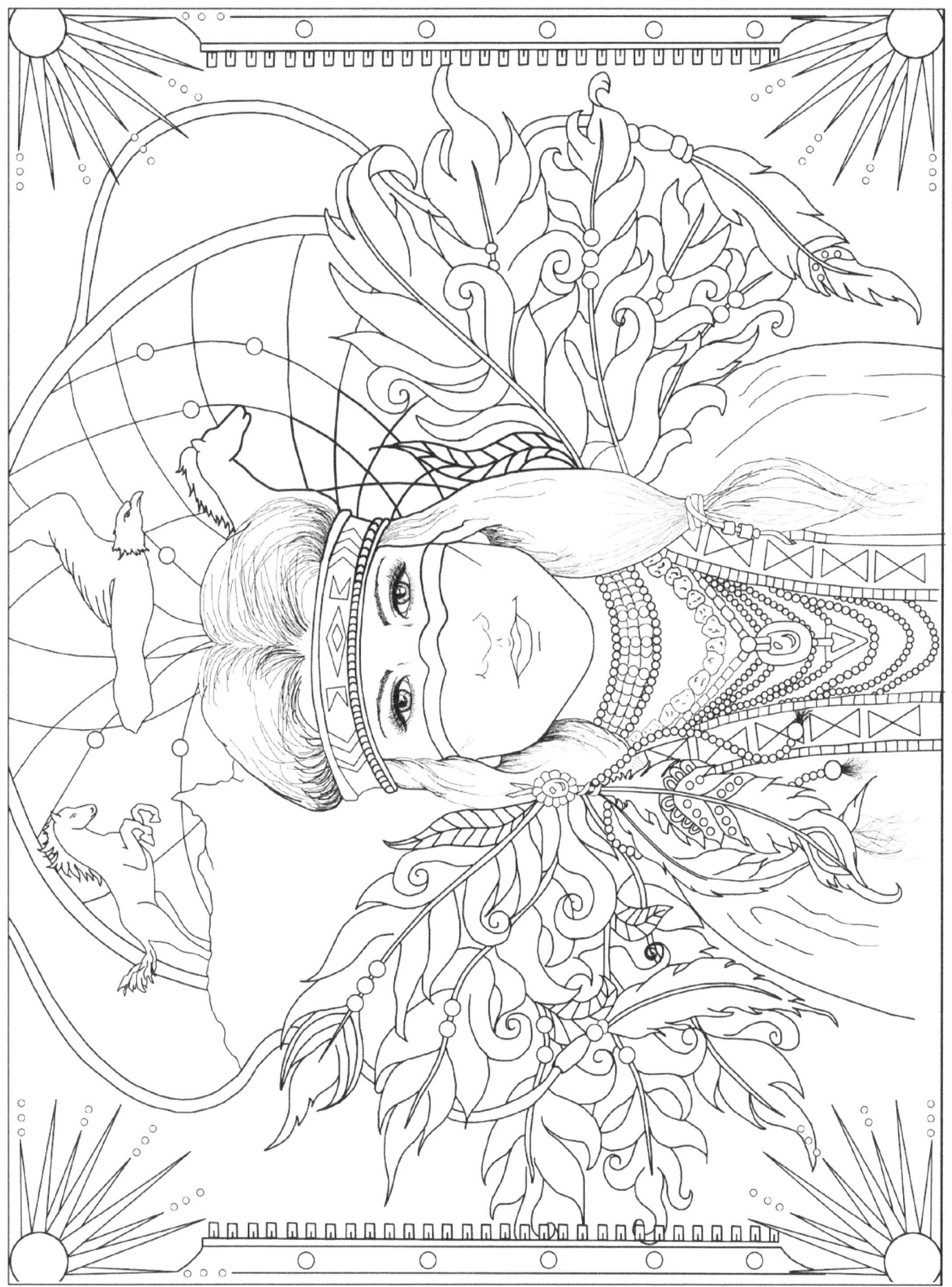

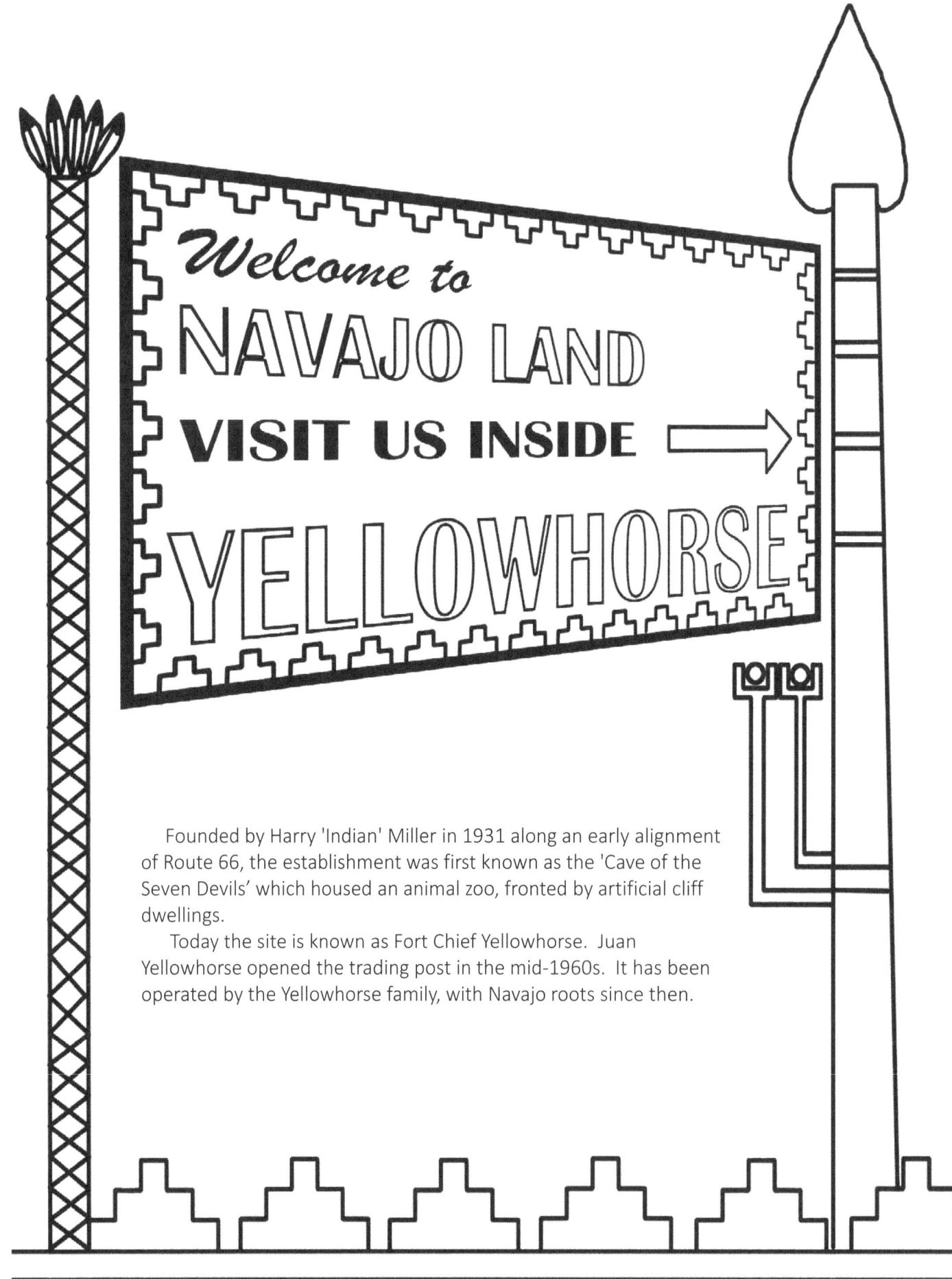

Founded by Harry 'Indian' Miller in 1931 along an early alignment of Route 66, the establishment was first known as the 'Cave of the Seven Devils' which housed an animal zoo, fronted by artificial cliff dwellings.

Today the site is known as Fort Chief Yellowhorse. Juan Yellowhorse opened the trading post in the mid-1960s. It has been operated by the Yellowhorse family, with Navajo roots since then.

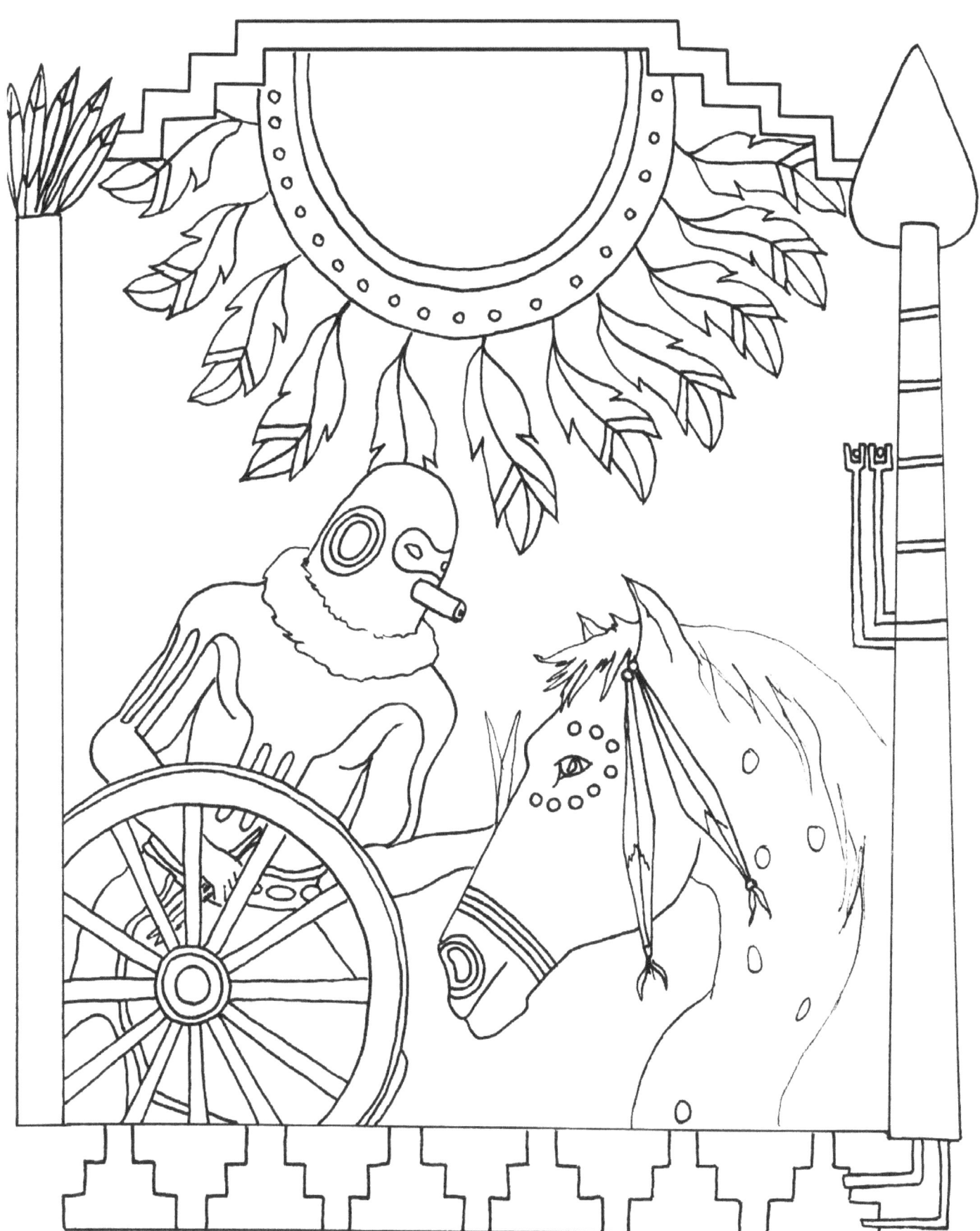

Painted Desert Trading Post

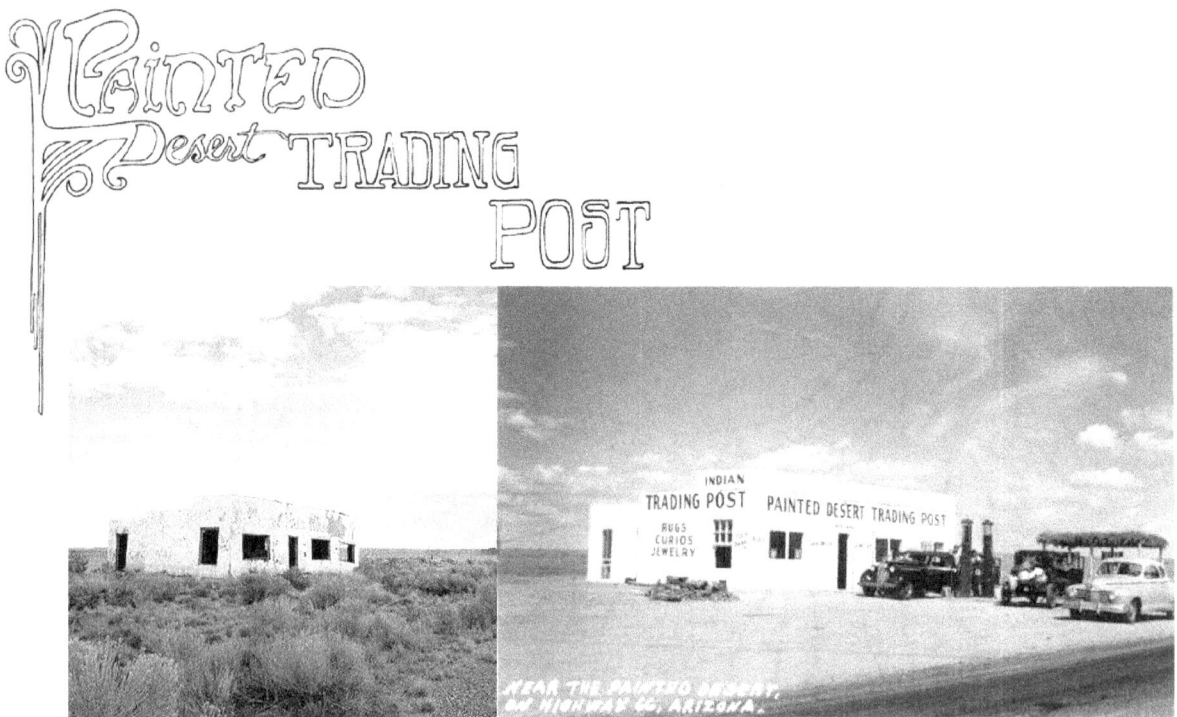

Dotch Windsor and his first wife, Alberta, opened the Painted Desert Trading Post along Route 66 during the early 1940s. Even along the Mother Road at the time, it was a remote outpost with no electricity or telephone service (gravity pumps dispensed fuel). It closed by the late 1950s after being bypassed.

The long-abandoned ruins of the Painted Desert Trading Post, located several miles from Interstate 40, remains mostly inaccessible except for the most dedicated explorers of old 66. The iconic building became unstable as cows walked through it. This building as well as many other iconic locations along Route 66 were on the endangered list and it was out of time. Until a group of Route 66 roadies pulled together and formed Route 66 Co-op with the sole purpose of saving and preserving buildings such as this for our future generations to enjoy.

Even though much work was done during the first session it will still take another 2-3 weeks of work to complete all that needs to be done. Raising and stabilizing the back corners of the building as well as the connecting walls, replacing roof and ceiling timbers and the metal roof, and pouring a concrete foundation in places where the old foundation had washed out are the three major tasks that we hope to do this year. If the weather cooperates, and we are able to have enough Co-op members and volunteers to do the work then the rebirth of the Painted Desert Trading Post will be a reality.

The path to preservation requires a lot of physical labor and money. The group has organized "work weeks" at the PDTP for cleanup, stabilizing the trading post to forestall any further decline in the condition of the building. Man power and financial assistance is always needed. If you would like to help physically or financially contact Rich Dinkela, Jim Ross, or Mike Ward.

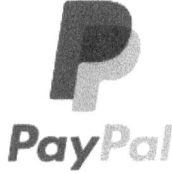

Donations are excepted at anytime. To help save the Desert Trading Post make your donations to

https://www.paypal.me/pdtp

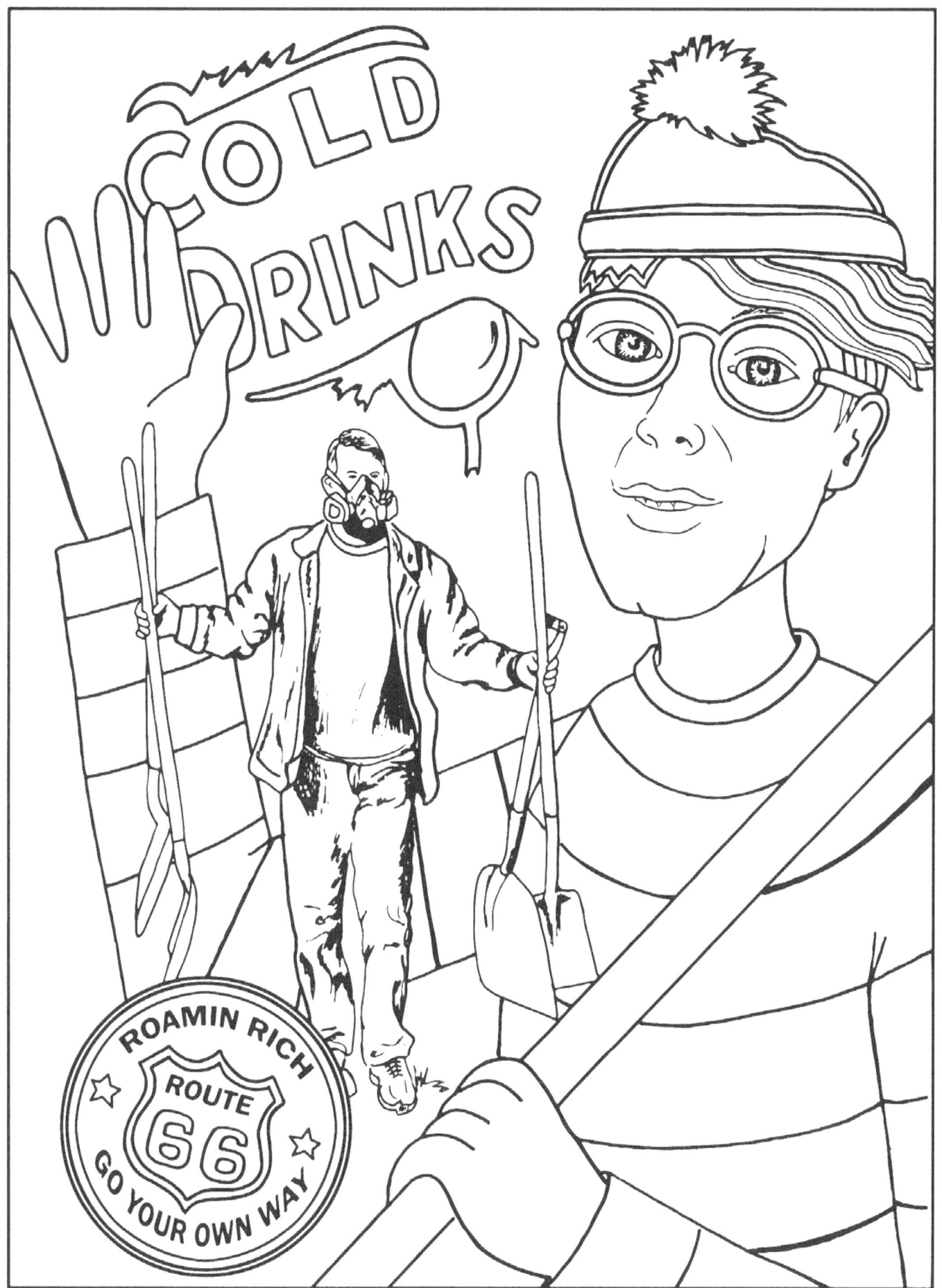

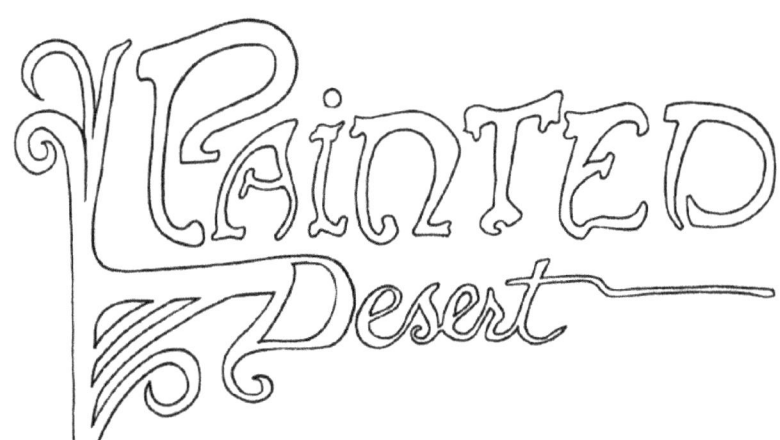
Painted Desert

    The Navajo and Hopi people have inhabited the region for hundreds of years however, the desert was not named until Coronado sent an expedition west to find the Colorado River. Instead of crossing the Colorado River he crossed the Little Colorado, discovering a breath taken view of a wonderland of colors he named "El Desierto Pintada" - meaning The Painted Desert.

    The Painted Desert is a natural wonder, millions of years in the making. Volcanic eruptions, earthquakes, floods and sunlight all combined together created the most breath taking view. The layering of clay and sandstone stacked on top of each other reflect the setting sun of Arizona. This beautiful display of radiating colors have enticed artist and travelers for many years.

    The Painted Desert, along with the Petrified Forest became a National Monument in 1906 by President Theodore Roosevelt.

       For the experience of a lifetime, don't miss the amazing sunset display of the fiery color striations within the rock formation and mesas.

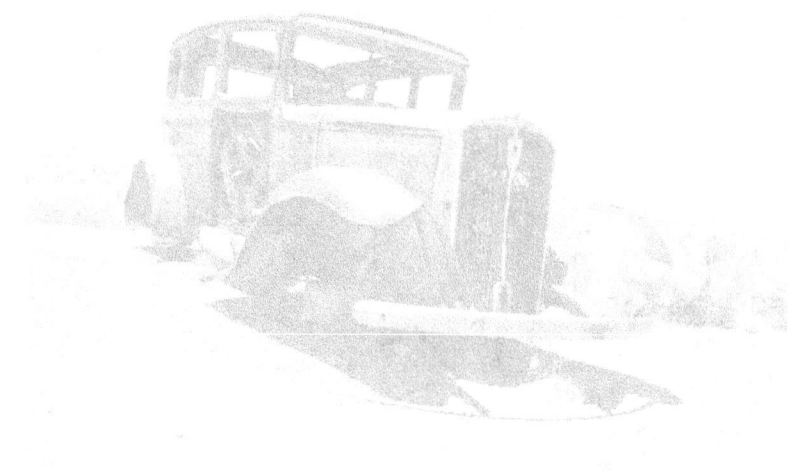

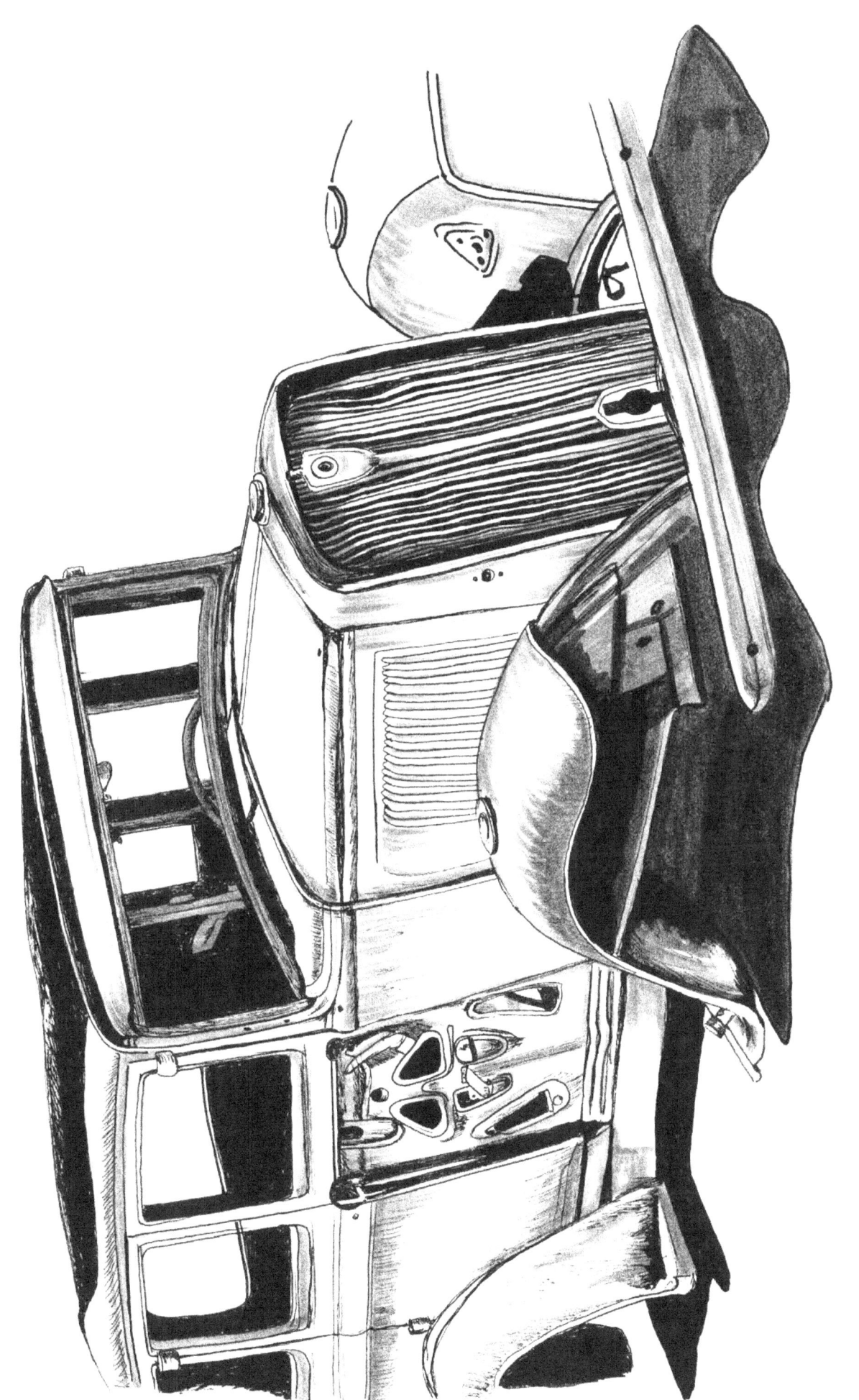

Adhere your selfie in the painted Desert / Petrified Forest

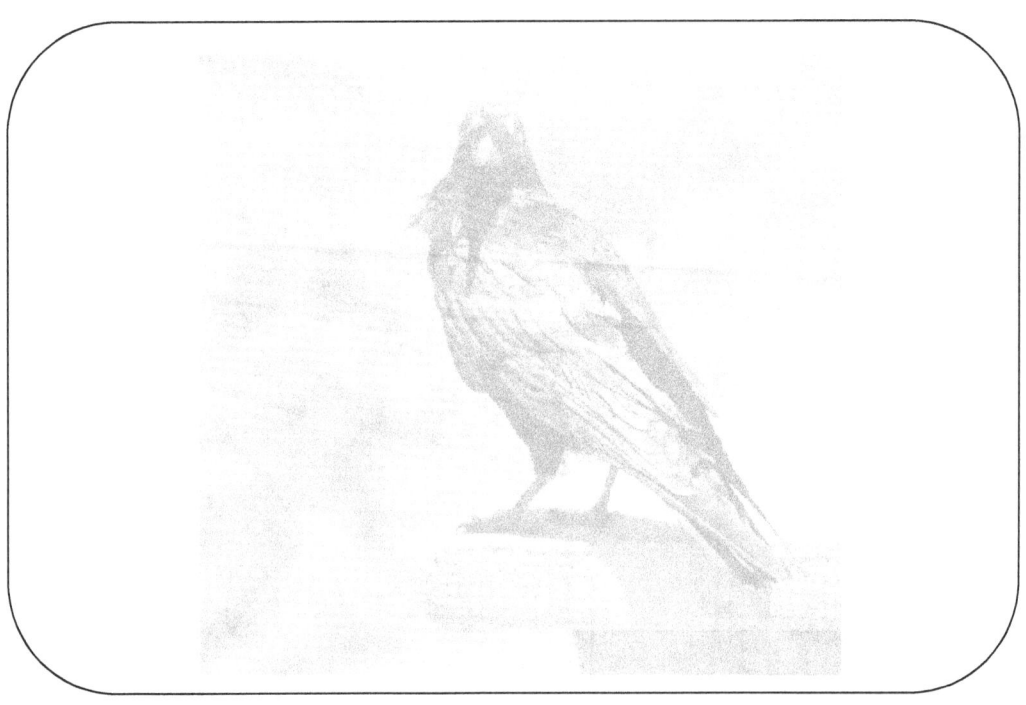

Step into the National Forest Gift Shop and obtain a date stamp from the wonderful park forest rangers, Stamp it here...

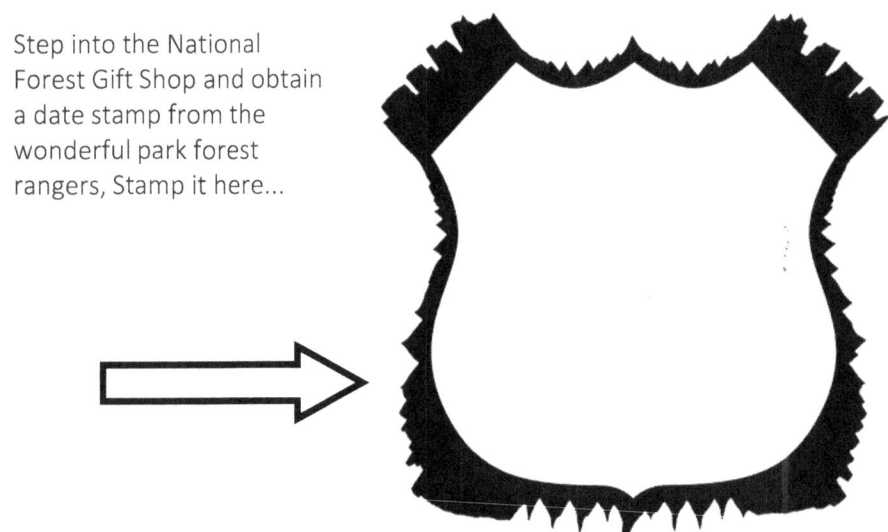

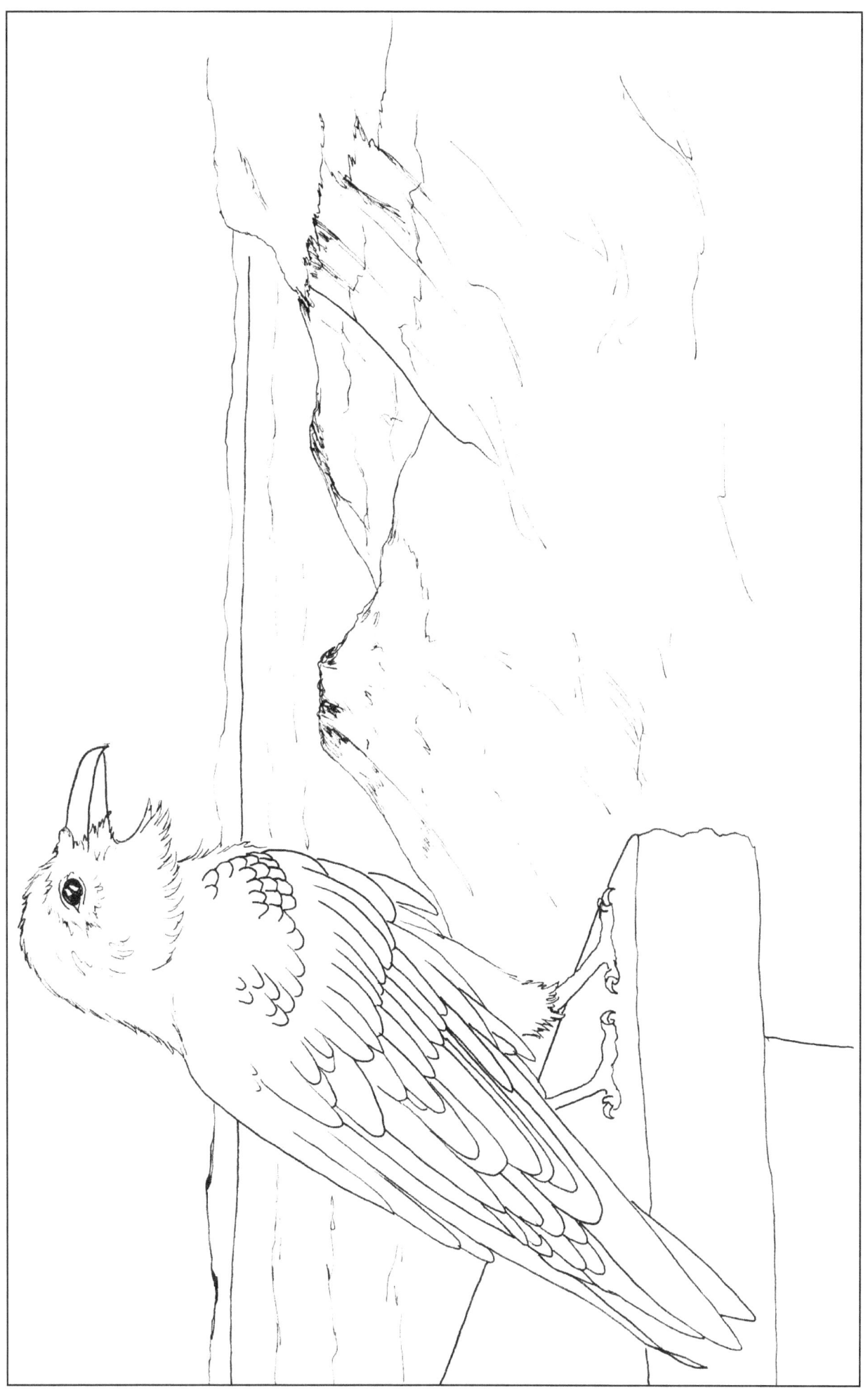

Navajo

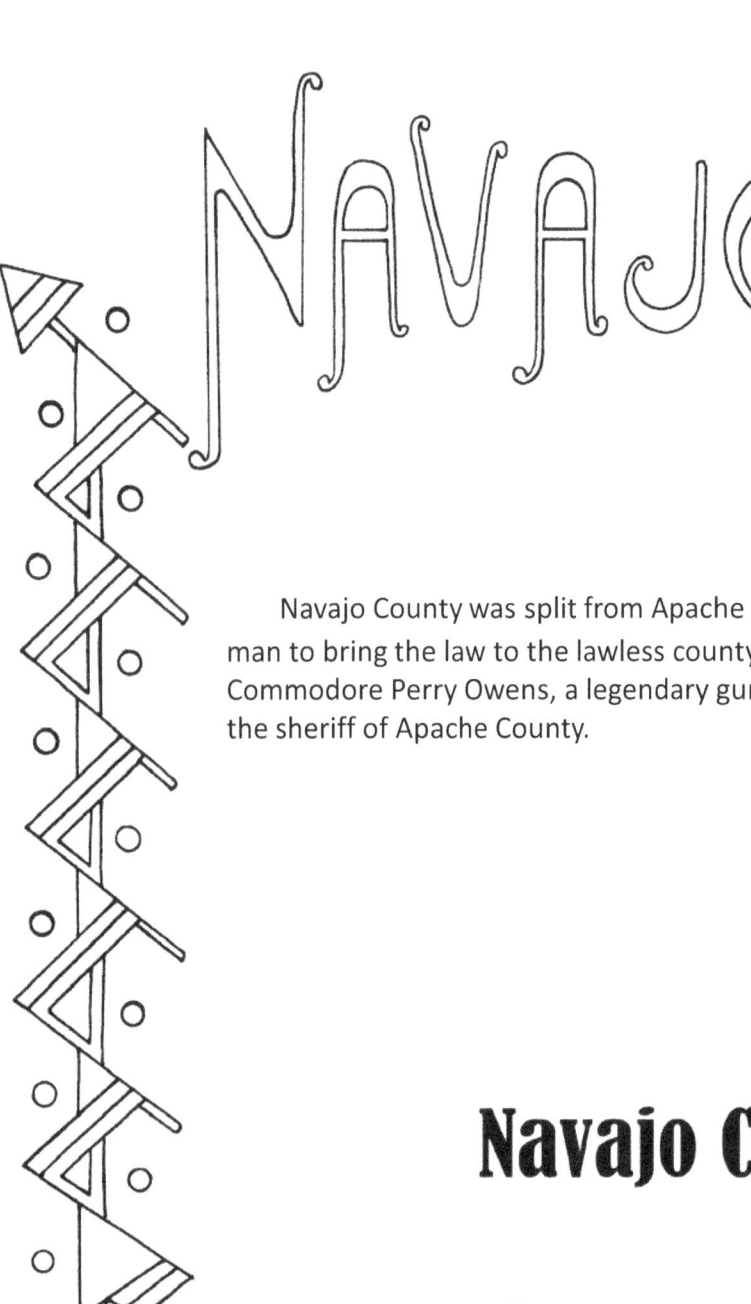

Navajo County was split from Apache County March 21, 1895. The first man to bring the law to the lawless county of the wild west was Sheriff Commodore Perry Owens, a legendary gunman who had previously served as the sheriff of Apache County.

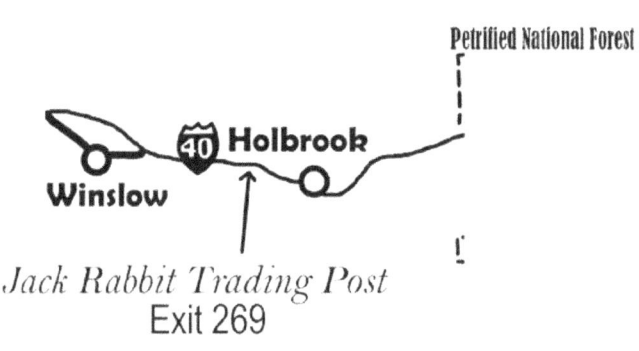

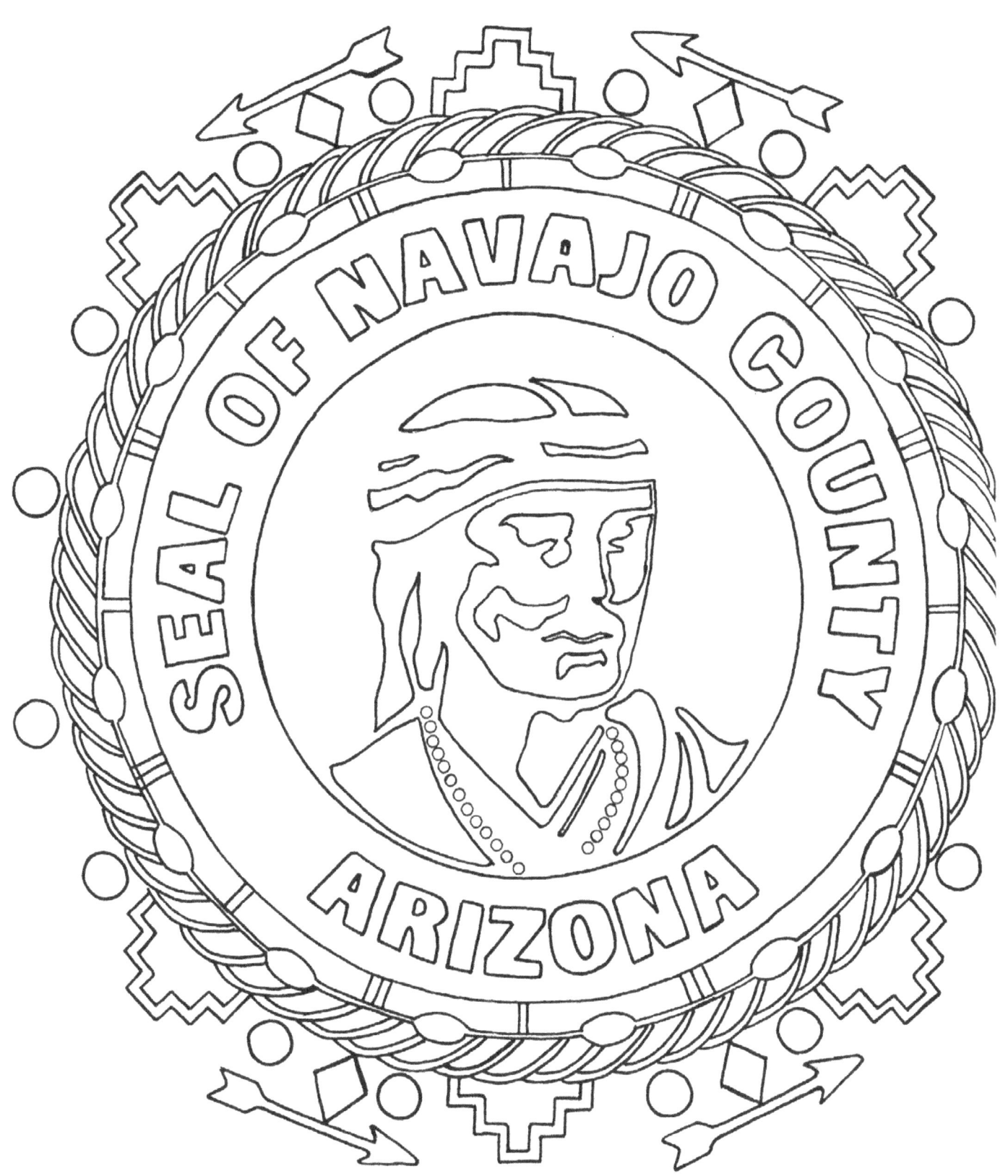

Code Talkers

After Japan bombed Pearl Harbor in 1941, the U.S. Marines needed a secret language to transmit communications. The brave Navajo Indians from Arizona enlisted and by using their native tongue, they were able to save countless lives. The young Navajo men were known as the Navajo Code Talkers. The oral code that they created was un-decipherable by the enemy, fulfilling a crucial role during World War II. There were more than 430 code talkers, "who answered the call of duty following the Pearl Harbor attacks."

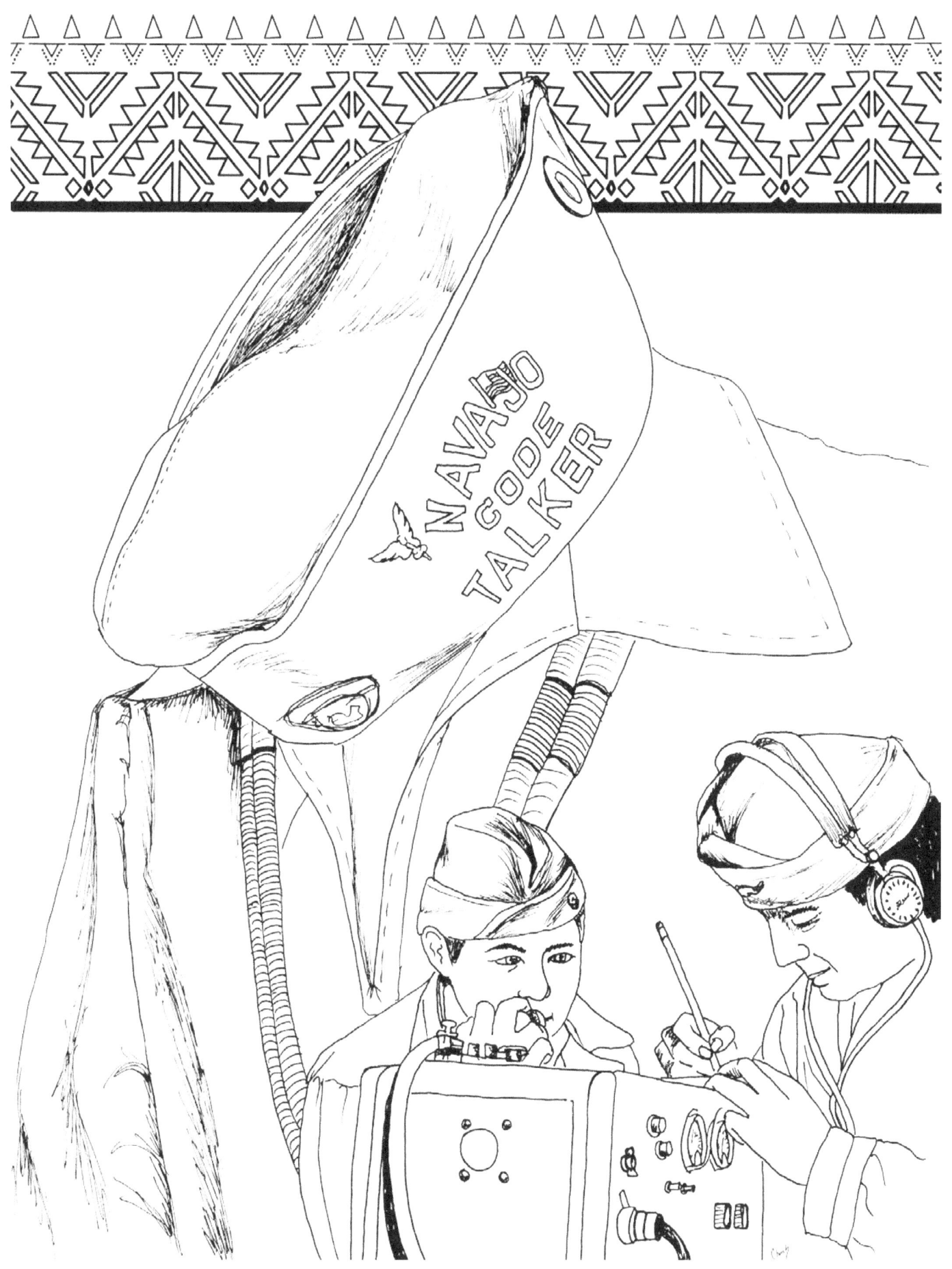

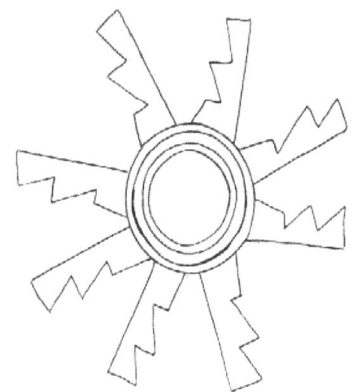

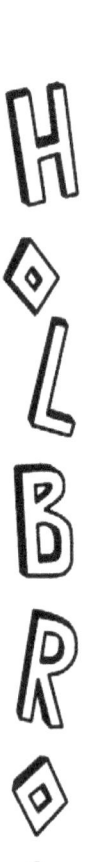

The land was known as Horsehead Crossing, the railroad saw it as a trade center. A decision was made and the tracks were laid in 1881, the following year a railroad station was built and a small town was developed. The small settlement was named after the first chief engineer of the railroad H.R. Holbrook. A year later a post office opened with James H. Wilson the postmaster. Holbrook was a typical wild west town complete with gambling, painted ladies, lots of cowboys, cattle ranchers and railroaders. The town was lawless resulting in it earning the name, "Bucket of Blood".

Many of the cowboys in the area worked for a not so popular cattle company called Aztec Land and Cattle Company also known as Hashknife Outfit. The company employed some of the roughest, fighting, thieving bunch of cowboys who thought nothing of gunfighting, rustling, robbery and even murder. There wasn't a stagecoach or train safe in the area. During this time, (1886) the Holbrook Times recorded 26 shooting deaths on the streets of Holbrook in one day. There was a desparate need for law and order for the wild town of Holbrook that was known as a town too tough for women and churches.

Commodore Perry Owens was the man to tame the wild town. He brought the law in 1887 with one of his first encounters to be Andy Cooper a cattle rustler. Andy Cooper wasn't his real name, in Texas his name was Andy Blevins but an outstanding warrant for murder aided in his changing his name and heading west. Owens went to visit the Blevins family home while they were eating Sunday dinner, of course Blevins refused to come out. It wasn't a very long standoff, Andy's half-brother John took a shot at the Sheriff, the sheriff retaliated with both six-guns, sending bullets in both Andy and John. The minute-long battle ended with an additional death of Sam Blevins and Mose Roberts. The site of this short-lived gun fight stands at Central Avenue in Holbrook.

Even with Holbrook nearly being destroyed by fire in 1888, the town continued to grow and rebuild and gaining the county seat in 1895. The court house was constructed and still stands today as Holbrook's Visitor Center and Museum. The courthouse is a must stop in Holbrook. The friendly staff will provide maps, directions, information on Navajo County's past, and give you a tour of the haunted jail cell. During the summer months, the Native American dancers offer free performances weekday evenings on the historical courthouse lawns.

The town remained pretty wild and the only county seat without a church for many more years.

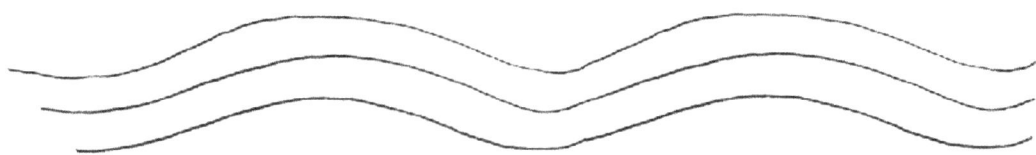

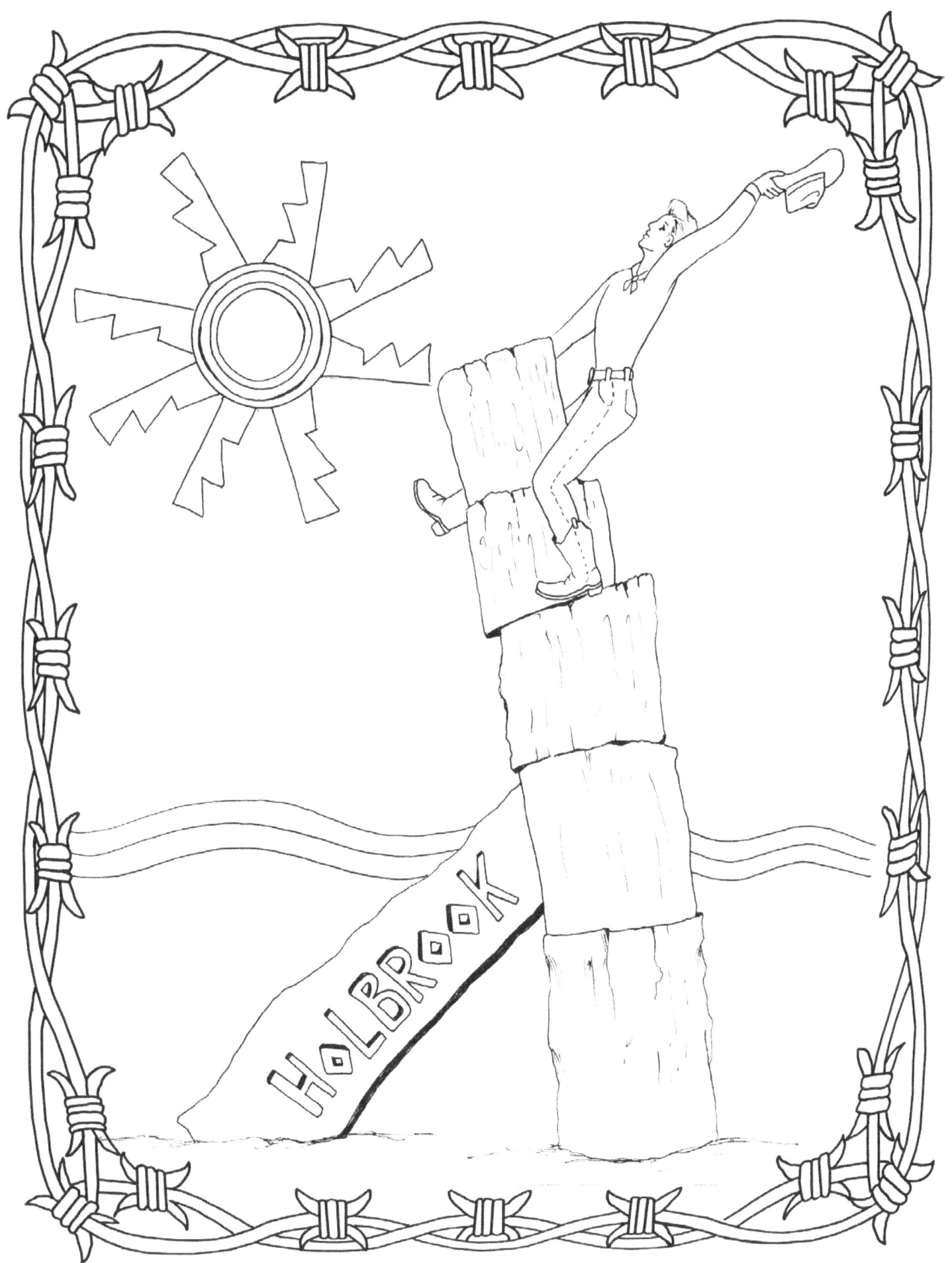

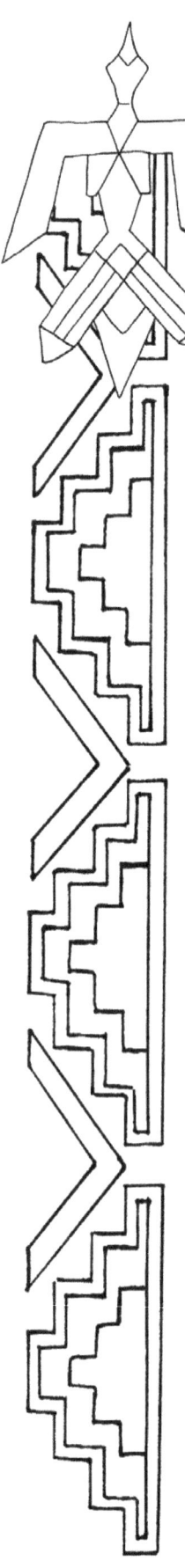

Painted Desert Indian Center

Exit 303

Native American tourist gift shop entices with Indian dwellings and dinosaurs.

Use this space for photos, stickers, post cards.

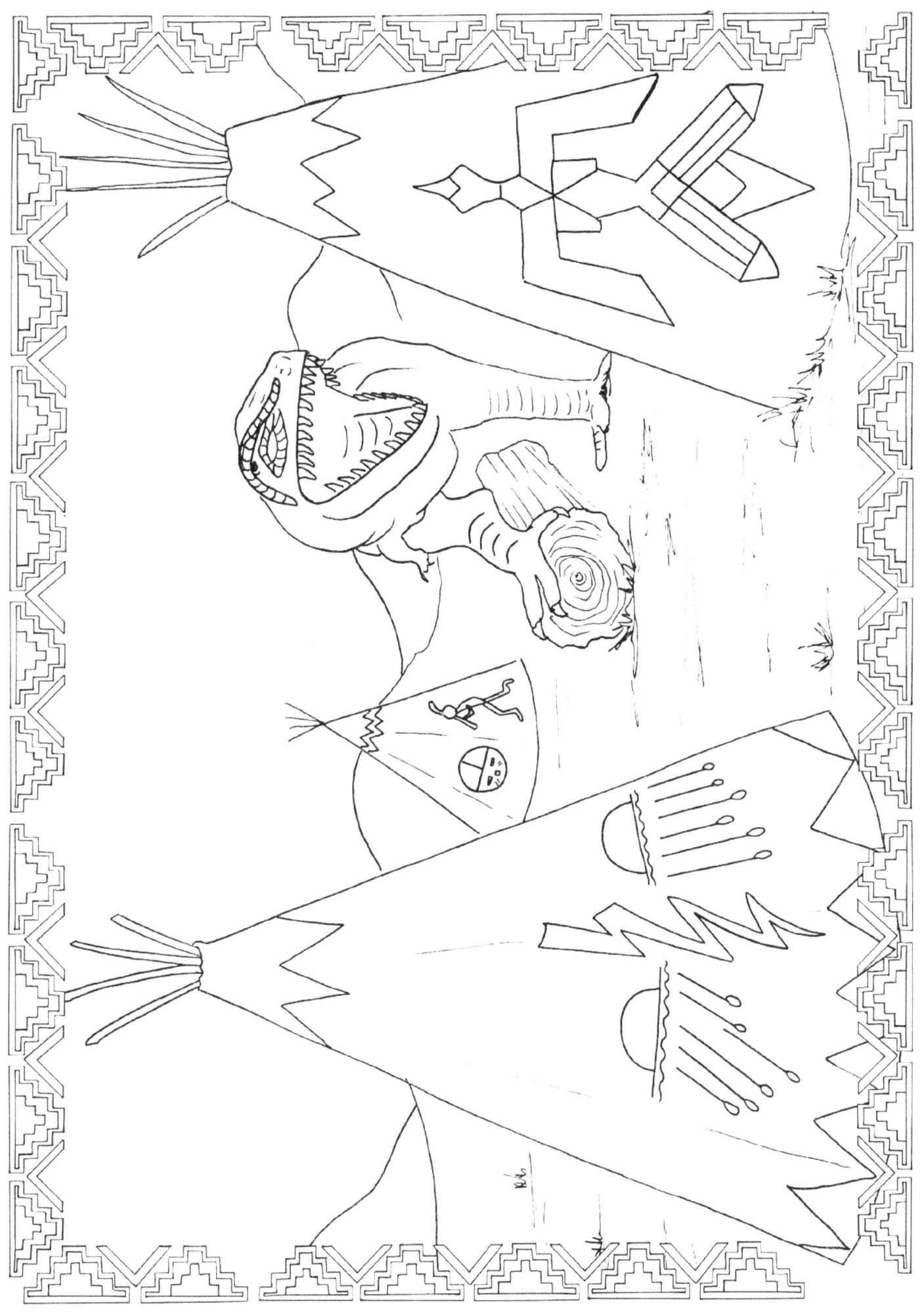

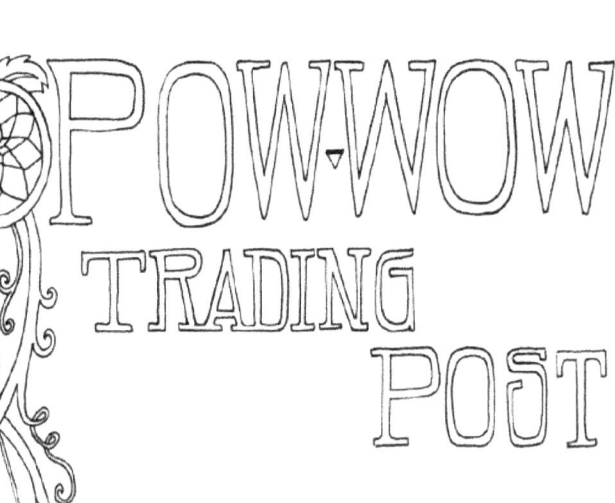
POW-WOW TRADING POST

If you want to capture someone's attention you go big. The large Kachina sign once displayed the word "Motel" spent many years attracting travelers for the night now says "Rocks". The trading post may have changed over the years but what hasn't changed is that it still caters to Roadies and still sells geological curios and jewelry.

Use this space for photos, stickers, post cards.

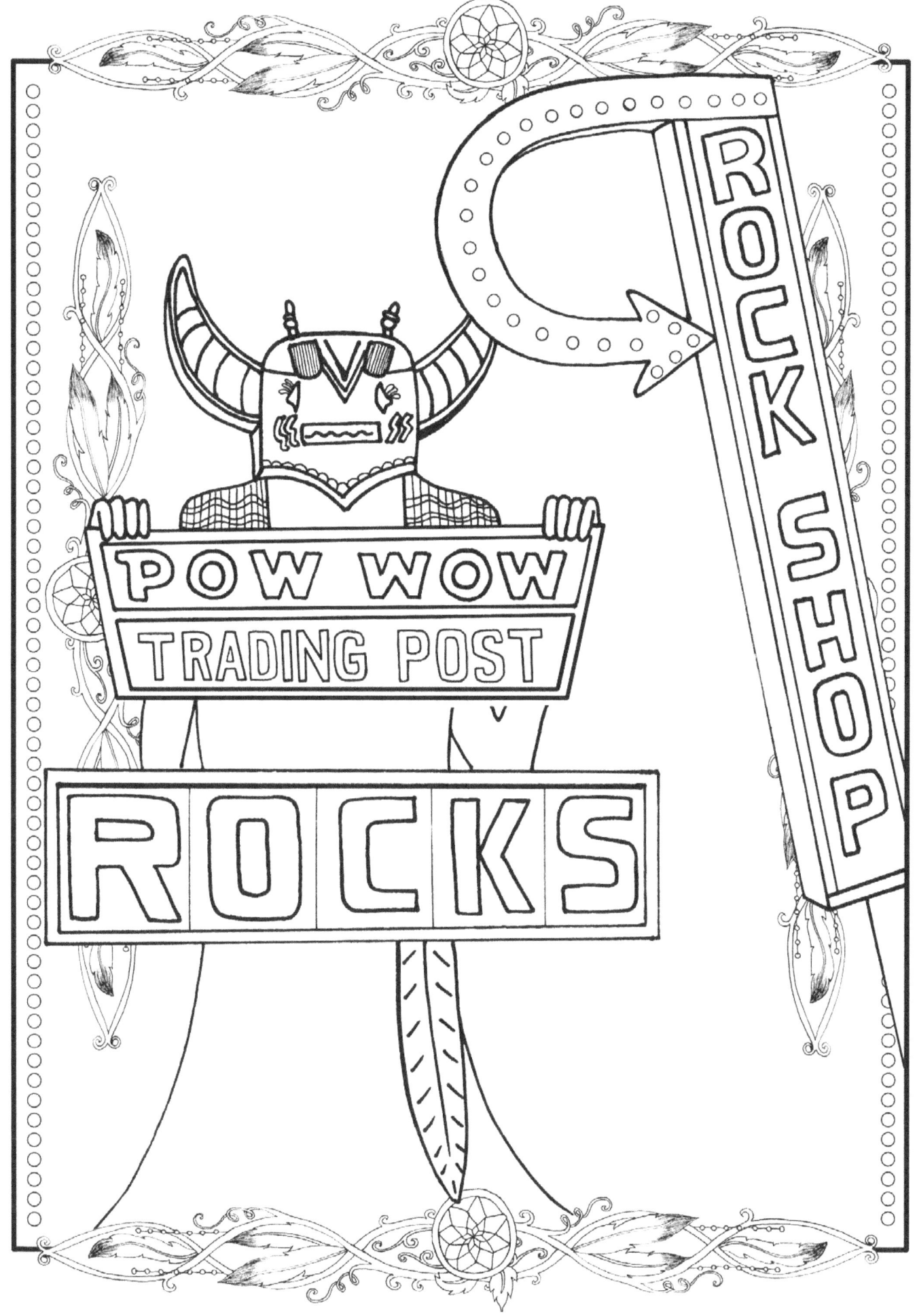

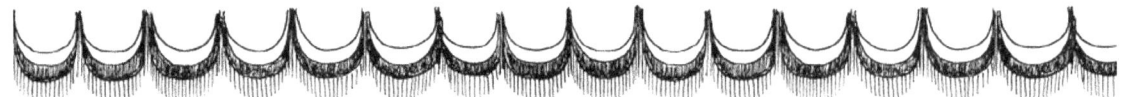

Rainbow's Rock Shop

Large piles of petrified wood and smaller specialty rocks scattered around and in between the feet of the dino's of Rainbow's Rock Shop. Owner Adam Luna took twenty years to build his fleet of dinosaurs out of cement and reinforcing rods.

Throughout the property displays, hand painted signs explaining the geologic forces to people.

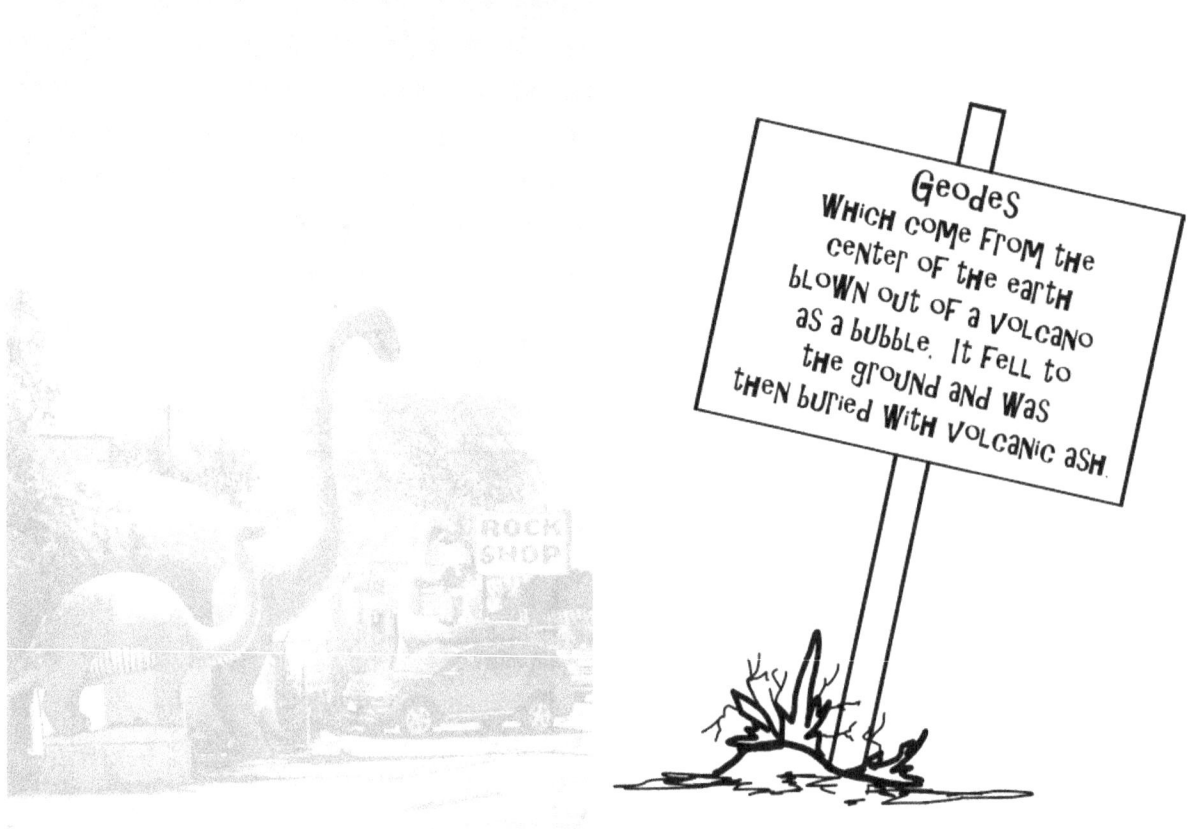

Geodes which come from the center of the earth blown out of a volcano as a bubble. It fell to the ground and was then buried with volcanic ash.

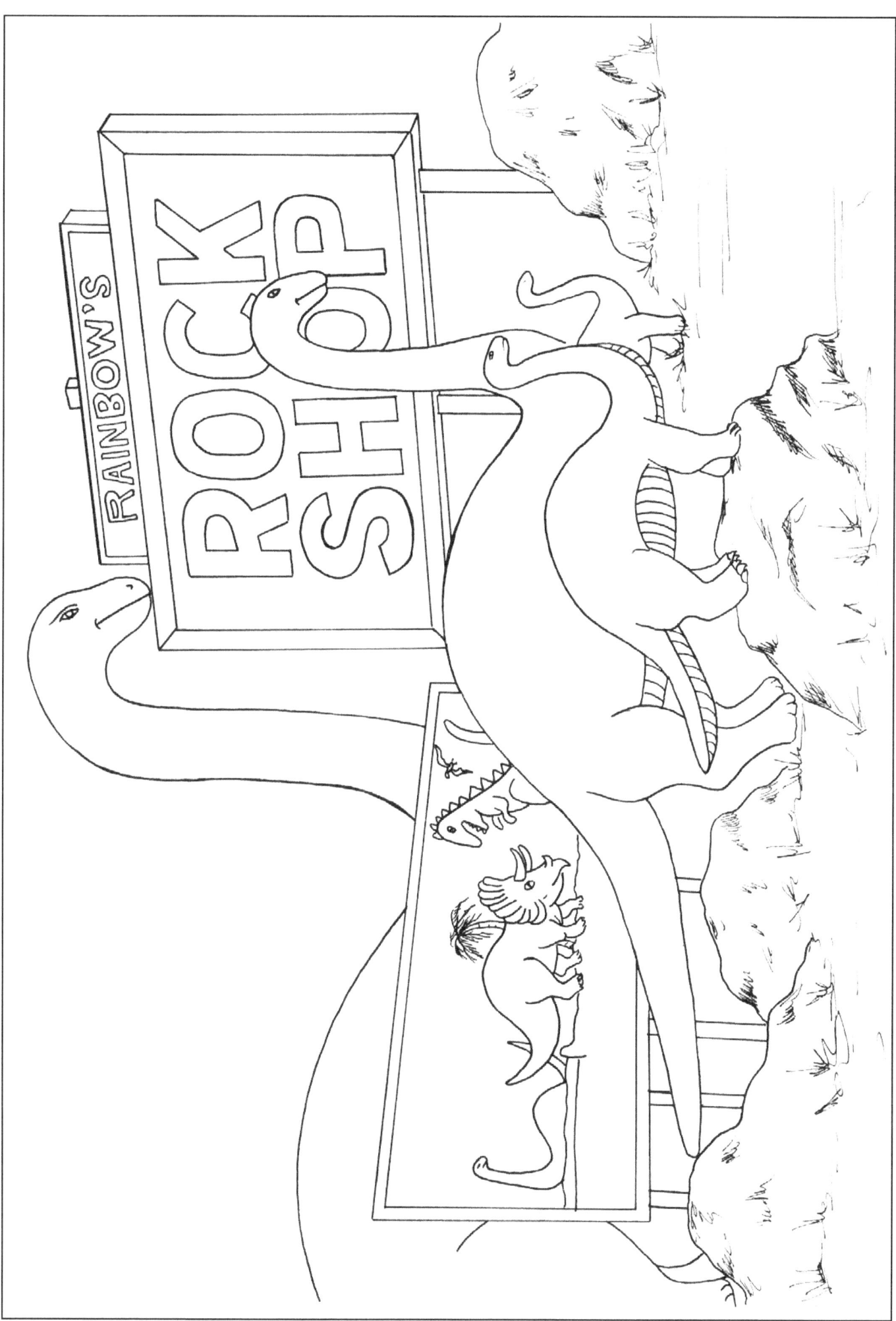

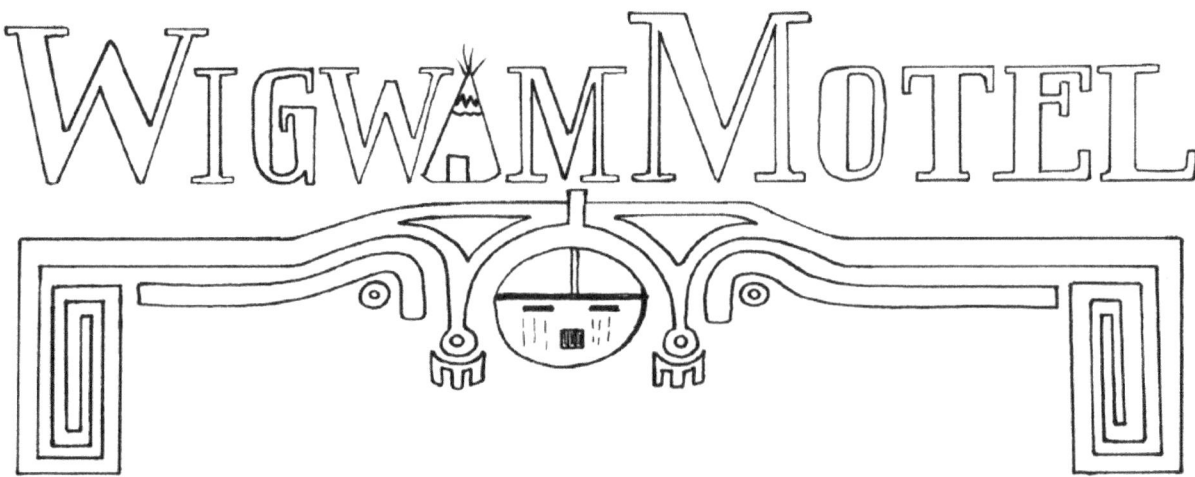

Wigwam Motel

Wigwam Motel is more than an iconic place along Route 66, it is a chance to sleep in a teepee, well a teepee look alike that is. The idea of a wigwam complex was the brain child of Frank A. Redford, a man from Horse Cave, Kentucky. He came up with the idea after visiting the Sioux reservation, his dream became reality and was patented in 1936 as the Wigwam Village.

The whole idea of a wigwam complex also fascinated another man, Chester Lewis. Mr. Lewis was awe struck by the oddly- shaped cabins so he set up a meeting with Frank upon which they came up with an agreement. Lewis was allowed to build a village of his own as long as Frank received the proceeds from the radios in each room (dime for a half hour play).

In 1950 Wigwam Motel in Holbrook was opened with 15 teepees on three sides, the fourth was the office and a Texaco gas station. Each teepee houses a tiny bathroom, shower and a bed within the round structure. The same year the seventh and final Wigwam Motel was built in San Bernadino, California.

For the next twenty-four years, the Wigwam welcomed visitors with its exhortation of *SLEEP IN A WIGWAM* until Holbrook and Route 66 was bypassed in 1974 resulting in the closure. Following Chester's death in 1986 his widow and children Paul, Clifton and Elinor, decided to renovate and reopen. After restoring the original hickory furniture and fittings, installing air conditioners, TV's and WI-FI the motel reopened in 1988. Classic vehicles adorn the grounds, which also included Mr. Lewis's own Studebaker.

The Lewis family continues to run the Wigwam Motel which since has been added to the National Register of Historic Places in May 2002. It remains as popular now as it was in the 1950s and booking is always advisable.

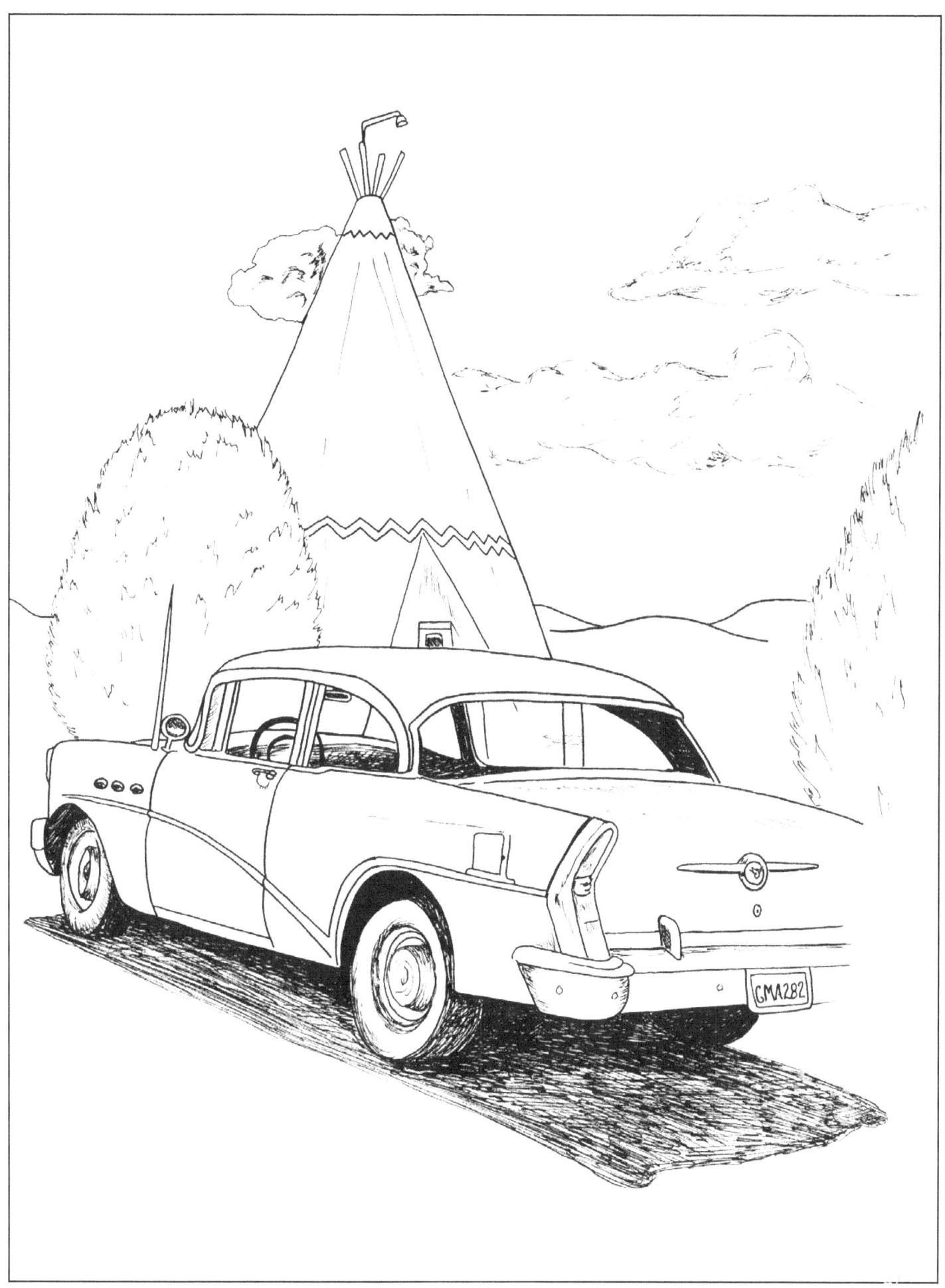

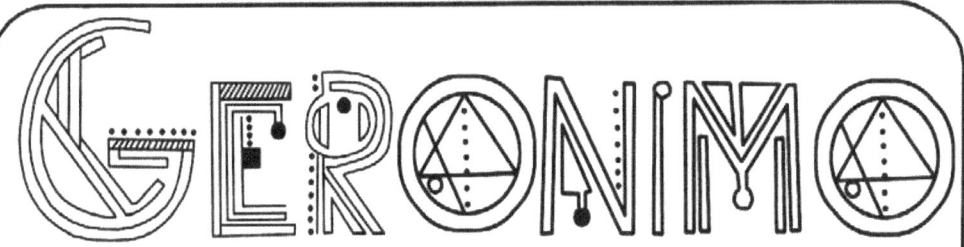

GERONIMO

A must stop as your traveling down Route 66. The Geronimo Trading Post displays many billboards along I-40 and Route 66 to draw in the tourist.

Geronimo Trading Post has American themed artifacts and houses the worlds largest petrified tree, of course half of it is under ground.

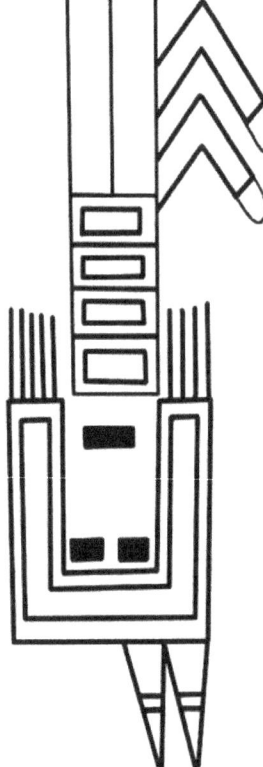
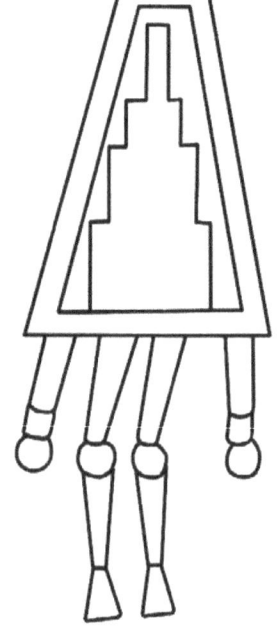

Use this space for photos, stickers, post cards.

APACHE
GIGANTICUS HEADICUS
PAINTED DESERT
ELTRAVADORE
GRAND CANYON
PEACH SPRINGS
FUN RUN
LAPOSADA
NAVAJO
WIGWAM
MOHAVE
BEALE
CURIO SHOP

DESERT
CACTUS
HACKBERRY
TRAINS
ANGEL DELGADILLO
CYRUS AVERY
ARIZONA
METEOR CITY
FLAGSTAFF
COOL SPRINGS
ROAD KILL CAFÉ
GALAXY DINER

PRONGHORN
ASH FORK
GERONIMO
HOLBROOK
WILLIAMS
KINGMAN
MOTHER ROAD
DIABLO
MR.D'Z
HUALAPAI
TOPOCK
BURROS
OATMAN

ROADTRIP
WINSLOW
YELLOW HORSE
SELIGMAN
TEEPEE
TRADING POST
JACK RABBIT

Answer key on page 140

Jack Rabbit Trading Post is located just outside of the town Joseph City.

The oldest Mormon settlement in Arizona. A band of The Church of Jesus Christ of Latter Day Saints settled in the area around the time of 1876. The band of 73 pioneers struggled obtaining water for their crops which resulted in many dams built over Little Colorado River. The first dam was built in 1876 over a period of 18 years. Ten other dams were built due to all of the previous damns being destroyed by the flooding season.

Naming the town started off with Allen's camp in honor of Captain William C. Allen, their leader. The town was renamed in 1878 to St. Joseph to only be changed yet again 45 years later to Joseph City.

When Route 66 was developed through the town, travel and traffic increased. This activity inspired James Taylor to build Jack Rabbit Trading Post in 1949. To promote his newly opened trading post James and a buddy traveled Route 66 to Springfield Missouri , plastering billboards all along the way. Dancing rabbits paired with dancing cowgirls could be seen for more than 1000 miles. Jack Rabbit Trading Post and the Men's Only Store in Winslow created the slogan "Here it is".

The "Here it is" slogan paired with the famous jack rabbit icon still adorn the highways being passed down from generation to generation. Cynthia and Antonio Jaquez run the post today with souvenirs, refreshments and even lemon cake.

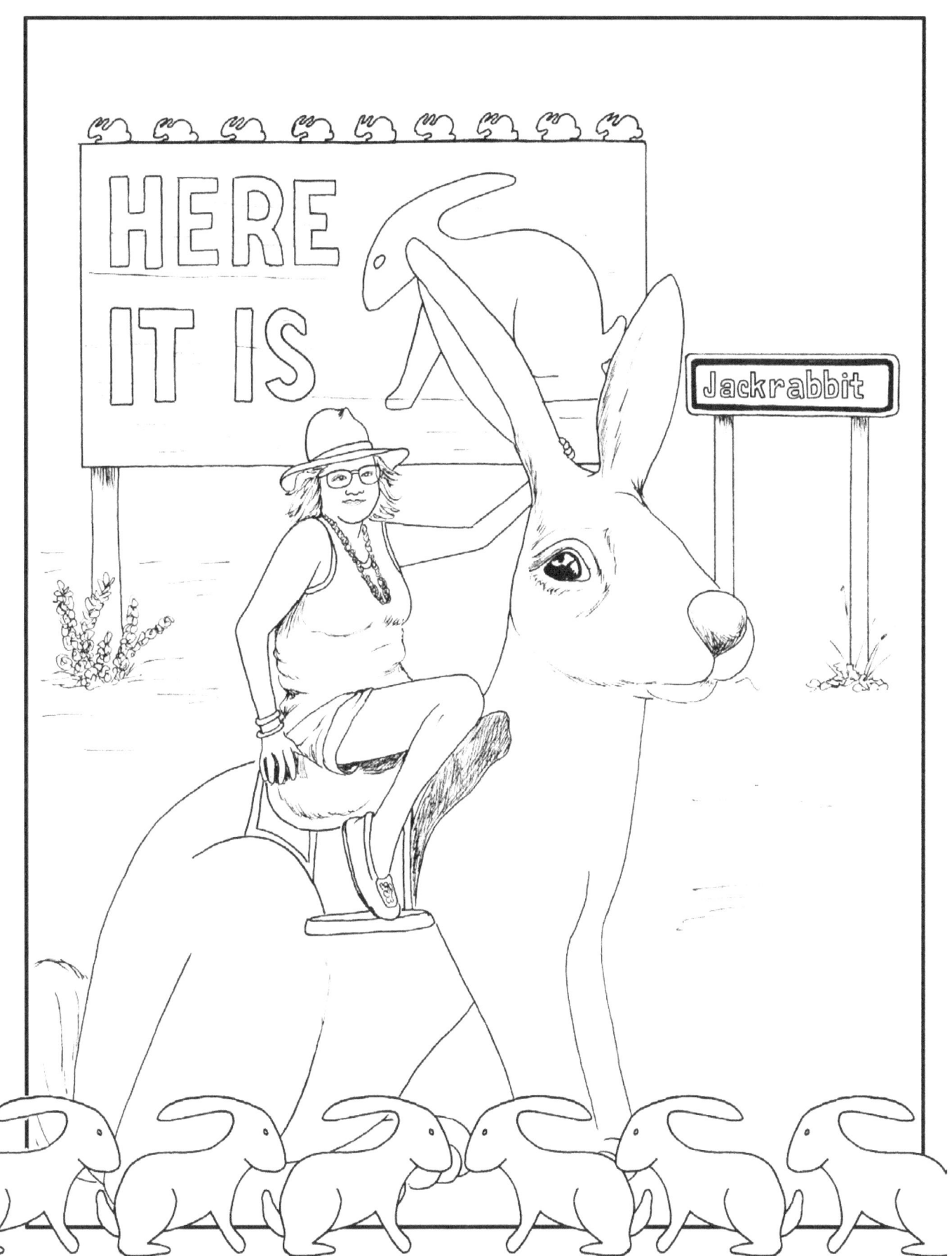

Selfie of you and the Rabbit! Or get a sticker/ stamp from the trading post.

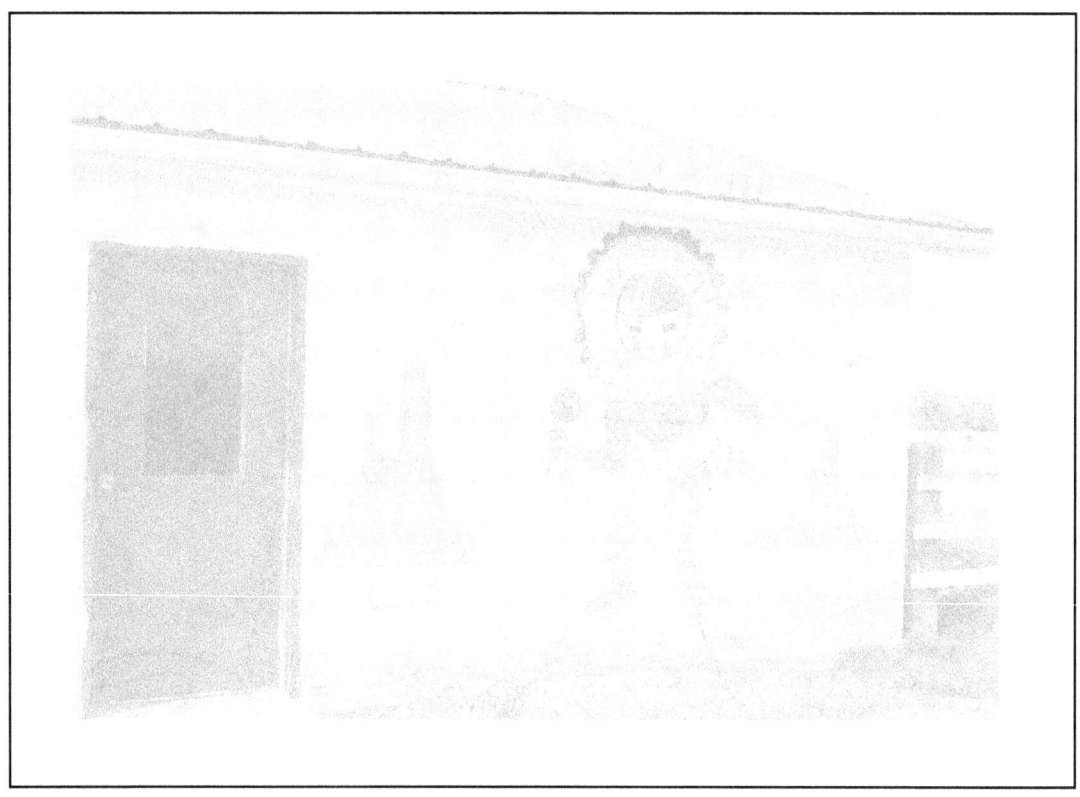

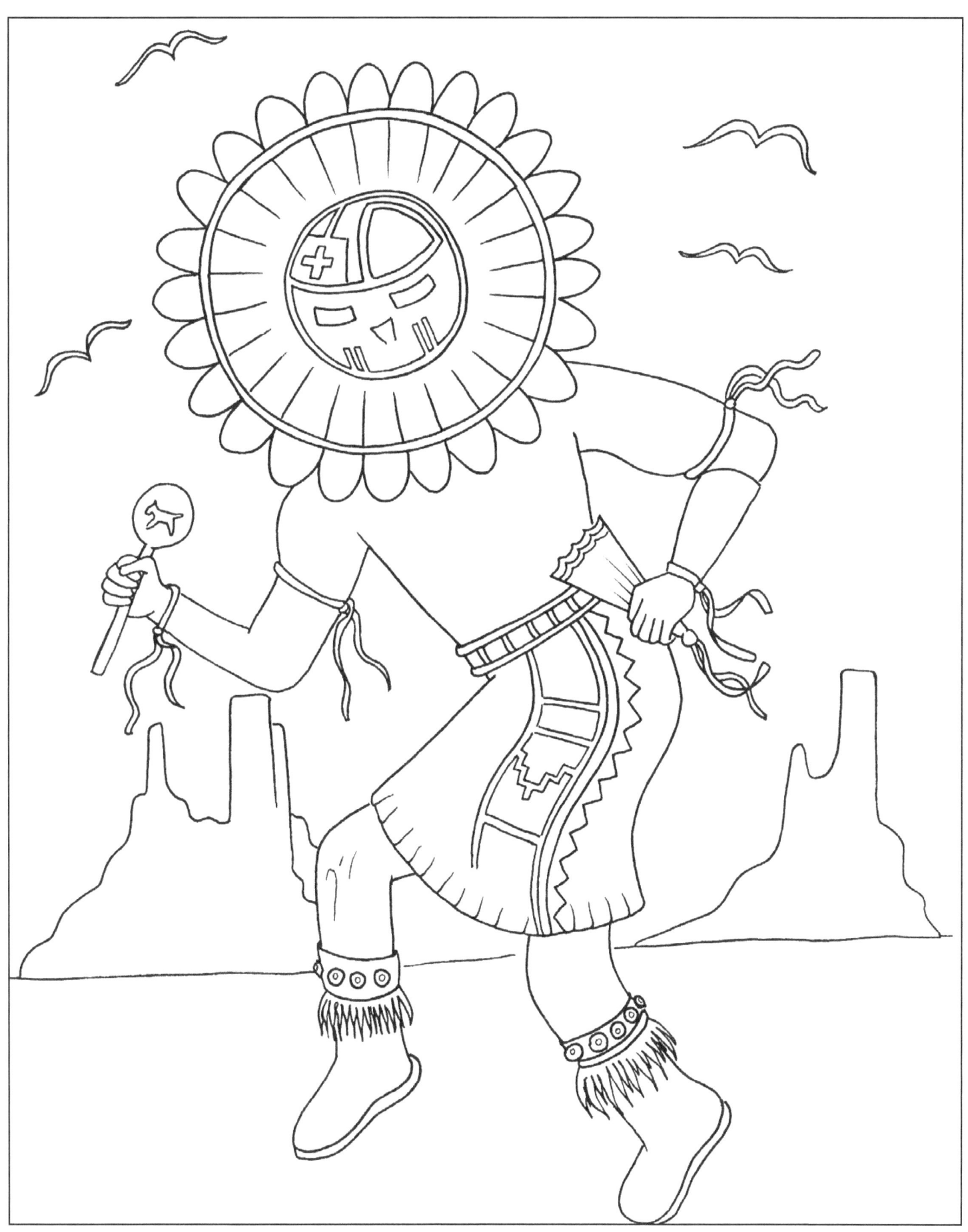

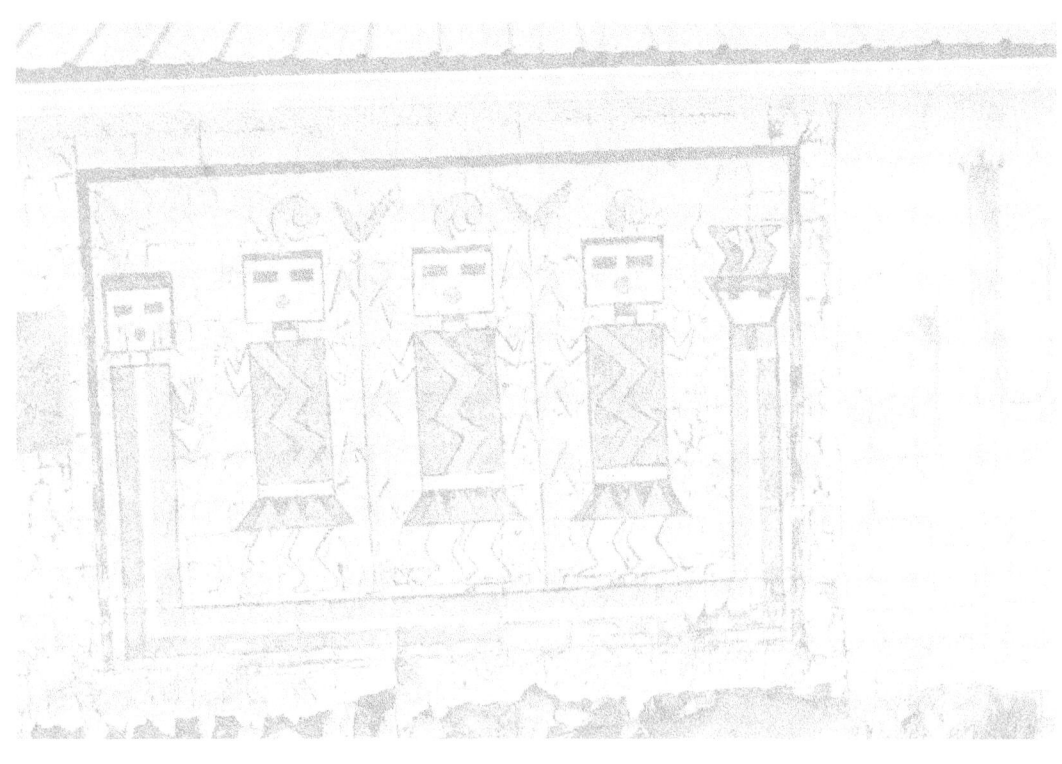

Use this space for photos, stickers, post cards.

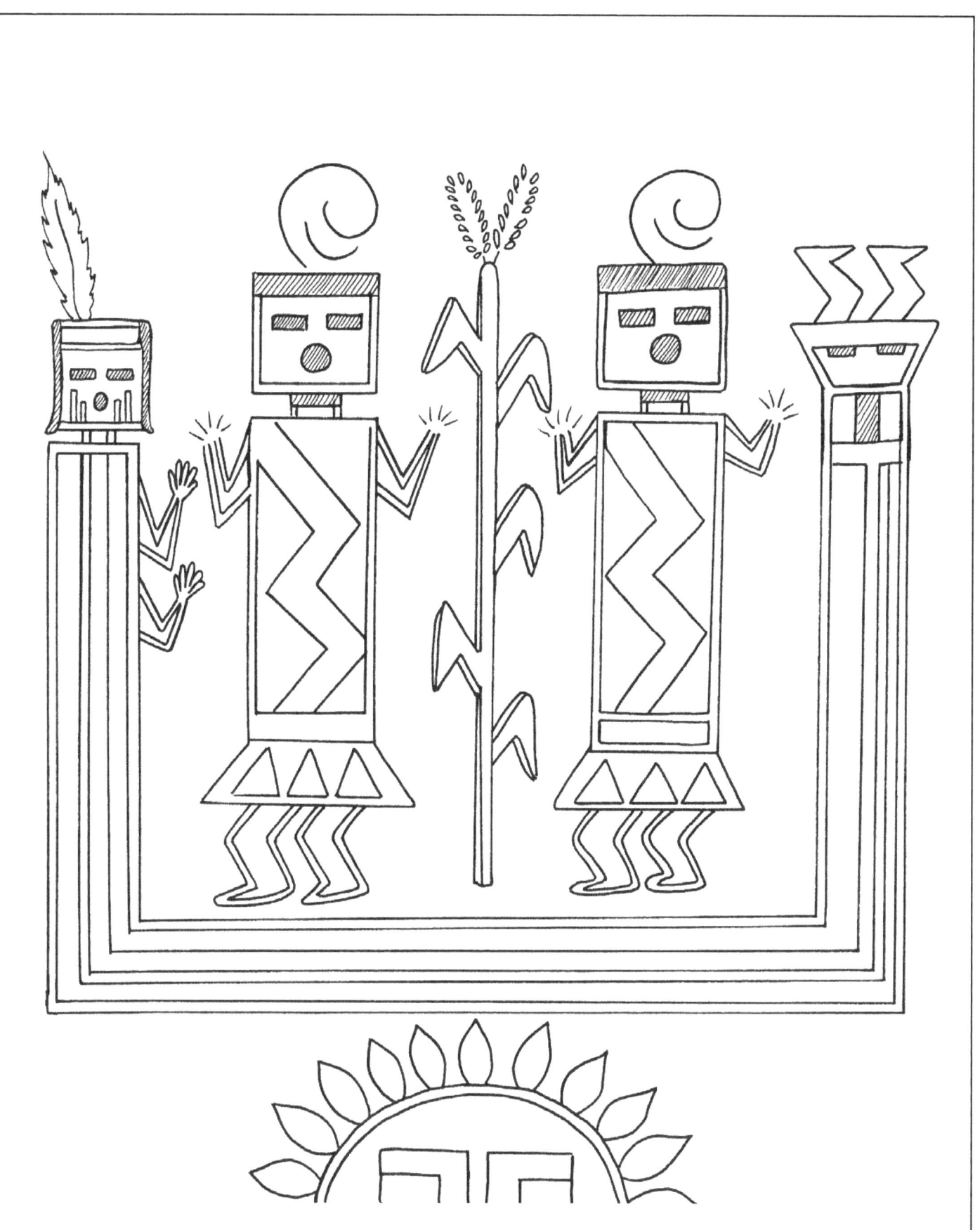

In the early 1880's a community developed for railroad purposes (water, trading etc.) The community grew into a town called Winslow. With at first only being a trading post, the little community grew, it soon became necessary for a Post Office. Once the first stone of the post office was placed on the ground the community had to have a name. It wasn't difficult to figure one out with the railroad President being General Edward Winslow.

A well known man of Winslow, who was instrumental in commerce development was John Lorenzo Hubbell. Developing relations with the Navajo, he was able to bridge the gap between the white people and the Navajo people, following of which he began building Navajo trading posts.

The Hubbell Wholesale Store of 1924 to 1948 still stands today.

Use this space for photos, stickers, post cards.

Find the hippie sculpture on the corner of Winslow and Arizona, Adhere it here.

Use this space for photos, stickers, post cards.

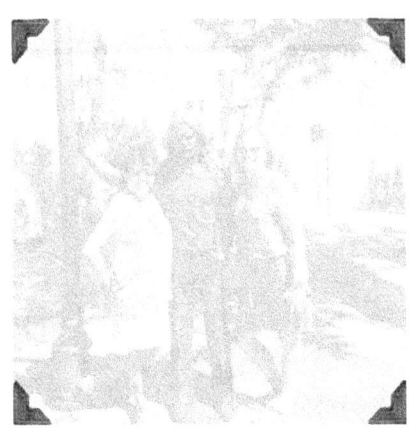

Adhere your selfie standing on the corner in Winslow and Arizona

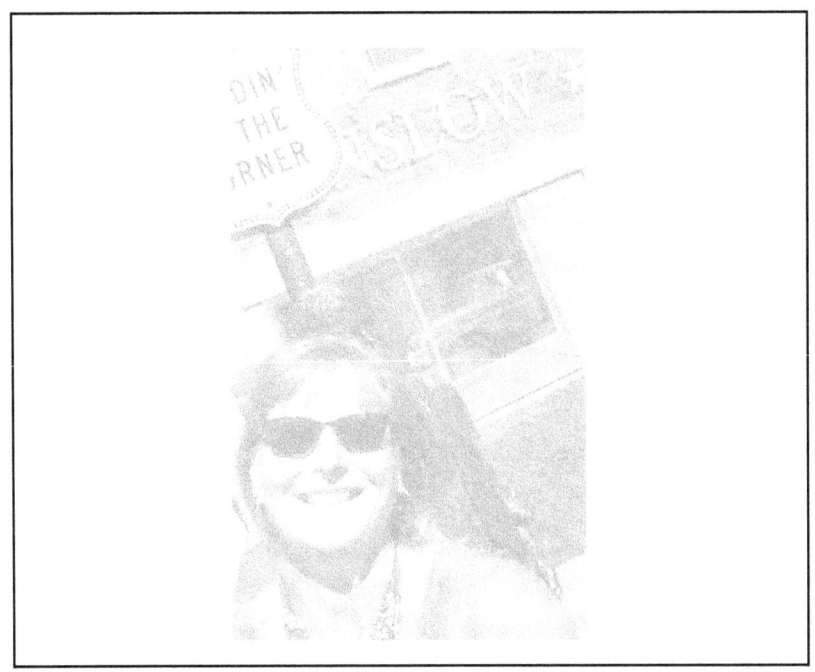

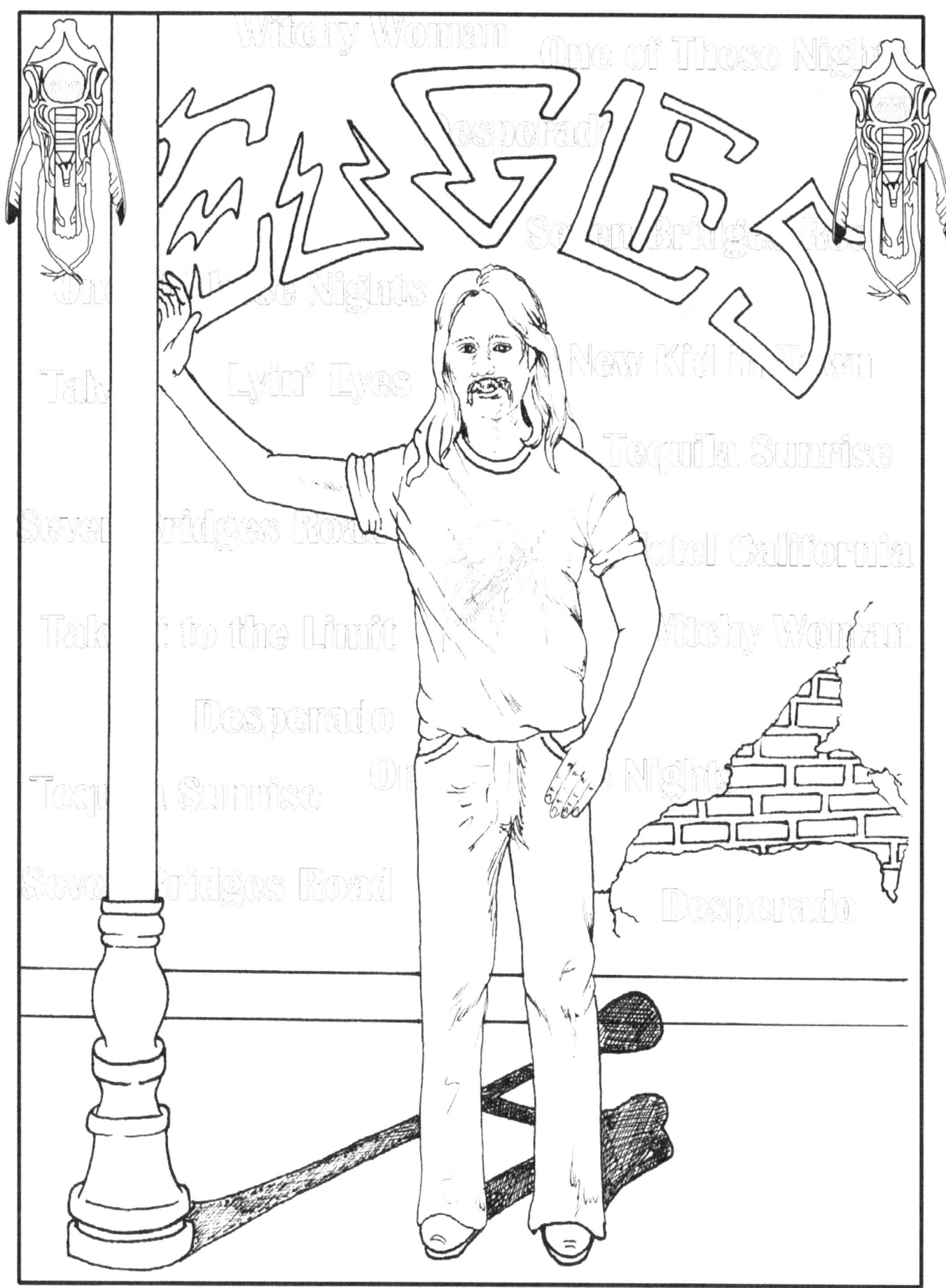

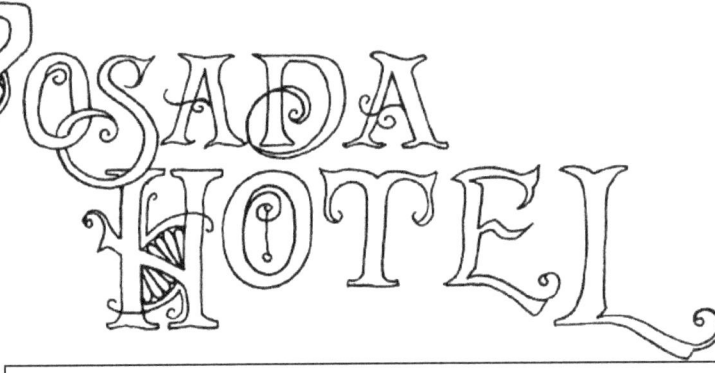

La Posada Hotel

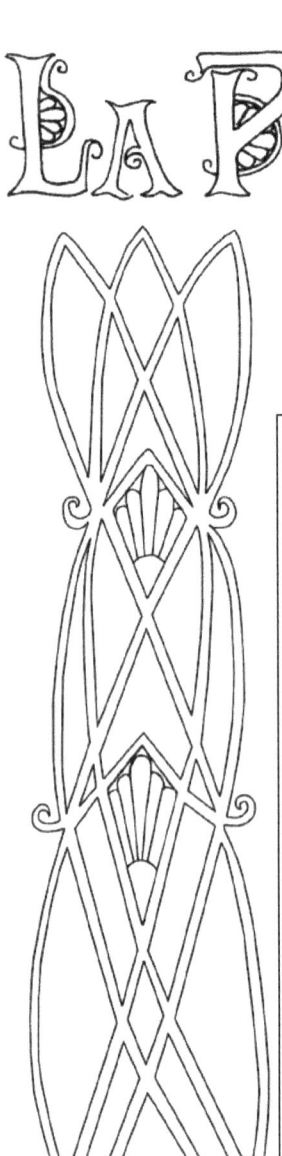

La Posada, Spanish for "the Inn", was Winslow's first Harvey House, opening in 1887. The Harvey Girls arrived three years after the opening. In 1914, a fire destroyed the building. Santa Fe Railroad rebuilt a larger version just a few months later.

In 1930 Fred Harvey and architect, Mary Colter's built the last grand hotel north of the tracks in the center of northern Arizona. The hotel was to be the finest in the Southwest with construction costs budgeted at $1 million in 1929. Rumors were in the air that the grounds and furnishings ended up being $2 million (about $40 million in today's dollars). Mary Colter considered the La Posada her masterpiece. She was not only the designer of the facility but she was responsible for the structures, landscape furniture, maids costumes and dinner china.

The old hotel did not go to waste, the Santa Fe Railroad used the first floor of the older house for division offices and the Harvey girls lived upstairs in the former hotel rooms.

La Posada had several good years, however, sadly in 1957 the hotel closed, the museum quality furnishings were auction off. Much of the building was nearly demolished, being converted into offices for the Santa Fe three years later.

In 1994, the once again abandoned La Posada was left for ruins, facing demolition. With no bank around willing to assist in loans for the historical building, locals took it in their own hands, organizing the La Posada Foundation in the early 90's. With determination and hard work the foundation was able to secure grant funds to assist in saving the building.

In 1997 Allan Affeldt and his wife, saw the 72,000 square-foot historic hotel appear on the national Trust for Historic Preservation's endangered list. Falling in love with the hotel and the unwillingness of letting a renaissance of American history be forgotten, the couple negotiated with the railroad. After three years, they were able to purchase the building knowing that the 12 million dollar restoration costs would be a challenge. With no experience in hotel management, the couple accomplished what once seemed impossible, transforming the once forgotten gem into a magical place and living museum.

Twenty –two years later, travelers can stay in the 54 art – filled beautifully restored rooms of La Posada's Hotel and Gardens, dining in its award-winning Turquoise Room. The hotel attracts railroad aficionados, architects, history buffs, Route 66 fans and travelers from all over the world.

Through this restoration, Mary Colter's architectural style has not been forgotten has created a fan base and has become the pride of the region.

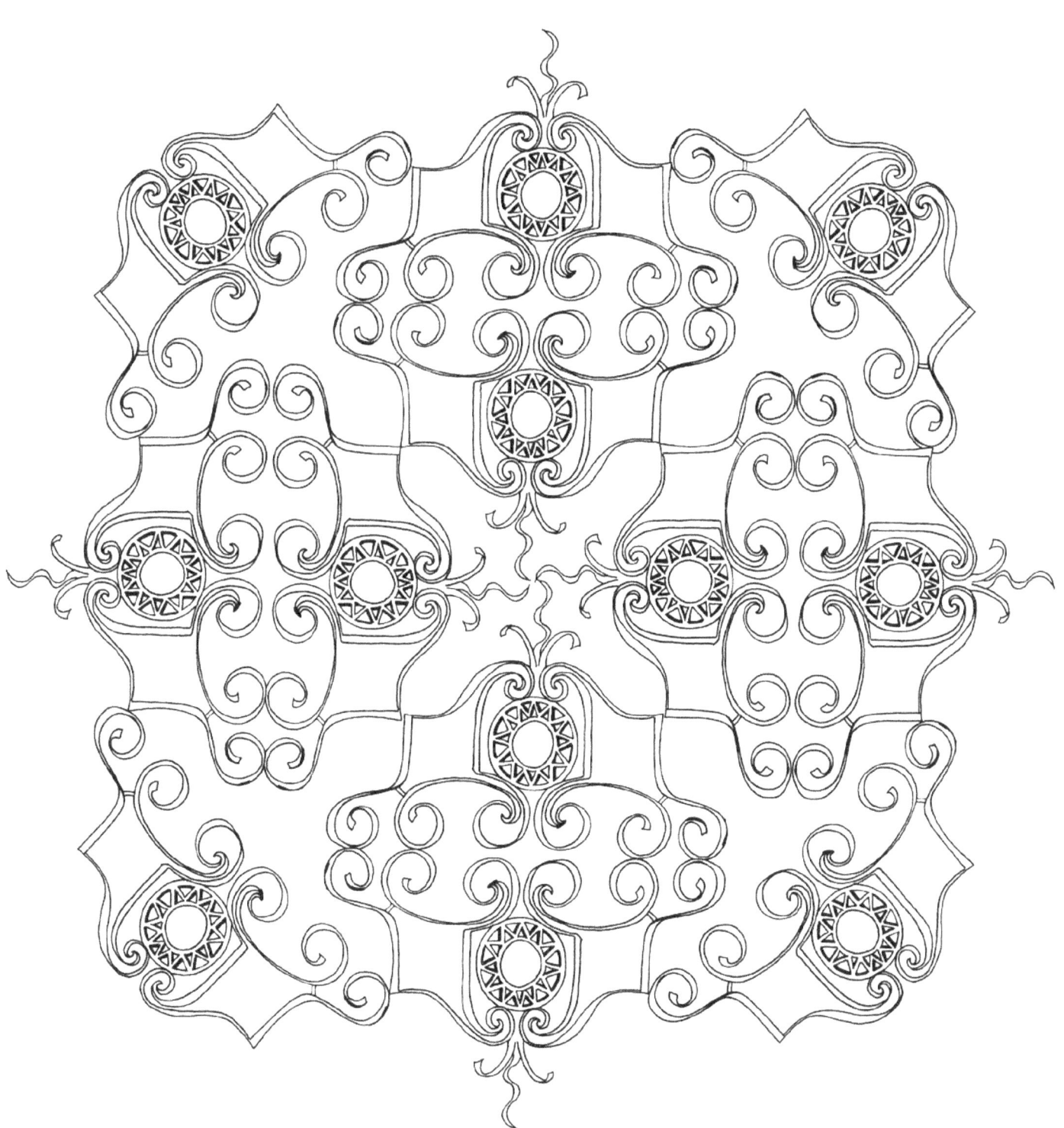

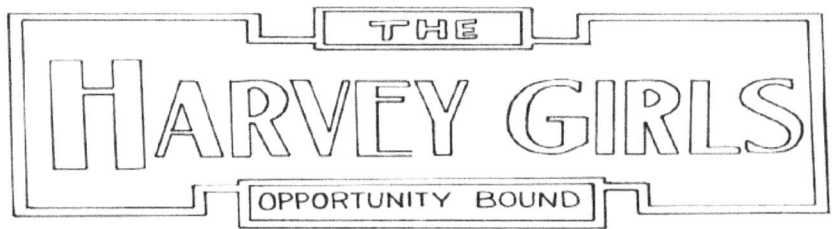

The man responsible for the nation's first chain of restaurants and hotels.

Arriving in New York from England in 1850, Fred Harvey at the age of 15, began his career in the restaurant business. During the Civil War, Harvey was working for the railroad as a mobile mail clerk, traveling from state to state. It is then that he noticed a need for a business that would offer travelers good food and personal service. He promoted his idea to the Santa Fe Railway president who agreed to let Harvey open a dining room in the Santa Fe Topeka depot in 1876.

A year late,r Harvey purchased the hotel in Florence and added restaurant accommodations to his hotel services. Meals were served on tables set with imported linens, silver table service and fine china personalized with his name.   His staff were all woman known as "Harvey Girls". These women who were known for their good looks, fine manners and efficiency, wore black shirtwaist dresses, black bows, starched white aprons and caps.

By 1891, there were 15 successful Harvey House restaurants. His Harvey Girls had the only reputable waitressing job for young women of its time.

When he died in 1901, there were 45 restaurants and 20 dining cars. The empire continued until the decline of the railroad.

Fred's slogan was "If you don't behave like gentlemen, you can't stay here and you can't come again. Now put up your guns and take a drink with Fred Harvey!"

Use this space for photos, stickers, post cards.

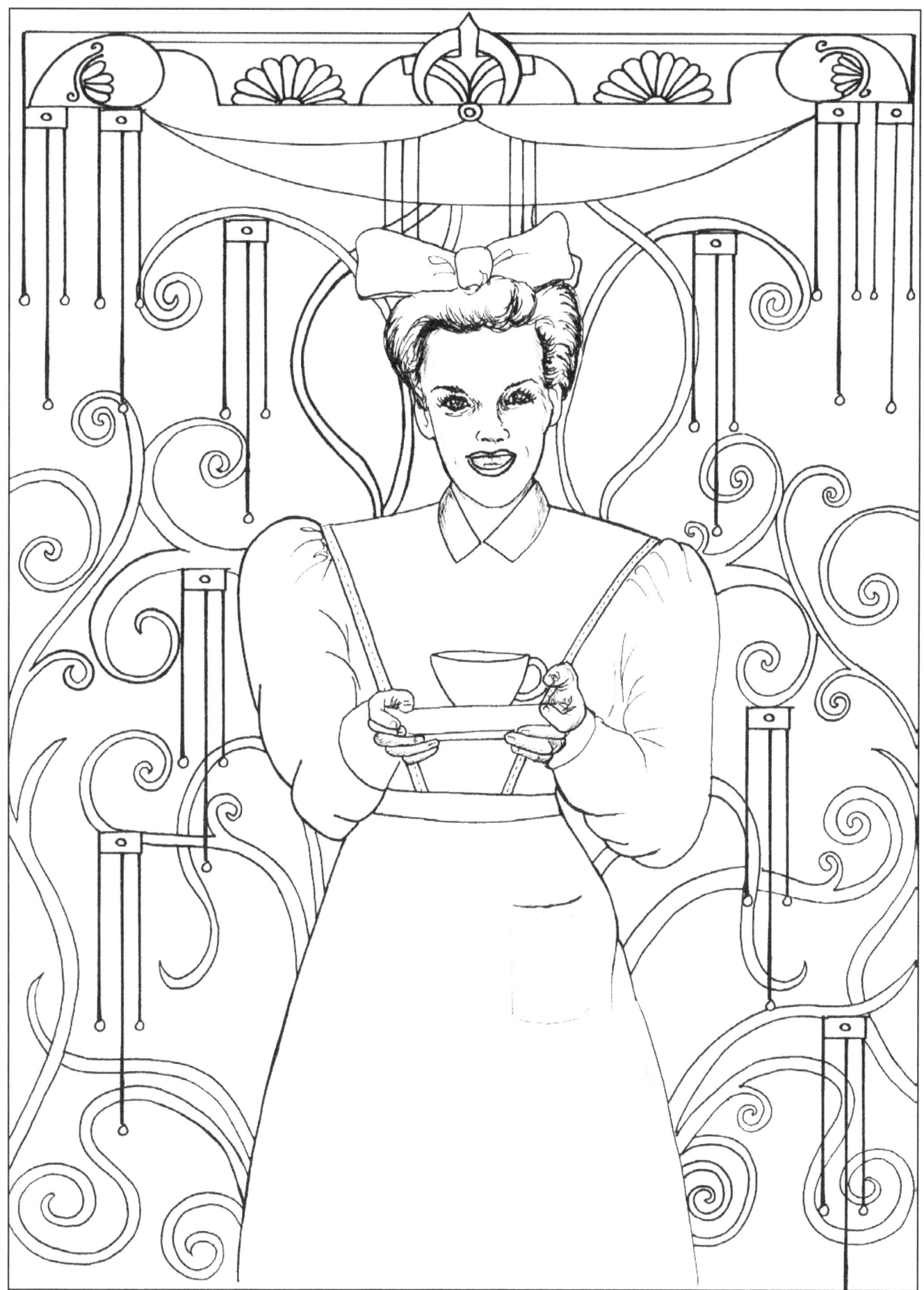

Standing on the Corner in Winslow, Arizona Gift Store

After standing on the corner of Winslow and Arizona, stop in the Winslow Visitor Center (In the historic Hubbell Trading Post)

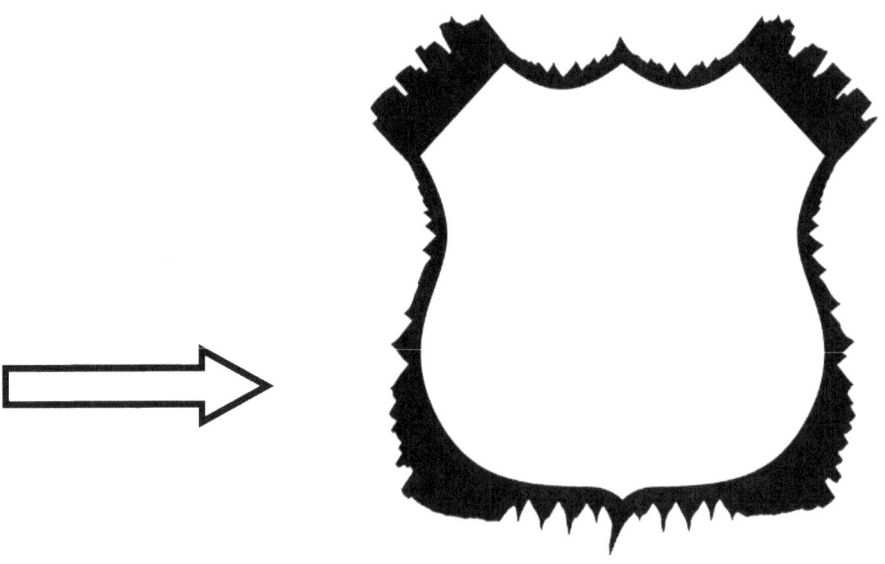

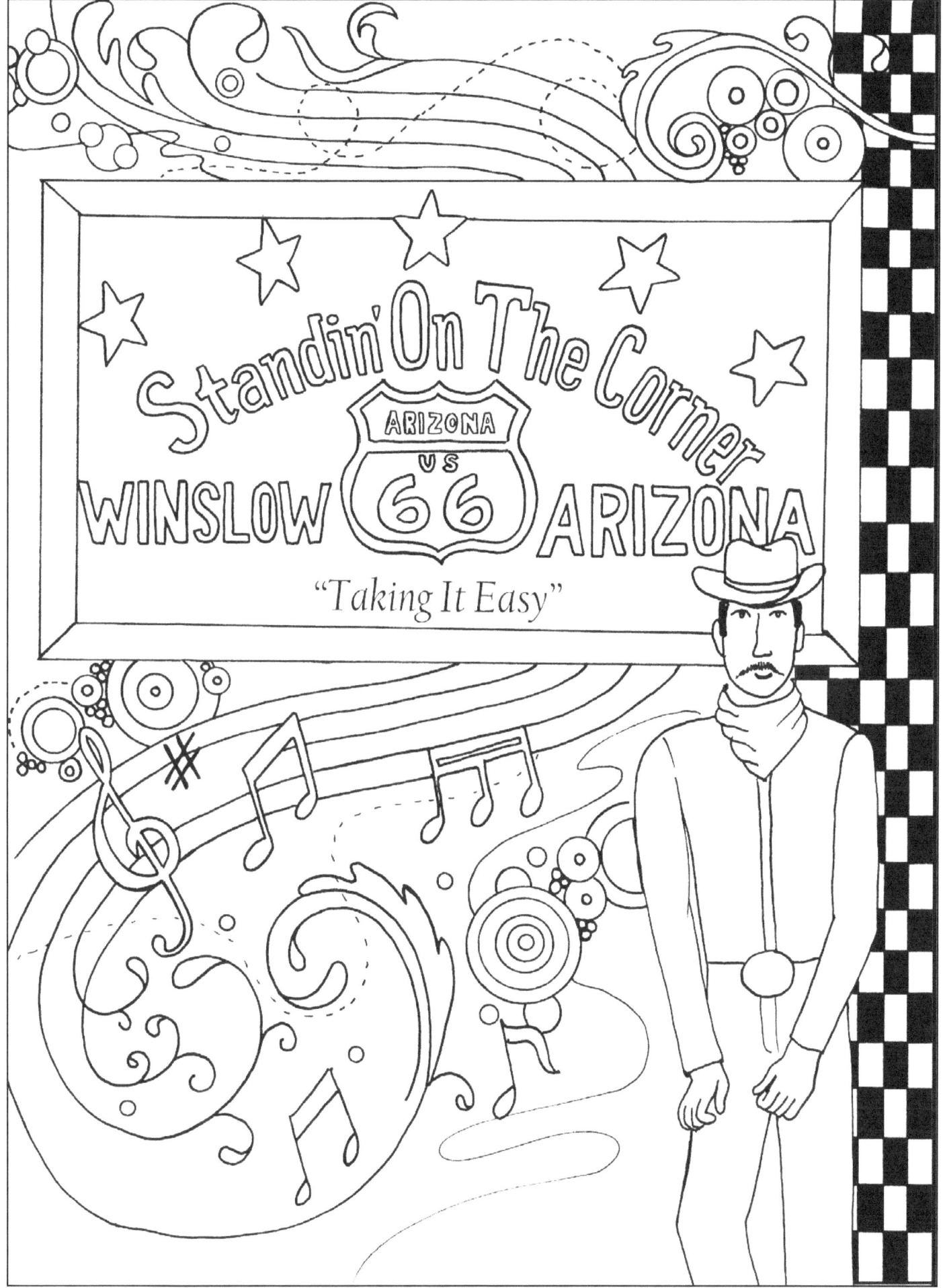

Coconino

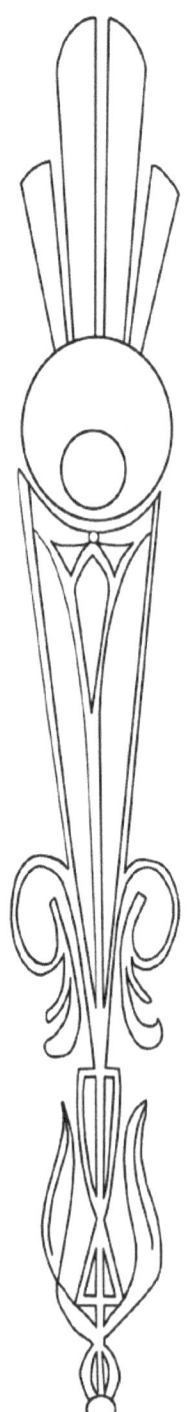

Coconino is the second largest county in the United States just behind San Bernardino. Coconino county separated from Yavapai in 1891 after the experience rapid growth due to the Atlantic and Pacific Railroad construction. The people of the northern reaches were very supportive of the separation, it would cut the travel in half to the county seat which was appointed to Flagstaff.

Today, 30 % of Coconino County is Native American tribes consisting of Navajo, Havasupai, Hopi and others. The county is rich in beauty and blesses with one of the seven wonders of the world, the Grand Canyon. The canyon is one of the deepest gorges on earth with an average depth of one mile and an average width of 10 miles.

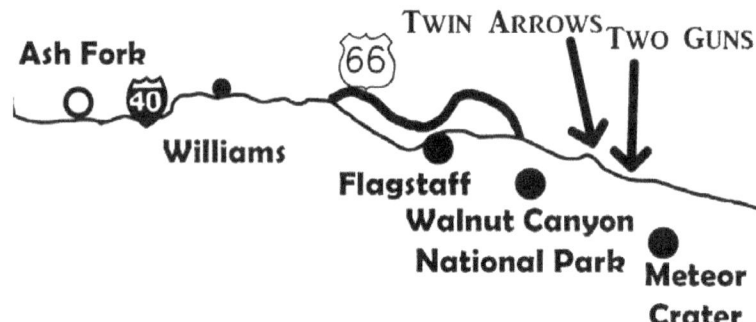

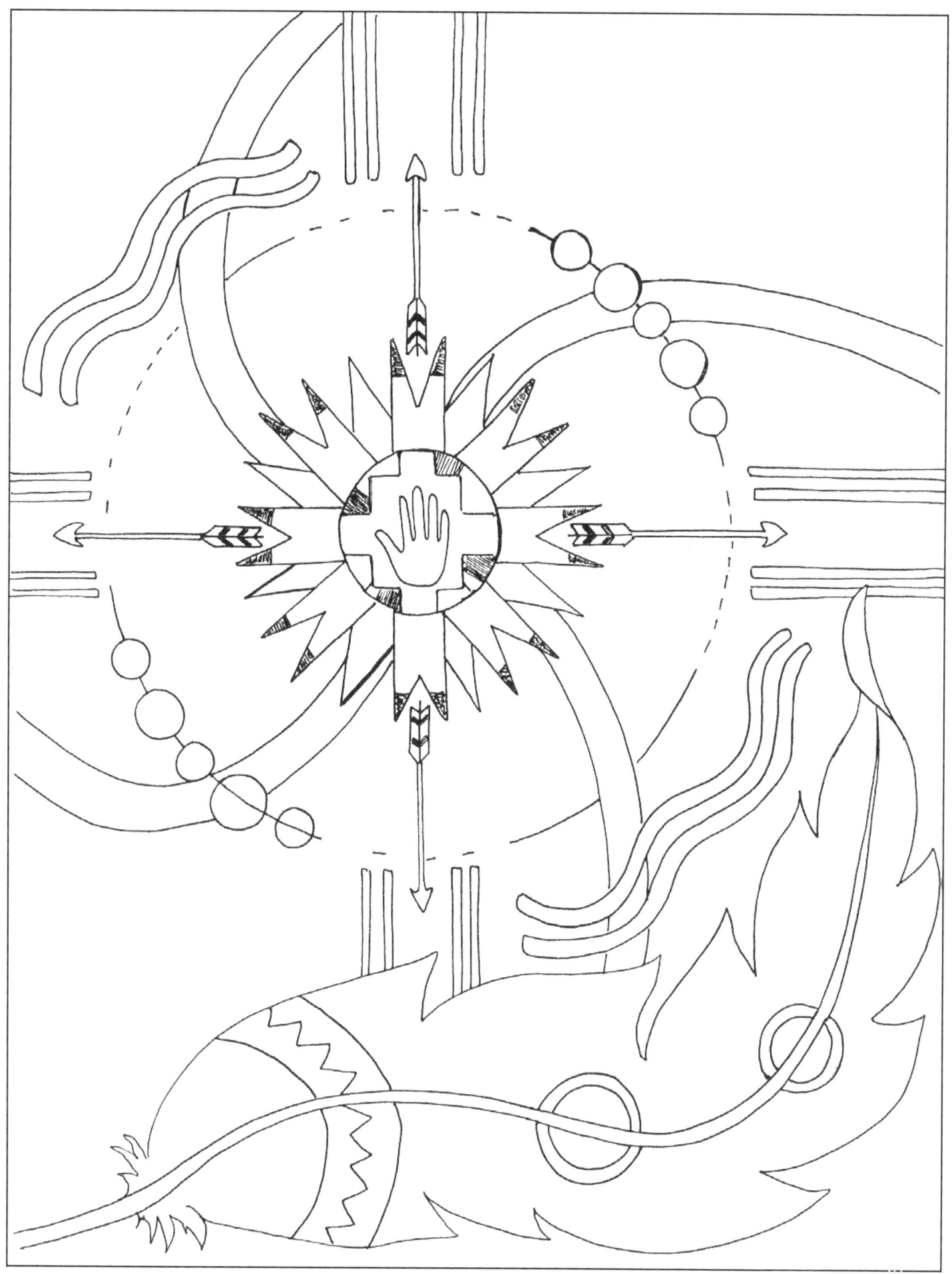

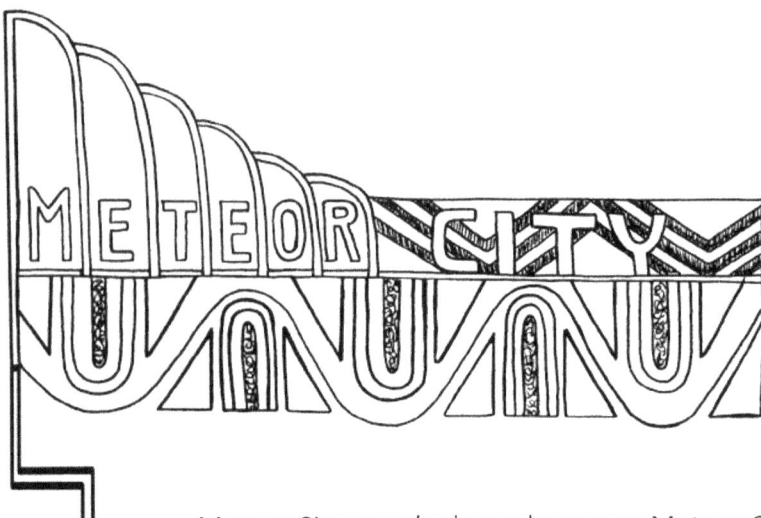

Meteor City wasn't always known as Meteor City or even a city at all, it started out as a trading post. The original trading post was built by D.M. Barringer in 1938, it started out with a gas station with the store following three years later. Along with many items for sell there was also a photo opportunity and a crater observation deck and for 25 cents, you could view the crater through a telescope.

The post did not gain its geodesic dome and the worlds largest dream catcher until 1979. The dome lured travelers off of Route 66 with the moto "Easy Off - Easy On".

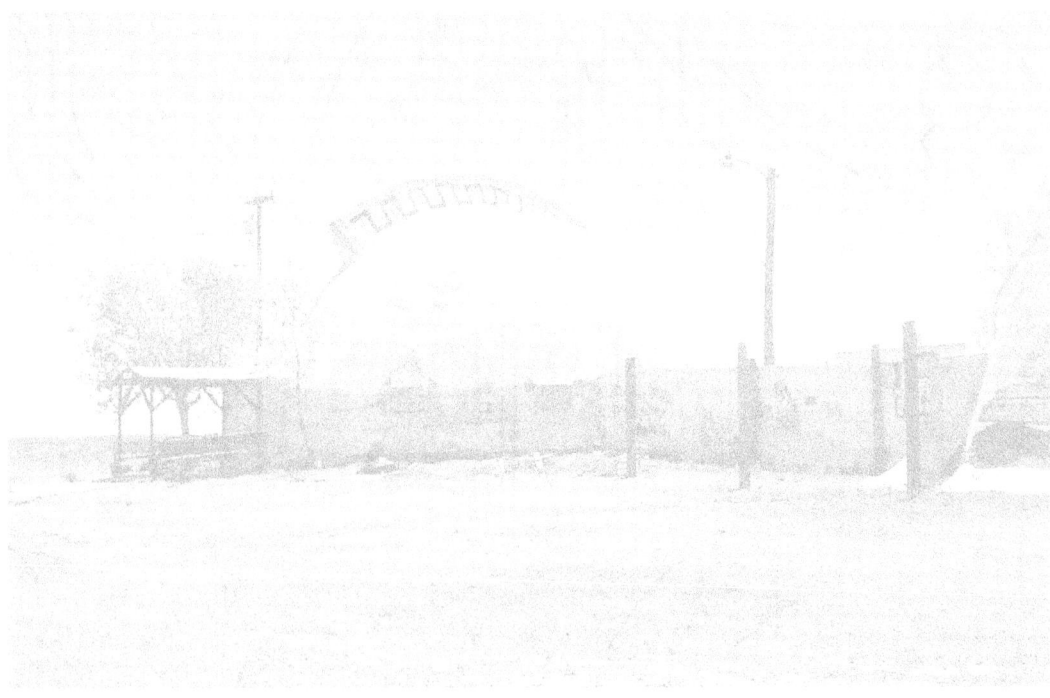

Use this space for photos, stickers, post cards.

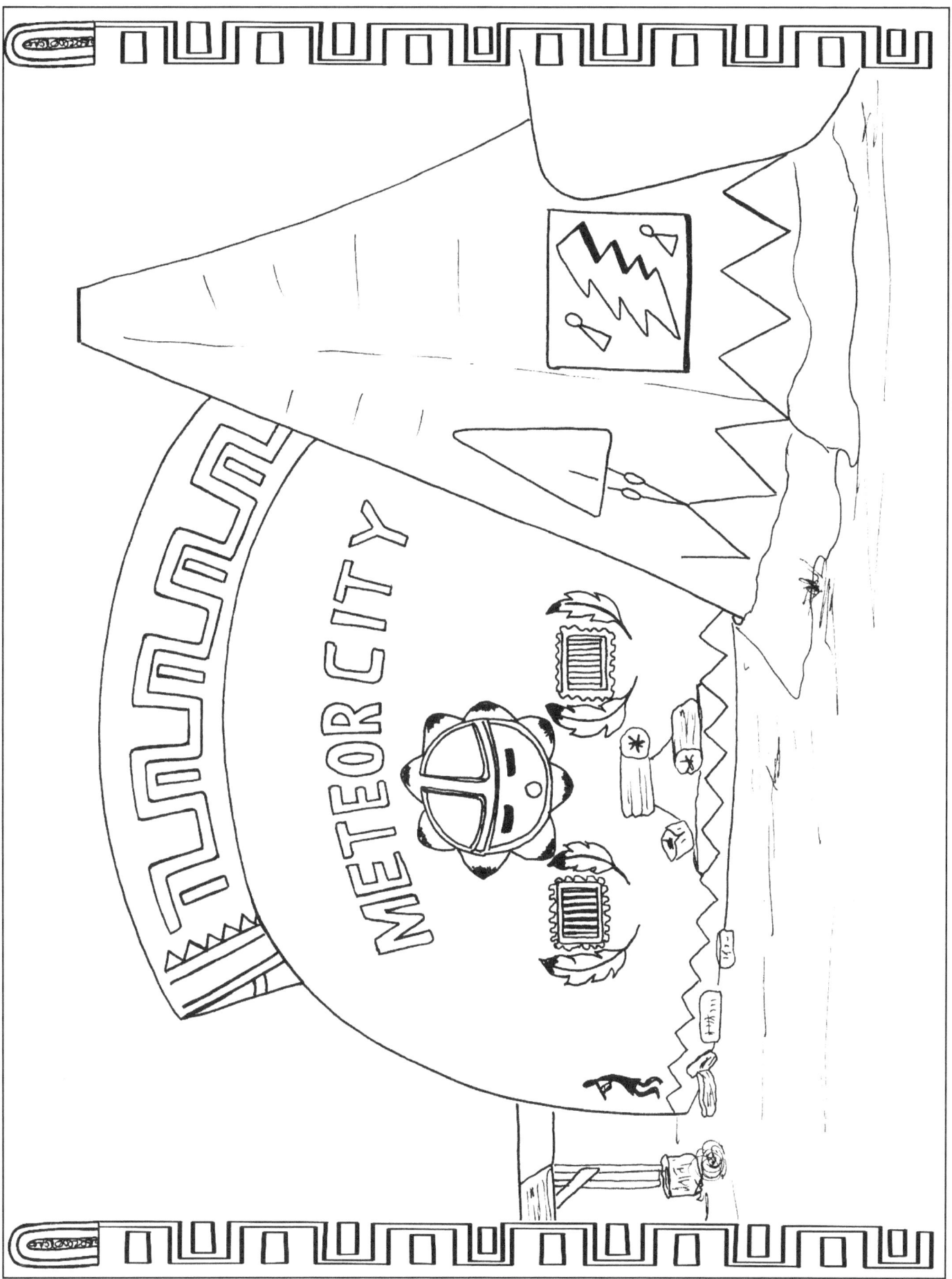

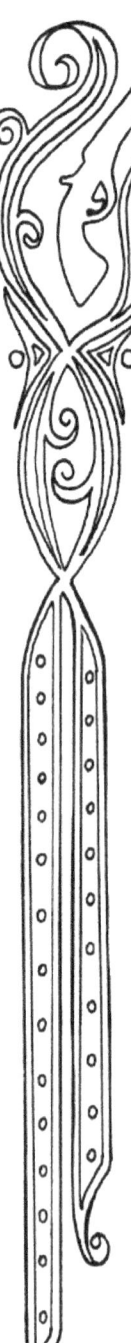

Two Guns

There are actually two ghost towns on this segment of land, Two Guns, and Canyon Diablo, one almost on top of the other. Two Guns has the look and even the feel of a historic landmark of the wild west, with its rusty barbed wire aligned with the road, ravines cutting through the middle of the town, bridges, abandoned KOA campground and gas station. Historical it is not, but what it does have is a brutal past that possibly cursed the land that Two Guns rests on.

The Wild West name Two Guns came from a the original inhabitant of the area, a wild, violent individual called "Two Gun" Miller. It is said that this eccentric hermit lived in a cave in nearby Canyon Diablo and was hostile to visitors. It is believed that his spirit lives in Two Guns. But the curse doesn't start there, it starts before Two Gun Miller. The story of the curse begins with the Apaches and the Navajos.

In 1878, the Apaches raided two Navajo camps along the Little Colorado taking their food and supplies and killing everyone in their path except for three girls, whom they took with them. Twenty five Navajo men went after the raid party, tracking them into Diablo Canyon; the Apache had seemed to have disappeared. The scouts felt warm air and heard voices coming from a crack in the ground. They realized it was the Apache raid party hiding in a cave right under their feet. They found the mouth of the cave in the ravine and began filling it full of wood and lit a fire. The Apaches tried to escape to only be killed at the mouth of the cave just like their two guards, they were trapped. The Apache tried to bargain with the Navajo warriors however when the Navajo realized that the three young girls were dead they stoked the fire even more. Knowing their fate, the Apache began to sing death chants as they killed their horses and stacked them in the entrance of the cave in an attempt to stop the heat and smoke. As the chants echoed into the ravine, the fire roared on. The next day, after the fire was completely out and the chants were silent, the Navajo went back into the cave to find all of the Apache horses dead, charred and stacked and 42 asphyxiated Apache warriors. The Navajo retrieved the stolen items and quickly left. From then on local tribes avoided the cave, considering it and the surrounding land, to be cursed. The bones of the horses and Apache remained in their cave until the trading post opened and the remains were sold off as souvenirs.

The Route 66 travelers were lured into Two Guns because of the Apache Caves, trading posts and even a small zoo. The original alignment of Route 66 crossed Canyon Diablo at the stone ruins of Two Guns along the rim of the Canyon. Looking closely, you can still see the Route 66 Bridge that crossed the canyon that gave early explorers such a problem and gained the canyon its name. The curse of the land continues, for neither Two Guns nor Canyon Diablo survived.

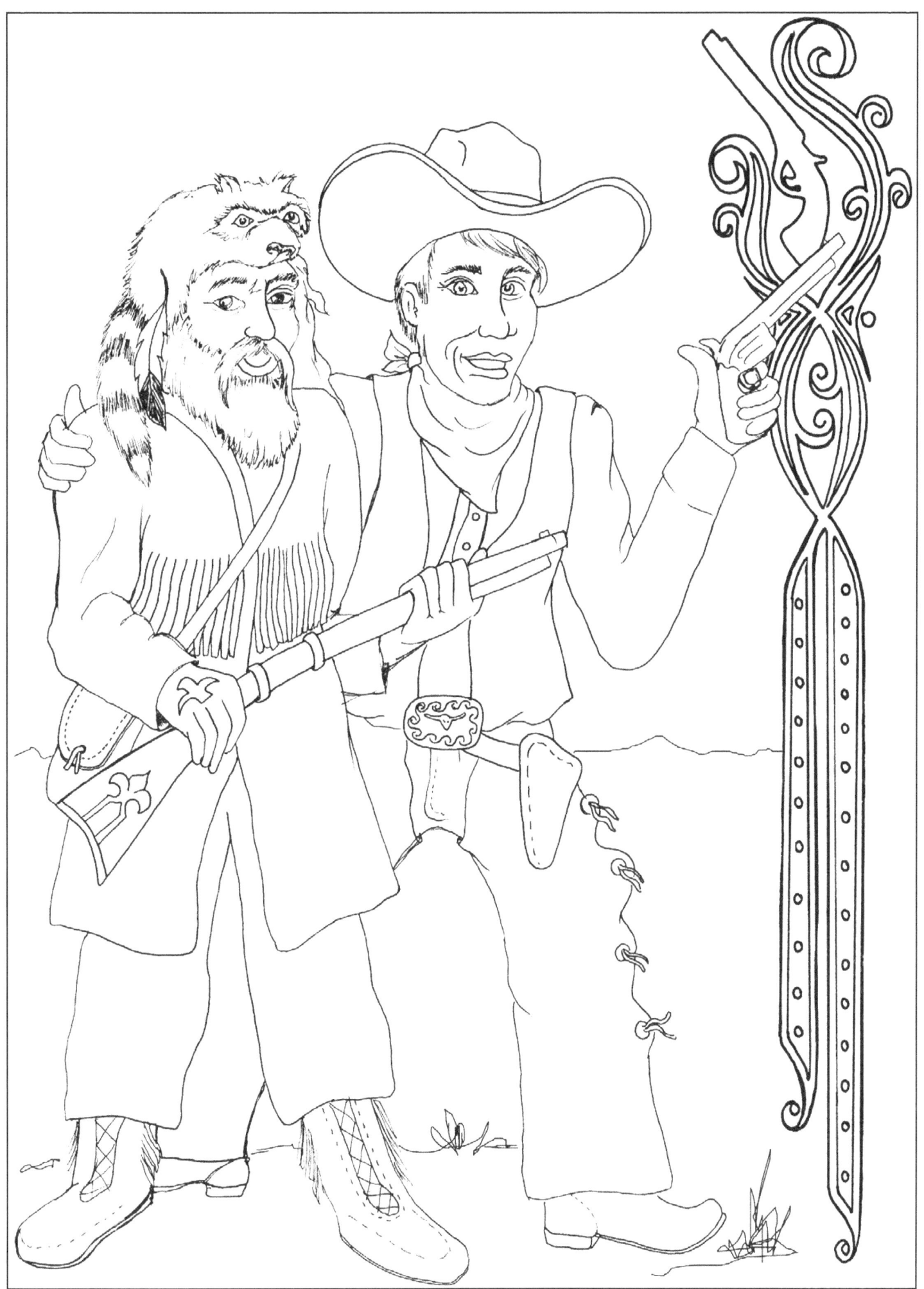

Canyon Diablo Shootout

The Wild West had many gunfights some memorable and some forgotten. Probably one of the most remembered gunfight between lawmen and bandits occurred on April 8, 1905 in the town Canyon Diablo which is now a ghost town.

Two young men in their mid-twenties, William Evans and John Shaw, rode into Winslow, Arizona April 7th 1905. The boys were tired of the hard life of a cowboy and were more interested in the easier life of banditry. Shortly before midnight the two dressed in their finest clothes, entered the Wigwam saloon, headed straight for the bar, and ordered a couple of shots of rot gut whiskey, which was common at the time. The two boys grabbed their shots, swung around from the bar facing the crowd, they immediately noticed a good size pile of gold and silver coins in the center of a poker game table in play. Setting their glasses down without even a sip taken, sauntered over to the poker table, and pulled their revolvers. They swiftly claimed the group of men's spoils of the game, estimated to be around $600 of silver coins. Without a single shot fired, the two men fled out the front door for their quick escape.

The bar keep immediately notified the owner of the saloon, which was also the deputy sheriff. After his investigation of the crime scene, Deputy Pete Pemberton notified the Navajo County Sheriff, Chet Houck, and Winslow's City Marshal, Bob Giles. Together they went after the young cowboys, now bandits. The trail was easy to follow, the two boys left the saloon so quickly that they had scattered a stream of coins. Following the coin path, the lawmen ended up at the railroad tracks. Assuming that the two fugitives jumped on a moving train heading west to Flagstaff, the lawmen boarded the next train hoping to catch up with them. Once they reached the depot in Flagstaff they realized they had been dupe. At some point, the bandits had jumped off the train, or possibly never even got on it. Disheartened the two law men headed back to the train depot, boarding the return train to Winslow. While on the train the sheriff received word that there was two suspicious men seen hiding behind some bushes along the railroad tracks, close by the Canyon Diablo turn. Almost a ghost town, Canyon Diablo was still known as the "toughest Hell hole in the West," even in 1905. This might have been a good reason why the two bandits went there for refuge as oppose to Flagstaff, where they would be more apt to get caught.

The sheriff had a gut feeling that the men hiding were the two ornery side winders. Not wanting to be fooled again, the sheriff waited until the train past Canyon Diablo before getting off. After having the conductor stop the train, the lawmen proceeded to walk back west towards Canyon Diablo. With the sun quickly setting, the lawmen arrived into town, proceeded to the small trading post, where they interrogated Fred Volz, the owner. Mr. Volz told the men that earlier that day he had seen two well-dressed men standing in front of the trading post looking like they had stirred up some trouble somewhere. No more did the words come out of Volz's mouth when the two desperados came strutting around the corner of the trading post. Looking up they shockingly saw the sheriff and the lawmen side kicks, they knew they had been spotted. The two bandits took to their heels, making a break for the train depot. The lawmen hot tailed after the bandits, swiftly closing in on the short distance. With only six feet in between them, the sheriff demanded them to submit to search. One of the bandits rapidly spit out, "No one searches us!". All four men, standing near face to face, suddenly went for their side arms. Shaw fired first, and in a matter of a few seconds twenty one shots had been fired by the group. With Evans wounded, Shaw tried to reload his pistol, however sheriff Houck managed one more round off that struck him in the head killing him instantly. Even with guns a blazon at short range the three-second bullet-flying explosion resulted in one fatality and three who suffered non life threating wounds.

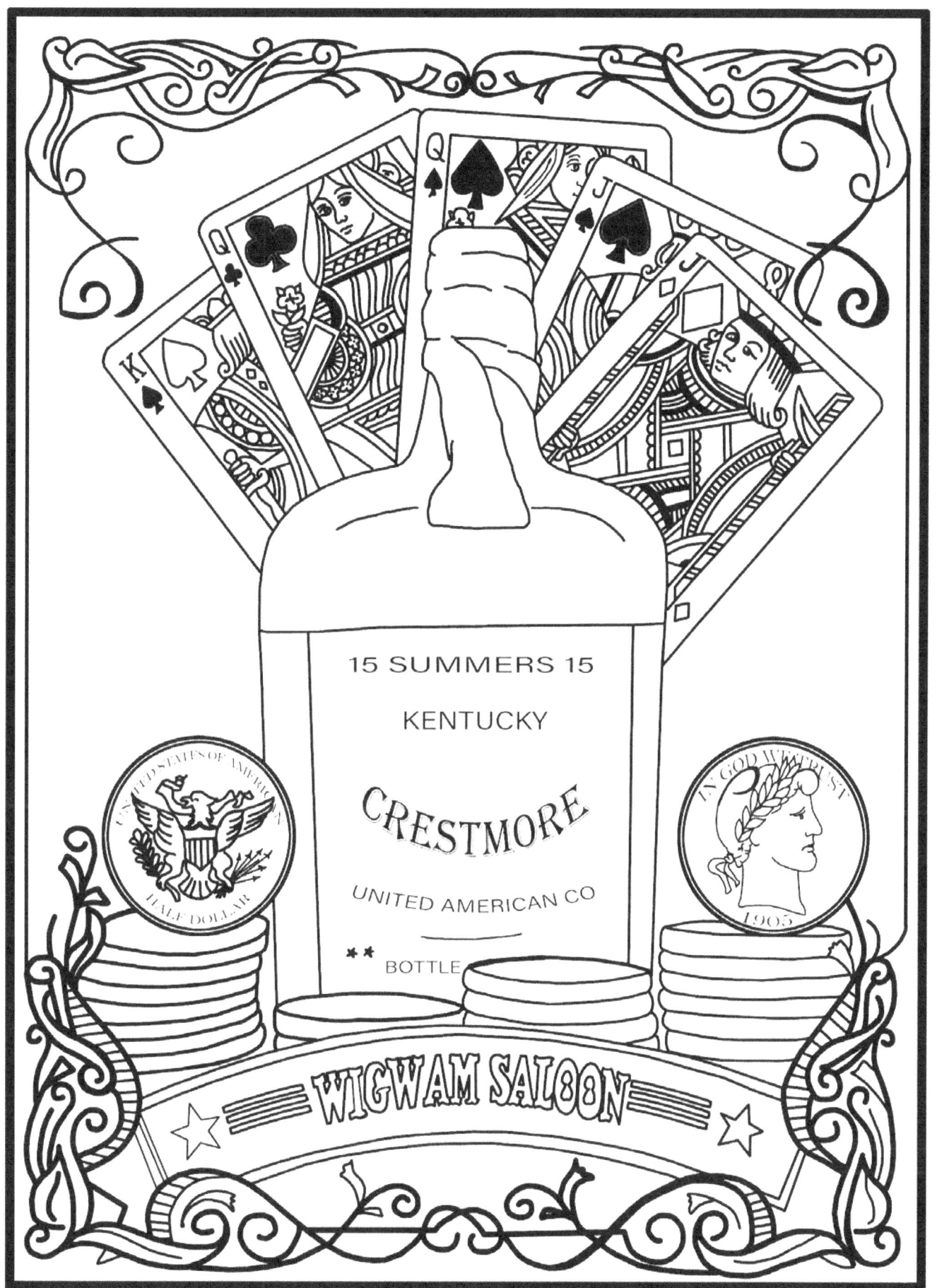

(Canyon Diablo Shootout continued)

The owner of the trading post just so happened to have a pine box readily available (after all, it was the Roughest Hell hole in the West). With no need for an undertaker, the sheriff put Shaw's body in the pine coffin and buried him in a shallow grave within the town cemetery. The wounded Evans was taken to the hospital in Winslow where he recovered and later was sent to prison for nine years.

The story does not end here! The following evening back at the Wigwam saloon, a group of drunken cowboys, were carrying on about the exciting event. One cowboy claimed that it just was not fair that poor ole Shaw did not even get his last sip of whiskey (remember he left it sitting at the bar). Laughingly the cowboys decided they were going to place their due respect to Shaw and give him that drink that he paid for. Staggering, the group grabbed their bottle of whiskey and hopped aboard the train heading to Canyon Diablo drinking the entire ride. At the break of dawn, they arrived at the Canyon Diablo stop, having a few more drinks then went to the trading post keeper, Mr. Volz, to borrow a few shovels from him. Mr. Volz was very appalled by the plan and refuged to assist the drunken cowboys. However, after some persuasion or fear, the shopkeeper reluctantly them use a couple of shovels but only if they took his Kodak Brownie camera and fired off a few shots. The old shopkeeper was thinking if he had a few photos of the bandit as proof of death that he might be able to collect bounty. The men took the shovels and the camera and headed off to the shallow rocky grave of Shaw's corpse. Once they had Shaw's coffin dug up they opened it and two of the cowboys reached in and lifted Shaw's body out. Leaning him up against the picket fence that surrounded another man's grave the cowboys were surprised to see Shaw appeared to be smiling as if he was pleased to get that last drink. Feeling horrified by Shaw's facial expression, the men quickly gave Shaw a "plentiful gulp of whiskey", took a few pictures, briskly replaced the body back in the coffin with a half-empty bottle of whiskey (they weren't in the mood to drink after a dead smiling man), said some prayers, reburied him and skedaddle on out.

As it turns out, unfortunately there was not a bounty for Shaw. The photos taken that early morning by the drunken cowboys never had the chance to be used to claim reward money, however they were not wasted. The photos made for great decoration and conversation pieces as they hung on the wall at the Wigwam saloon for the remaining years of the building, which was torn down in the 1940's.

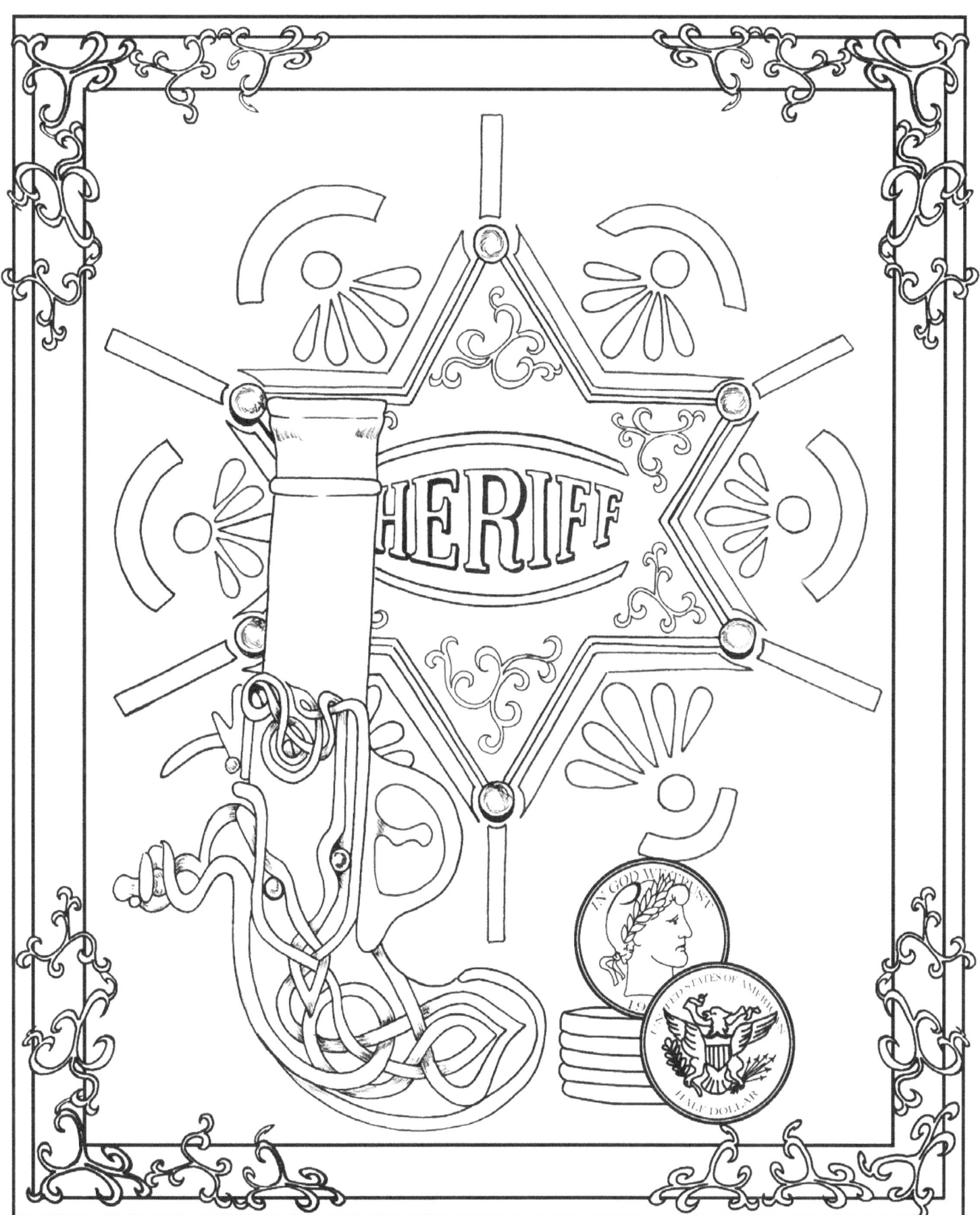

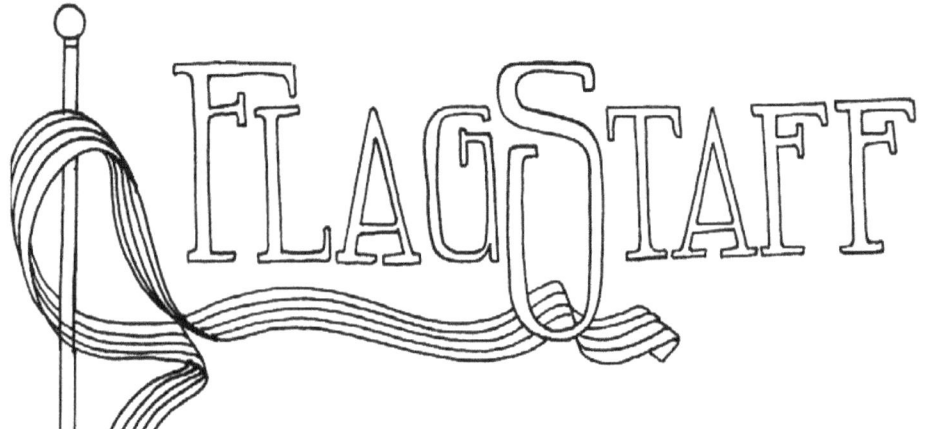

Flagstaff

Flagstaff is surrounded by desert, pine forests and mountains. Sitting at an elevation of 7,000 feet, Flagstaff is the highest point along route 66.

The city is named after a Ponderosa Pine Flagpole. The then town was settled in 1876, from the many ranchers, lumber mills and, of course, the railroad.

It took 52 years before Flagstaff was incorporated, not really growing and prospering until the 60's, when the town grew into a vibrant city as it is known today.

Use this space for photos, stickers, post cards.

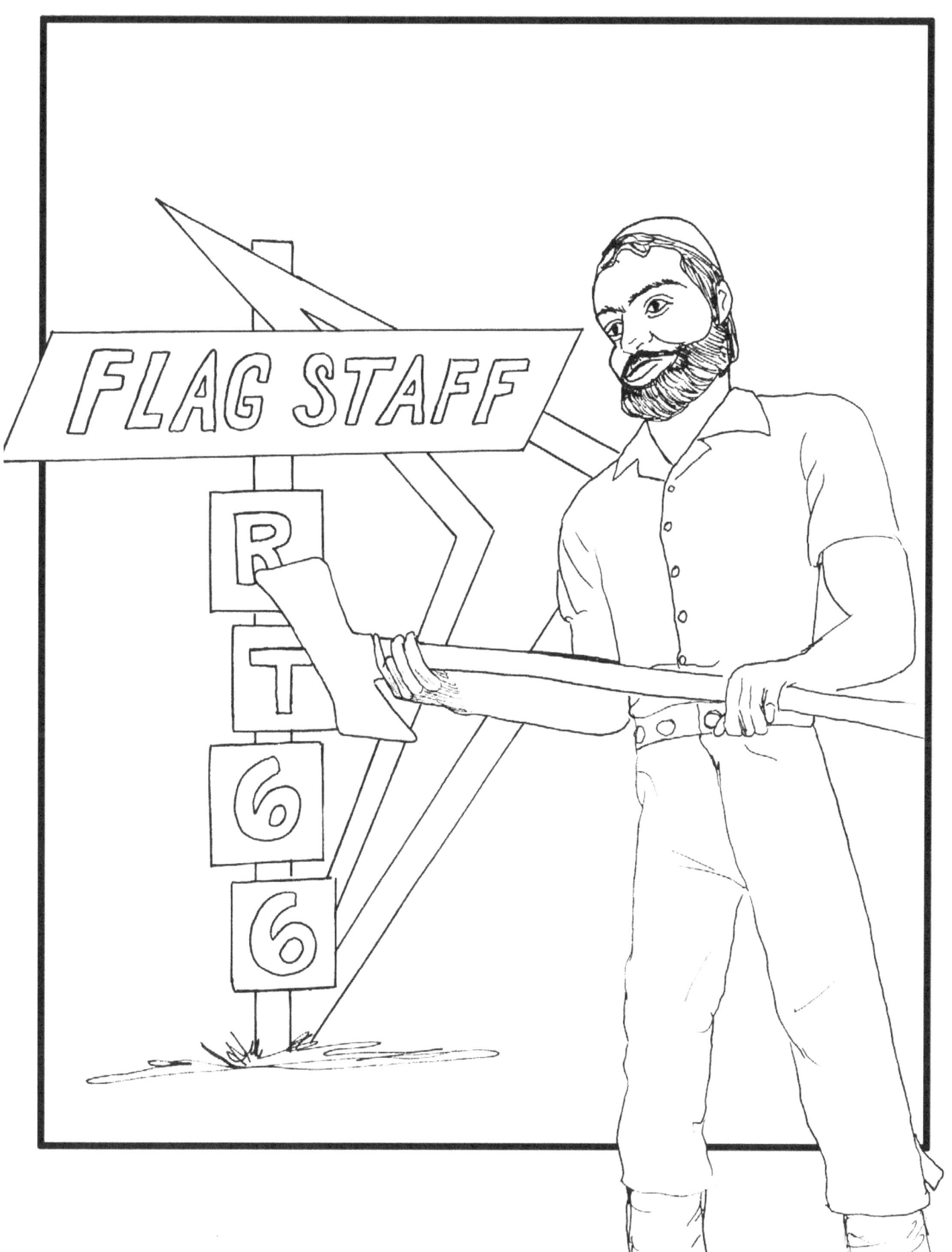

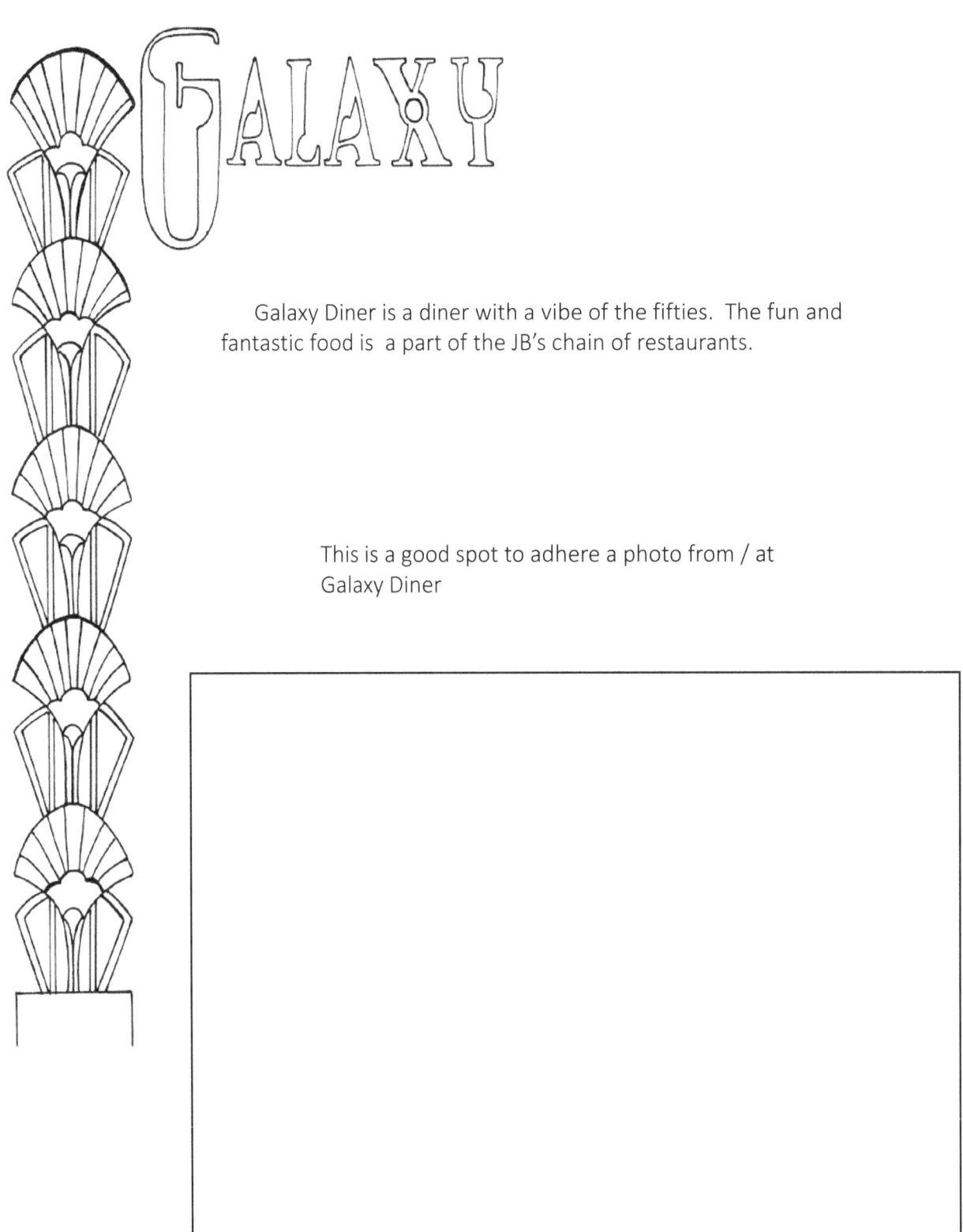

GALAXY

Galaxy Diner is a diner with a vibe of the fifties. The fun and fantastic food is a part of the JB's chain of restaurants.

This is a good spot to adhere a photo from / at Galaxy Diner

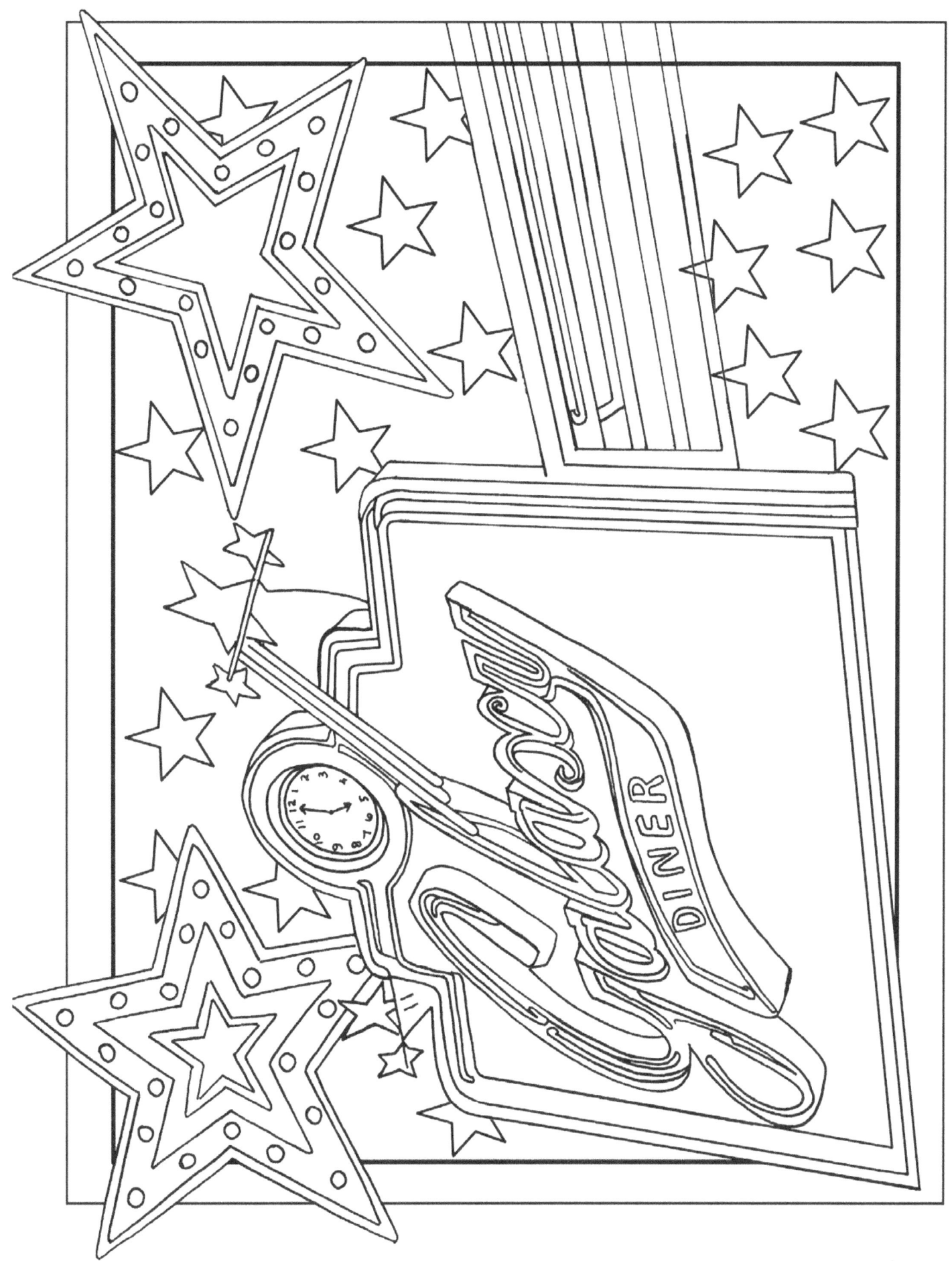

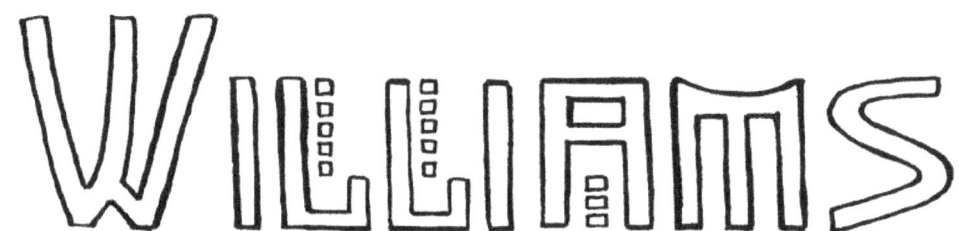

The Grand Canyon Railway (in the Historic Depot Gift Shop) is a good place to stop and get your book stamped and grab a few selfies to capture the moment.

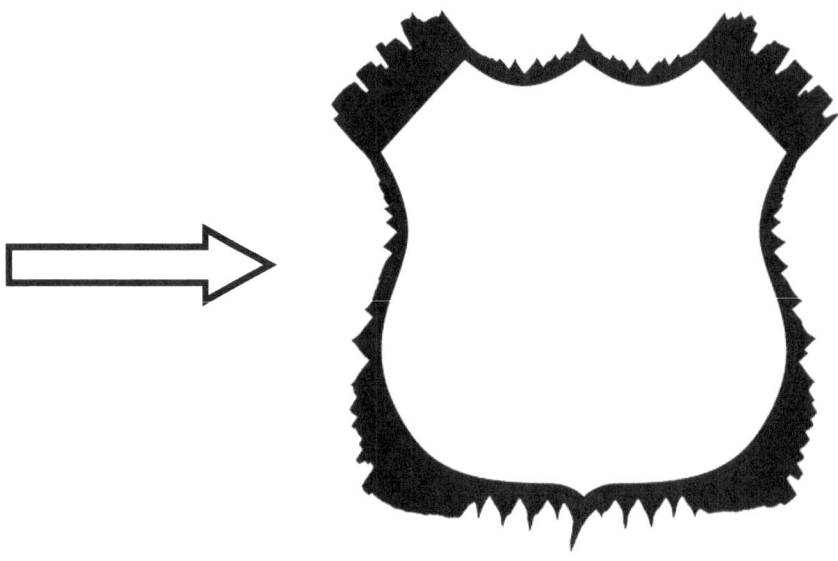

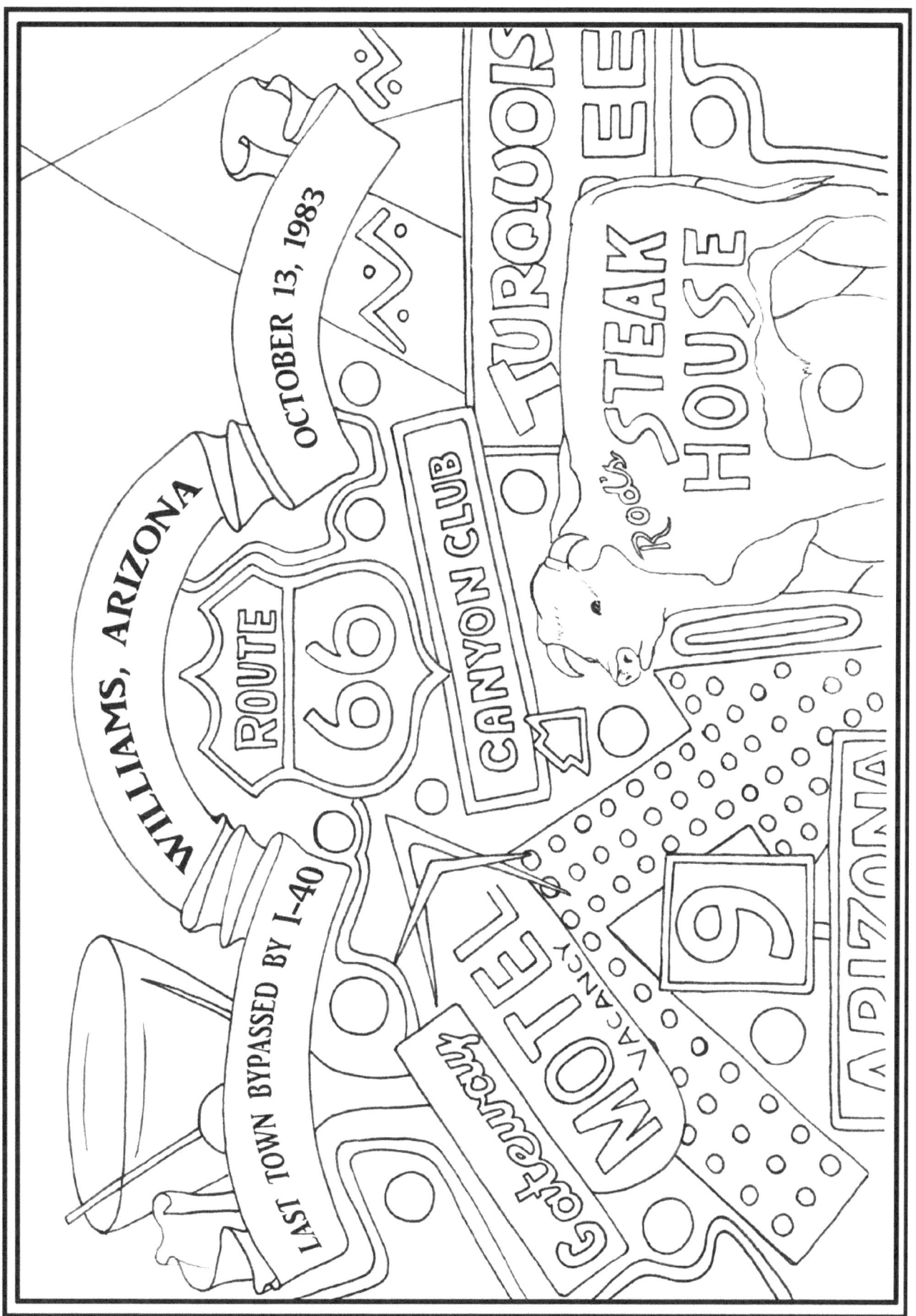

Adhere your picture of Smokey or a selfie with Smokey here, maybe even a sticker of him that you have found in the gift store.

Use this space for photos, stickers, post cards.

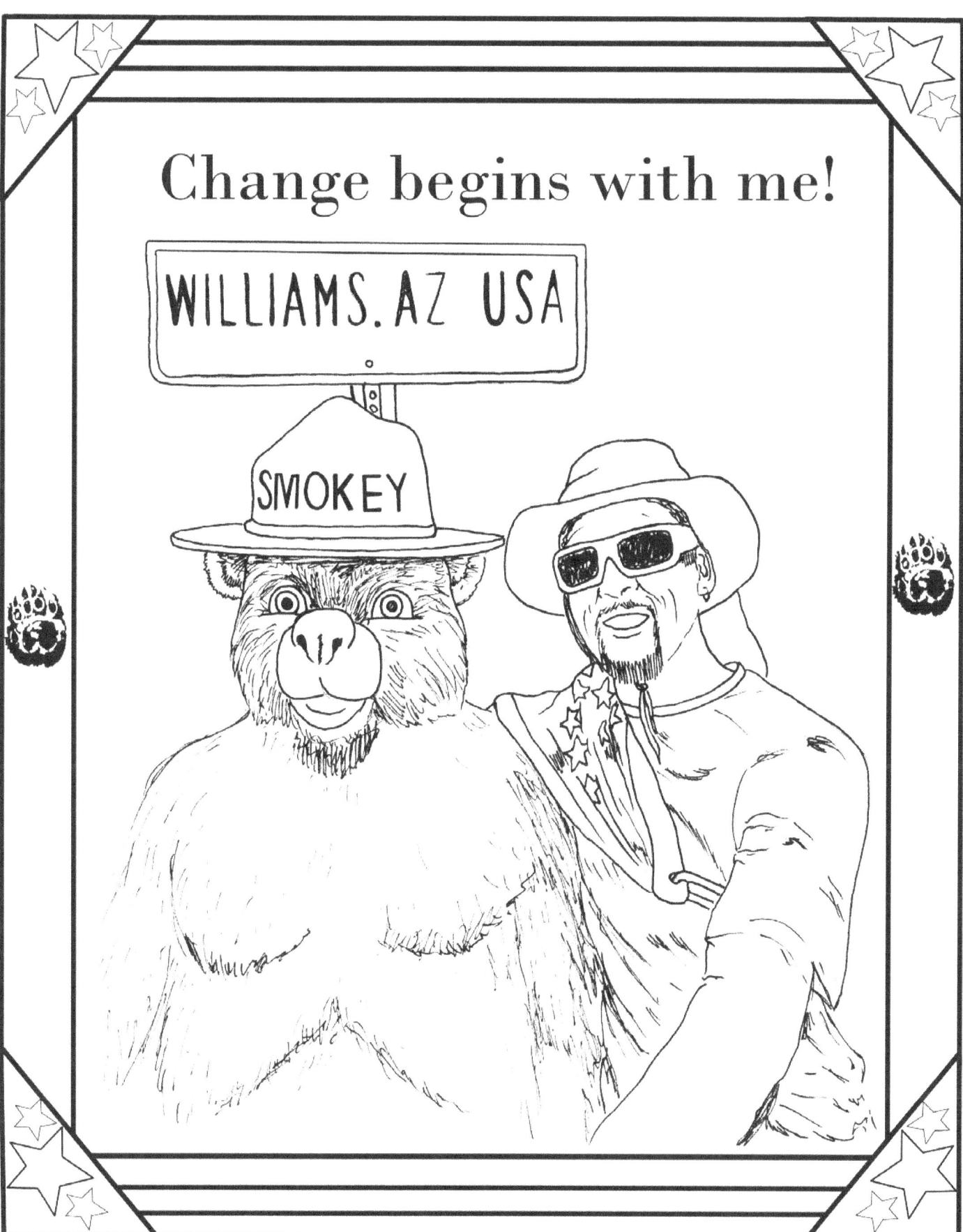

Twin Arrows

Another casualty of the Interstate is located a few miles east of Winona where old Route 66 started to climb into the wooded foothills of the Colorado Plateau. Twin Arrows Trading Post, just recently closed, with the price of gas frozen at $1.39 a gallon. The lonely arrows still appear strong, as if to continue luring travelers in stand silently with the dust of time rolling by.

Use this space for photos, stickers, post cards.

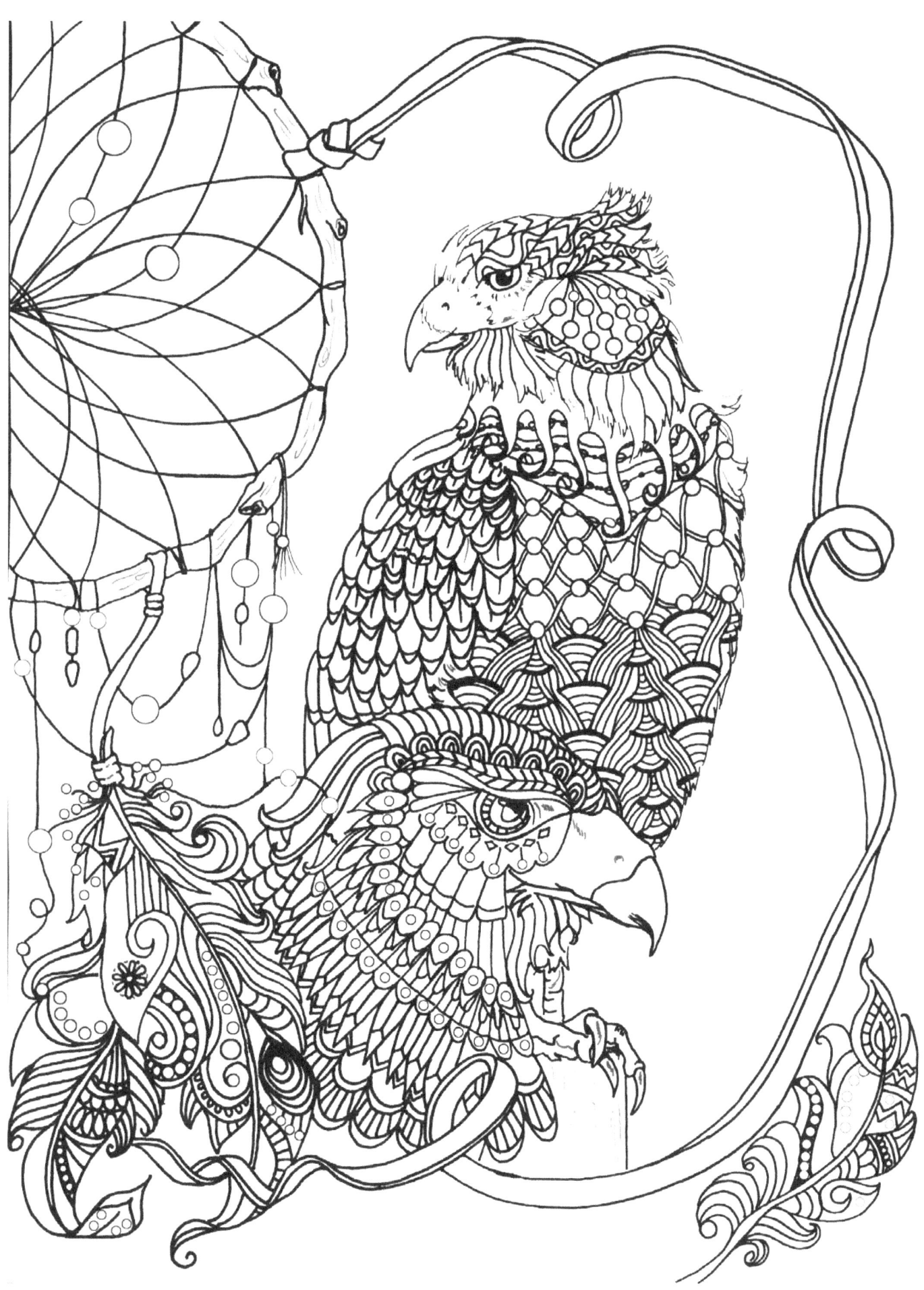

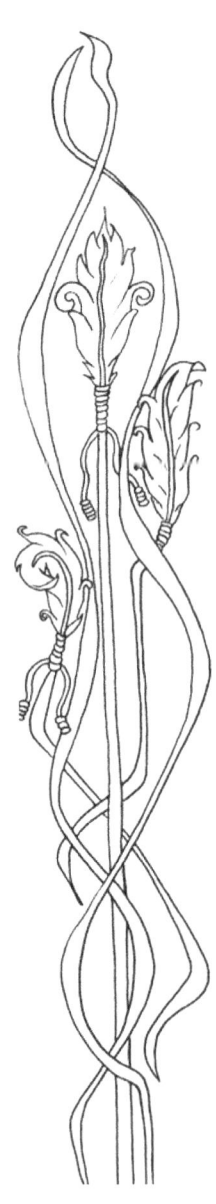
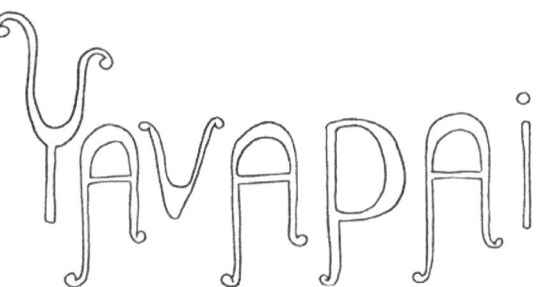

Mother of Counties

Yavapai County was one of the original four counties of Arizona formed in 1864 and was often called "Mother of counties" due to Apache, Coconino, Gila, Maricopat and Navajo counties all deriving from it.

Yavapai was named after the Yavapai Native American tribe

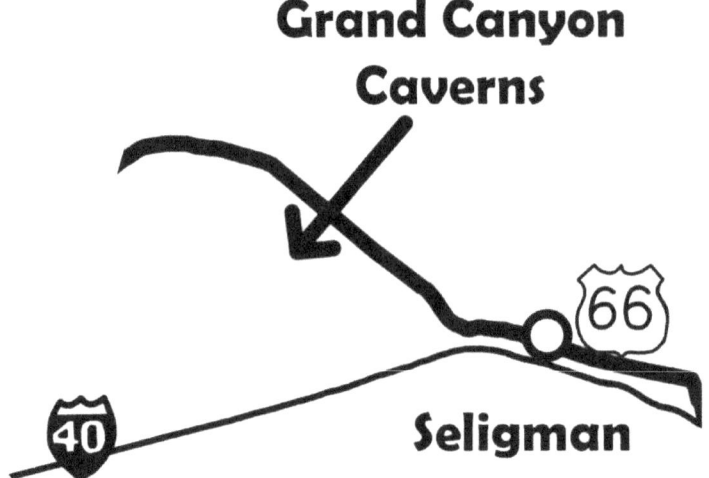

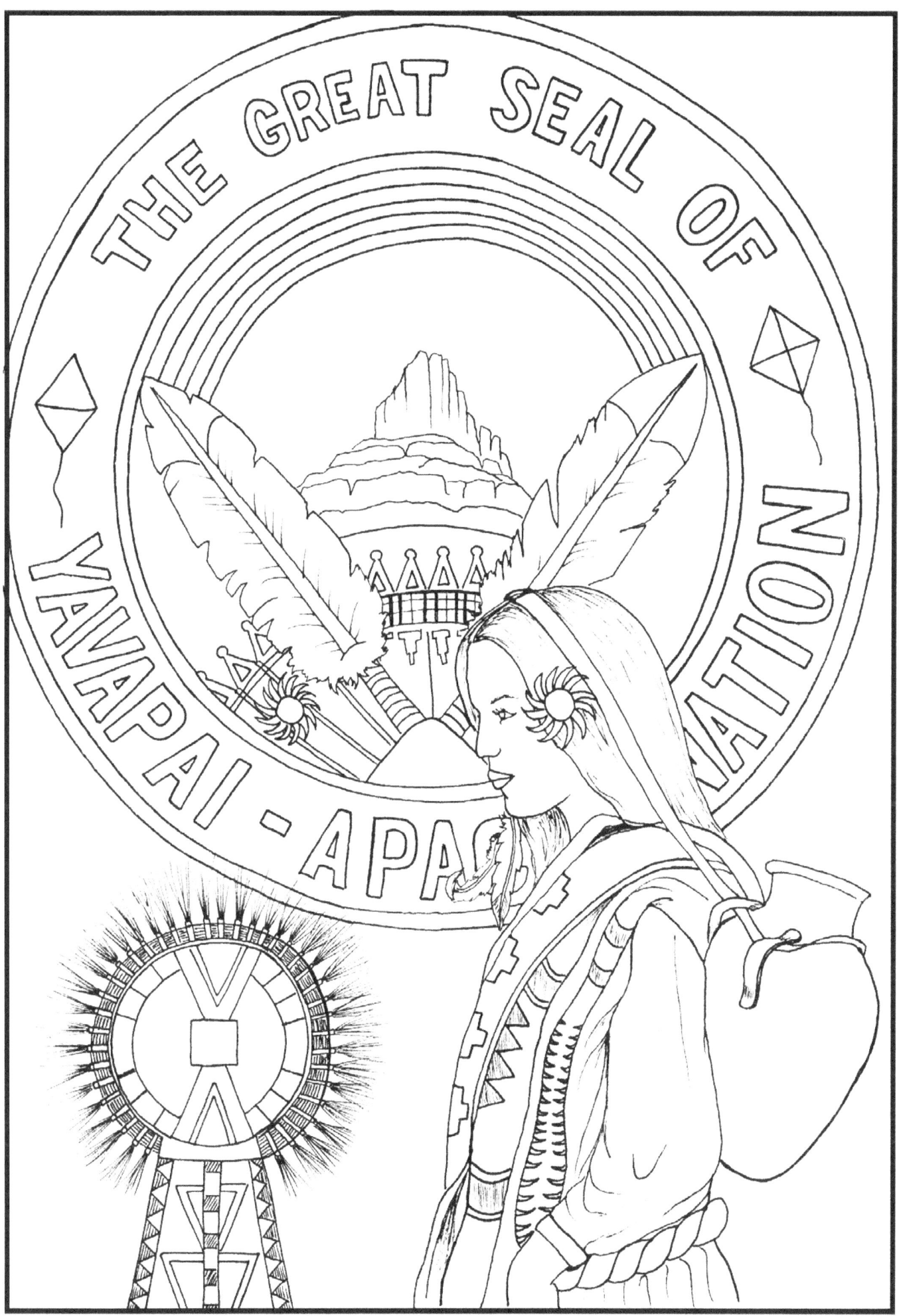

Old Trails Highway

Route 66 through Arizona proved to be a treacherous route and in some aspects, the deadliest. The "Mother Road" gave way to less flattering nicknames such as the "Bloody Highway" or "Death Alley."

In 1914, the road that was to become Route 66 was designated "National Old Trails Highway." In 1926, it became Route 66. One section in the Black Mountains, just outside of an old mining town of Oatman, now a ghost town, is a maze of hairpin turns and the steepest grades throughout the entire stretch of Route 66. It is so steep and dangerous that some of the earlier travelers would not even dare to drive it. Instead, they opted to hire the locals to navigate the winding grade. This section of the road is still open for travel today but is now called Oatman Highway.

An exciting event that takes place in Arizona is the Annual Historic Route 66 Fun Run. Rain or shine, the Fun Run goes from Seligman to Kingman and attracts more than 800 cars along with thousands of spectators from around the world.

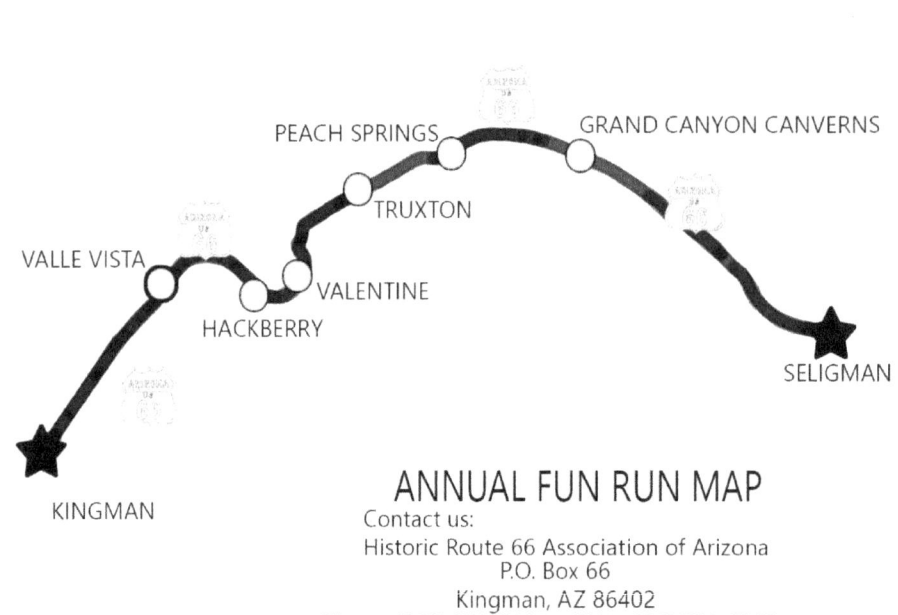

ANNUAL FUN RUN MAP
Contact us:
Historic Route 66 Association of Arizona
P.O. Box 66
Kingman, AZ 86402
Phone: (928) 753-5001   FAX: (928) 753-5852

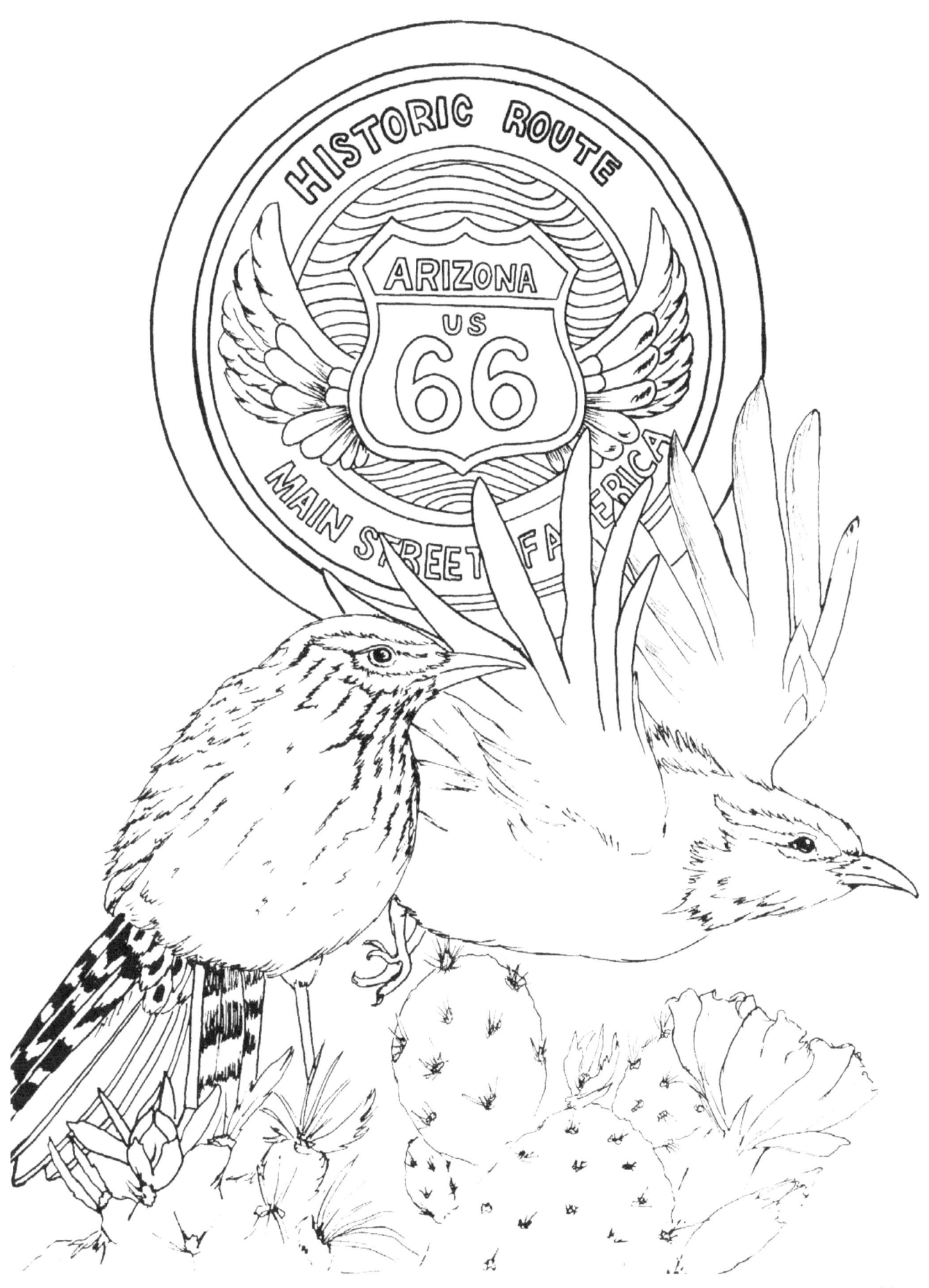

Seligman

The town site was on Beale's Wagon Road, originally being called "Prescott Junction" because it was the railroad stop on the Santa Fe mainline junction with the Prescott and Arizona Central Railway Company. In 1886, it was renamed Seligman, after Jesse Seligman, one of the founders of J.W. Seligman Co. of New York, who helped finance the railroad lines in the area.

Because of its flat land, Seligman became a large switching yard consisting of many tracks, and served as a large livestock shipping center for the areas ranchers.

Seligman was on the original US Route 66 from 1926 until its demise of 1978, when Interstate 40 bypassed it a few miles south. Seligman experienced its real heyday after World War II, when returning veterans and other motorists hit the road and made the Southwest a popular tourist destination.

The historic district includes the Pitts General Merchandise Store and the U.S. Post Office from 1903, the Pioneer Hall and Theatre and the Seligman Garage from 1905, and the Seligman Pool Hall from 1923.

In 1987, Seligman gained its name "Birthplace of Historic Route 66" due to the efforts of Seligman residents, who convinced the State of Arizona to dedicate Route 66 a historic highway. Seligman is the first stop heading west on the longest uninterrupted stretch of historic Route 66, running around 160 miles (260 km) to Topock.

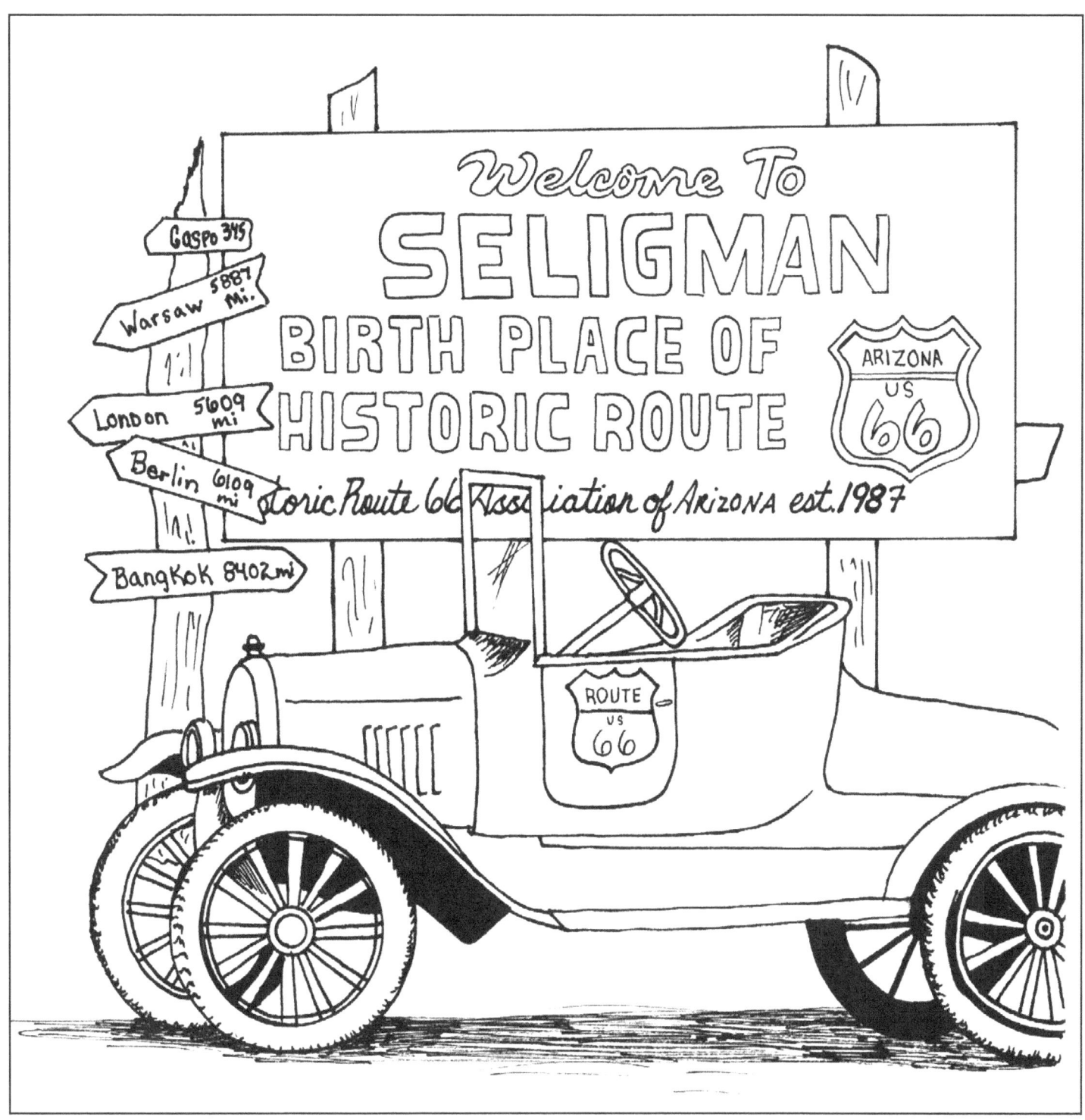

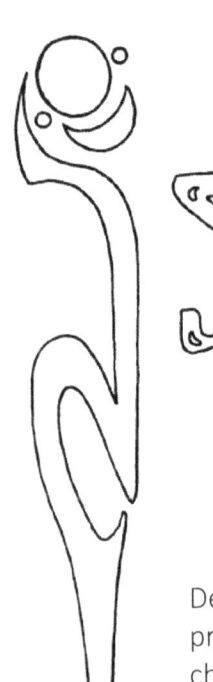

Snowcap

    Built in 1953, a showmanship drive In along Route 66, was a dream of Juan Delgadillo. On a limited budget and with mostly scrap lumber, Juan prevailed. He provided Route 66 travelers with not just a cheese burger but a cheese burger with cheese.

    Juan's cheesiness showed in his menu and the building. Hand painted warning signs such as "park at your own risk", " sorry we are open" adorn the building and parking lot.

    Juan's humor continues today through his son and daughter as they humor their customers with flying mustard, heaps of ice and dead chicken sandwiches.

Use this space for photos, stickers, post cards.

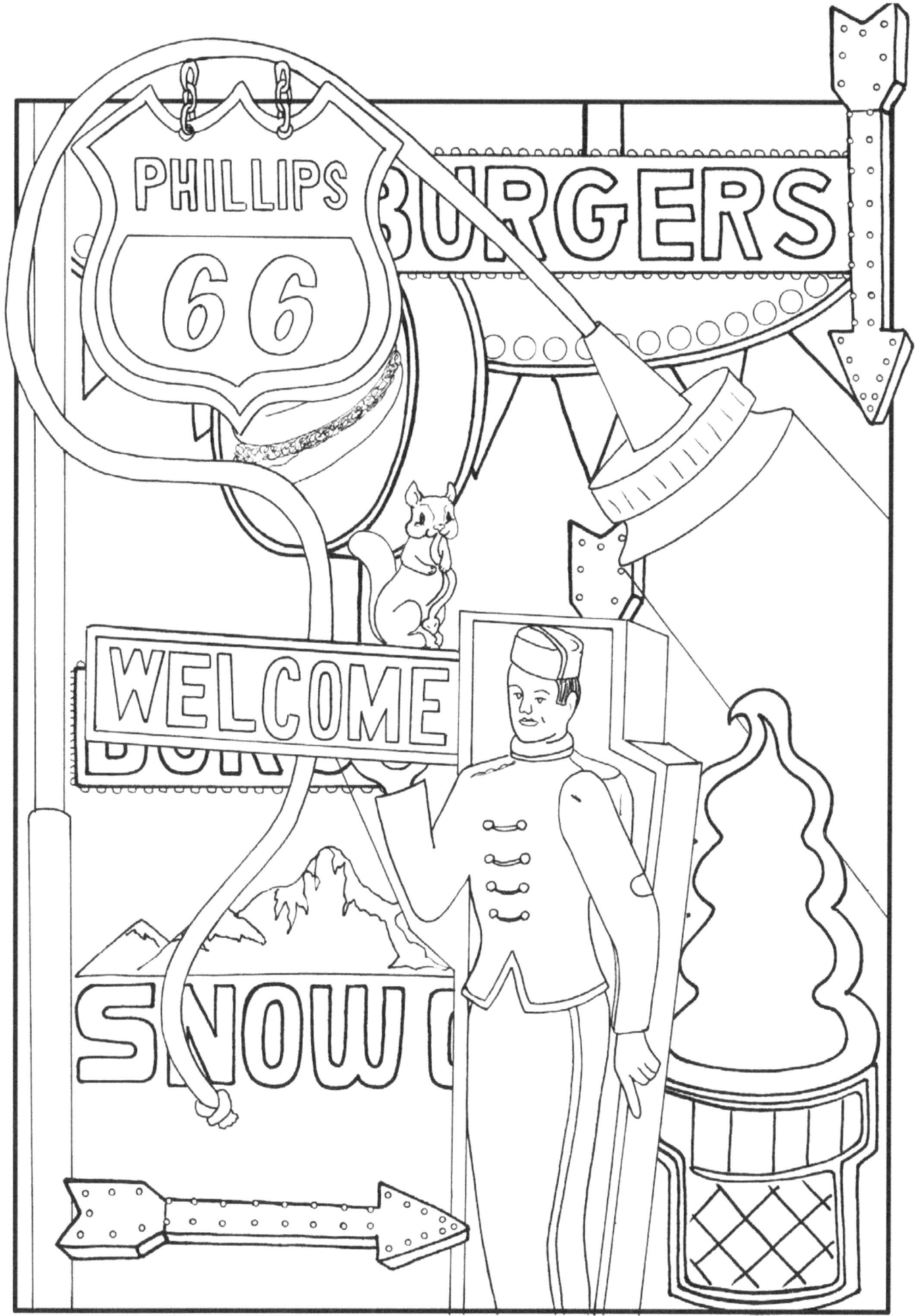

Angel Delgadillo

Angel Delgadillo, a barber from Seligman Arizona, dubbed the "Guardian Angel" of US Route 66 due to his countless hours and efforts to save his town.

Angel knew with the demise of Route 66, the town of Seligman would surely parish as well. Born in 1927 in the family home along Route 66, Angel was able to witness the effects of the Depression and World War I as the convoys of cannons, jeeps and trucks full of solders drove by.

Angel followed his father's footsteps and became a barber, opening his shop in the same shop as his father's barber shop and pool hall. In 1972, Angel moved his shop along the new alignment of Route 66, taking advantage of the traffic flow through town. The 9,000 cars traveling through Seligman each day brought prosperity to the Barber Shop / Pool Hall and other mom and pop operations along the route.

The day of reckoning came on September 22, 1978, when I-40 opened and suddenly the stream of cars stopped. No more were the 9,000 cars slowly cruising through the streets of Seligman. The once near impossible to cross street now was vacant. Slowly, businesses began to close, without the traffic to keep them alive, all was lost. After traveling to Flagstaff, Angel and his brother Juan noticed that the state had failed to put signage signifying the towns along the Interstate. Angel new he had to do something, he just couldn't stand by and watch the town that he loved and where he had lived his entire life disappear. He had a family to feed and a business to save, he had to do something. Angel declared "We the people must prevail and to do that we have to let the travelers of the new I-40 know that there are towns that are worth stopping for". Angel began to advocate for Seligman and all small towns along I-40. He met with state officials pushing for signage signifying the towns off I-40. Angel petitioned with state officials claiming Route 66 was a piece of American History that brought families together through leisurely road trips. The road was historical, memorable and needed to be labeled as so.

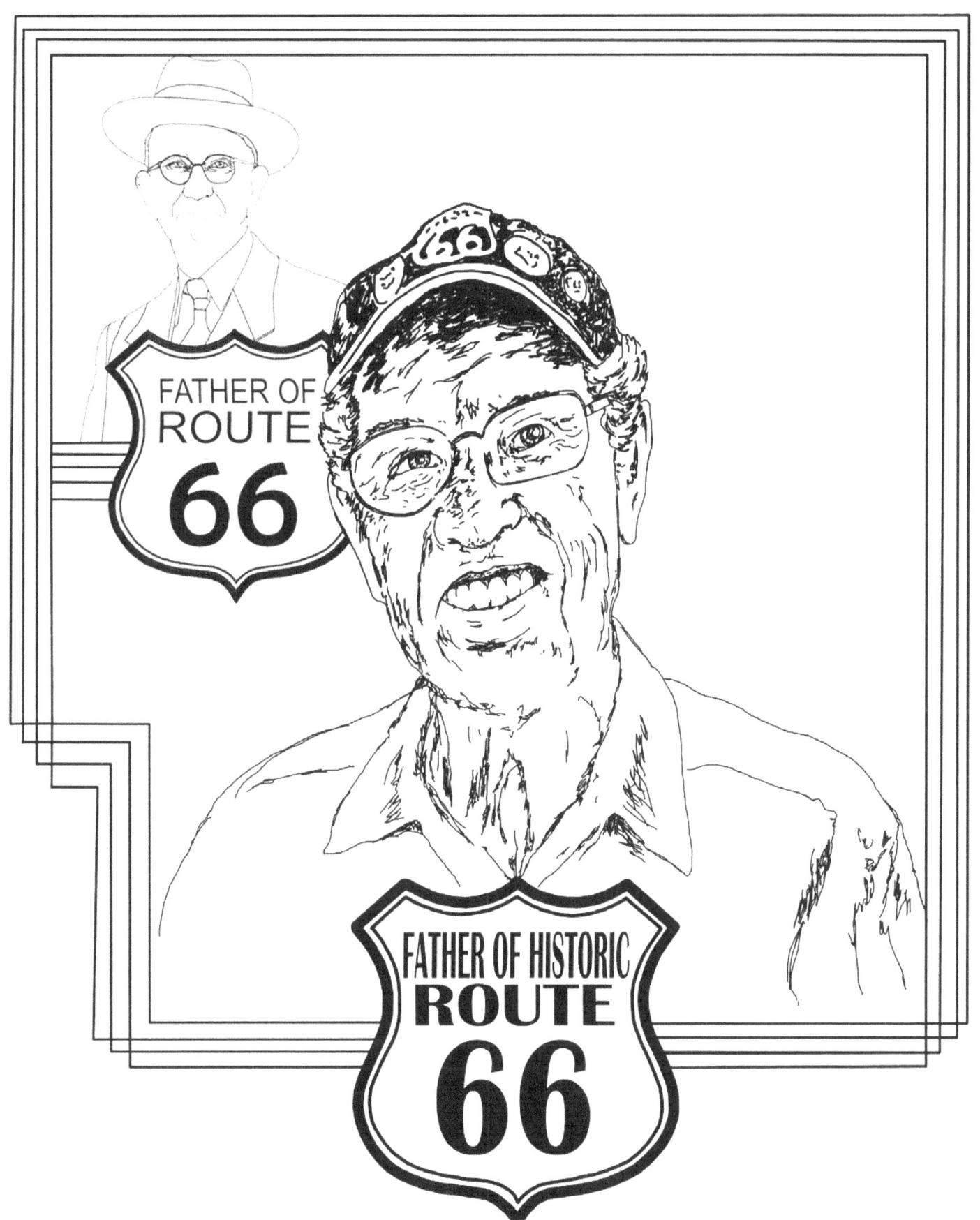

Angel and Vilma

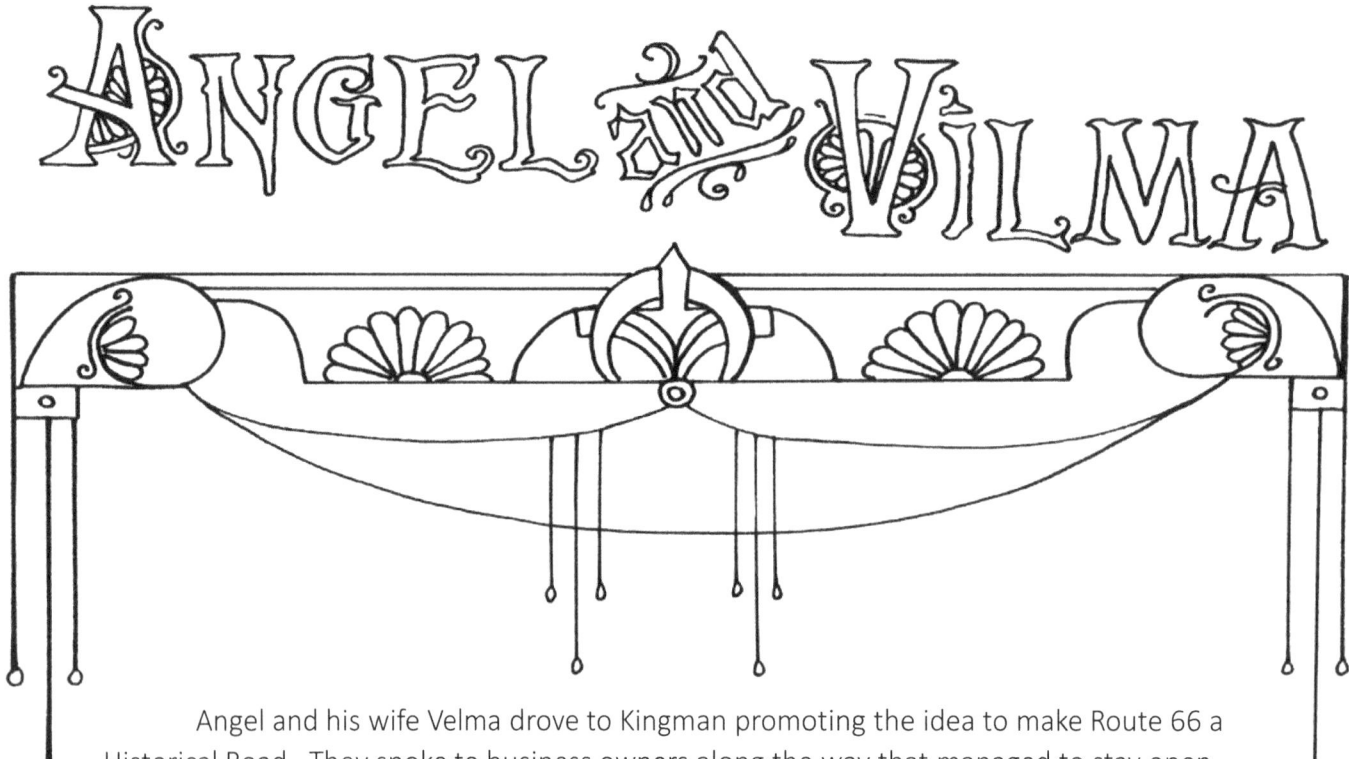

Angel and his wife Velma drove to Kingman promoting the idea to make Route 66 a Historical Road. They spoke to business owners along the way that managed to stay open through the desolated times. Angel needed the people to help him form an association to advocate and save the historical value of Route 66. The first Route 66 Association was formed with the goal of promoting the road as historical and worthy of recognition. Angel and Velma began selling a few pieces of memorabilia out of the Barber Shop / Pool Hall promoting Route 66, hence forming the first Route 66 gift shop. Interest grew in the cause of the nostalgia Route 66, people began requesting more memorabilia. The Association finally reached an agreement with state officials and in 1987, the state of Arizona reopened Route 66 titling it "Historic Route 66". This stretched of protected road is the longest continuous stretch of Route 66 being 159 miles from Seligman to the California border. A road dedication was held April 23rd, 1988 through the first annual "Fun Run" and car show from Seligman to the California border. A mere 153 cars showed up for the dedication and entertainment. The first "Kick Off" of "Get Your Kicks on Route 66" began. Today, the event continues with over 800 cars in attendance each year.

Because of Angel and the Association's efforts to keep 66 alive, associations have formed in each state and other countries, promoting Route 66. The associations work hard to promote the nostalgia of the old-time road, bringing back the leisurely travel through the scenic black top ribbon of Route 66.

Because of a man's desire to save his town and family, thousands of people come from all over nationally and internationally to travel Route 66 from Chicago to L.A.

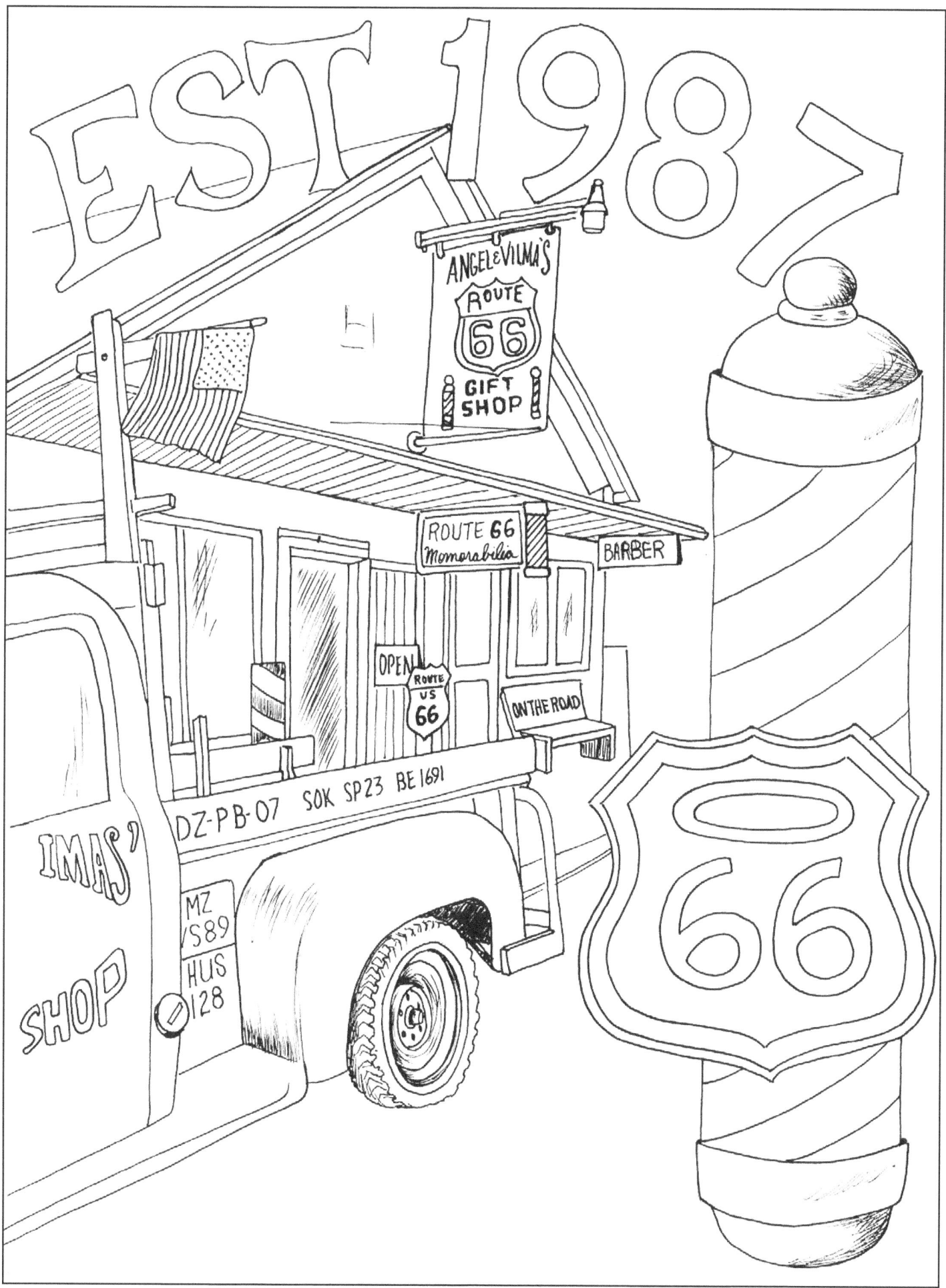

Angel and Vilma

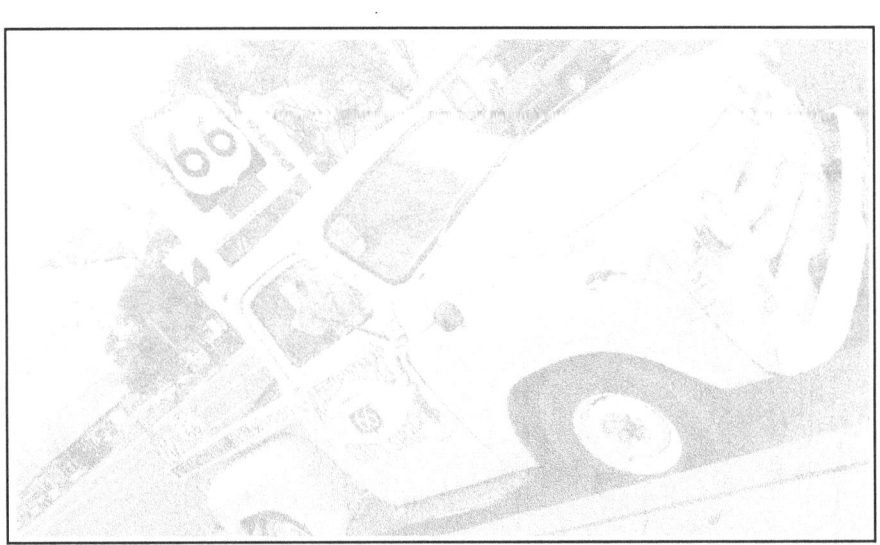

Stop in the Delgadillo's Route 66 Gift Shop for a selfie with Angel (or his life size cutout)
The amazing folks there will gladly stamp your book

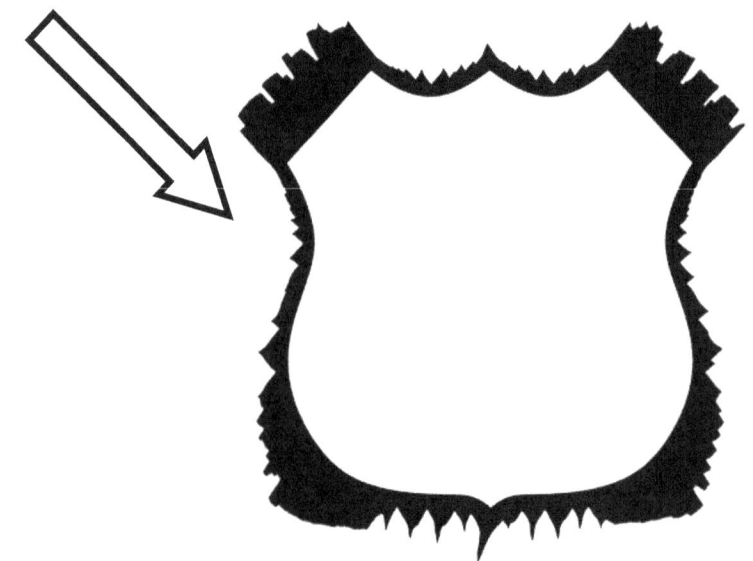

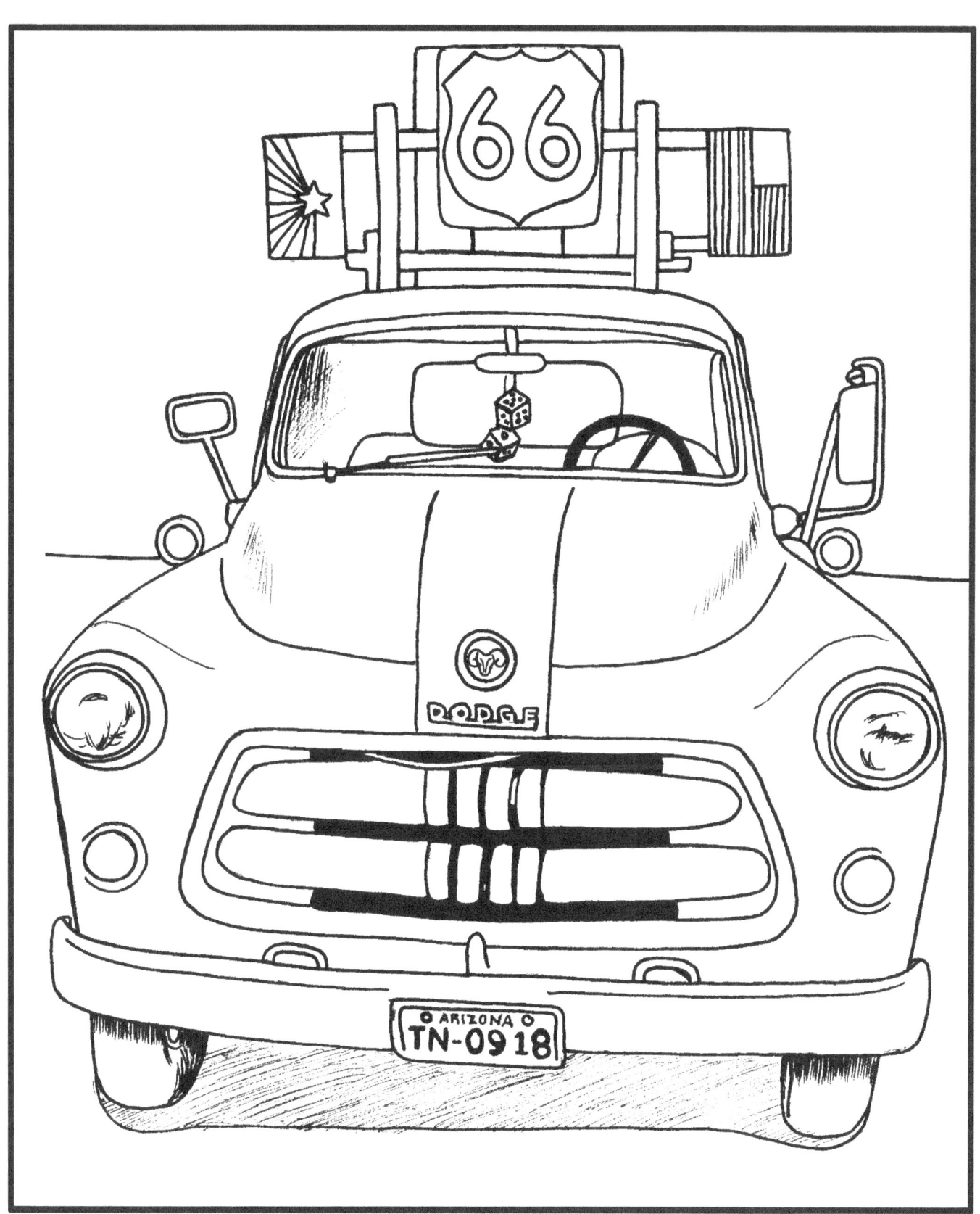

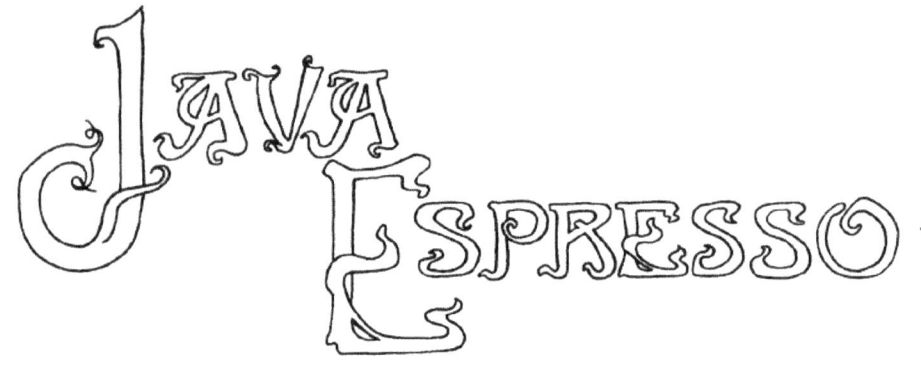

Sundries
Gift & Specialty Shop

Java Espresso has served old fashion malts, gourmet coffee and more since 1904. The building has been known through the years as Ted's Trading Post. Ted's was a place where plays were once enjoyed on the stage, and gitter bugging on the dance floor.

The preservation is key to this historic building now known for amazing artifacts and memorabilia.

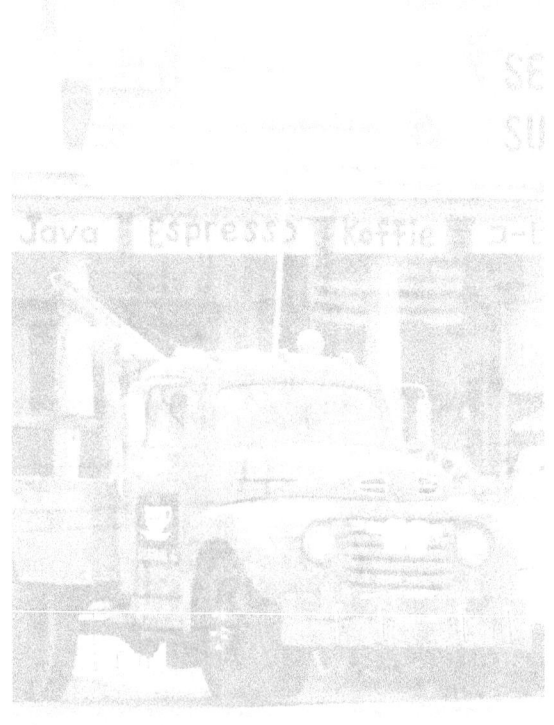

Use this space for photos, stickers, post cards.

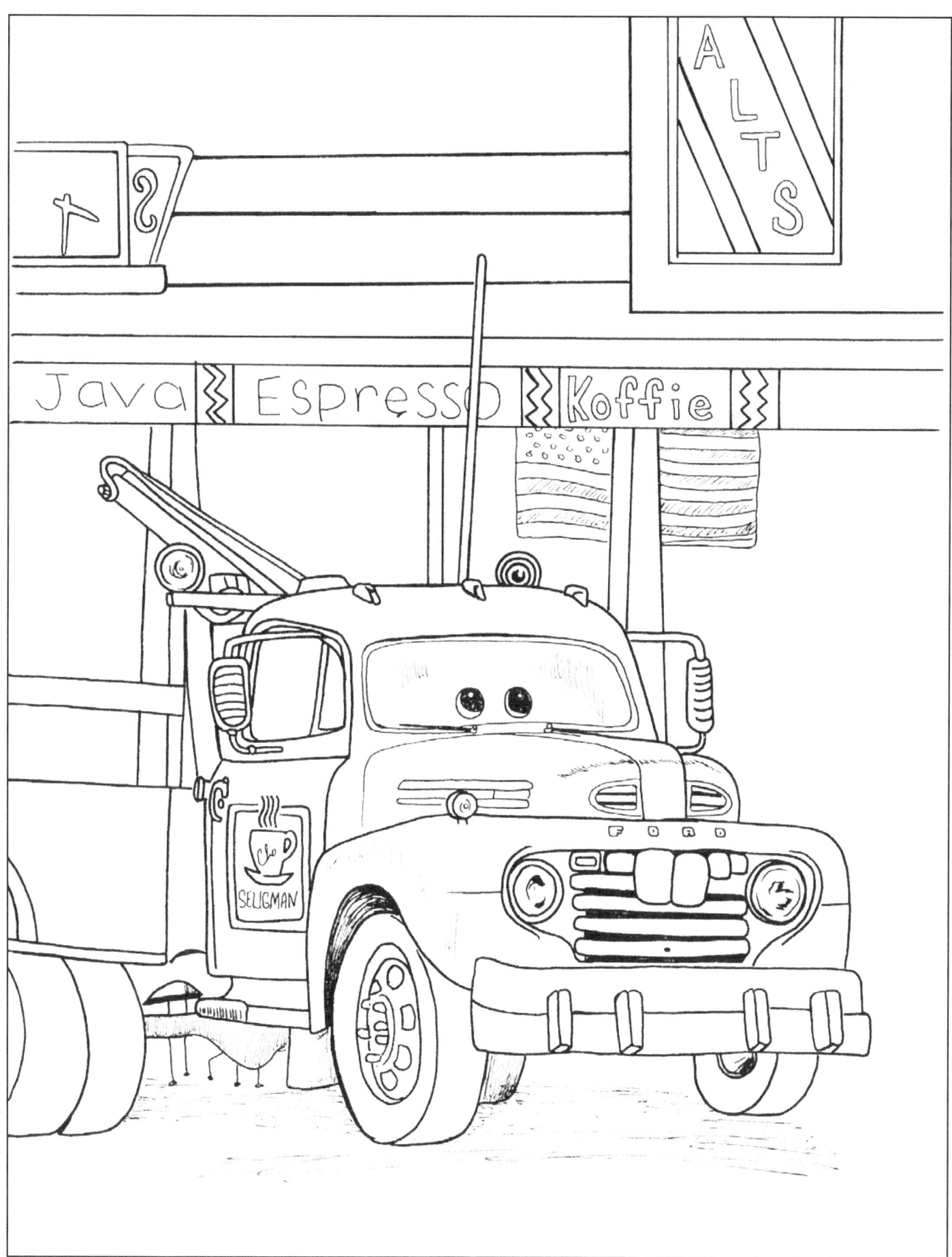

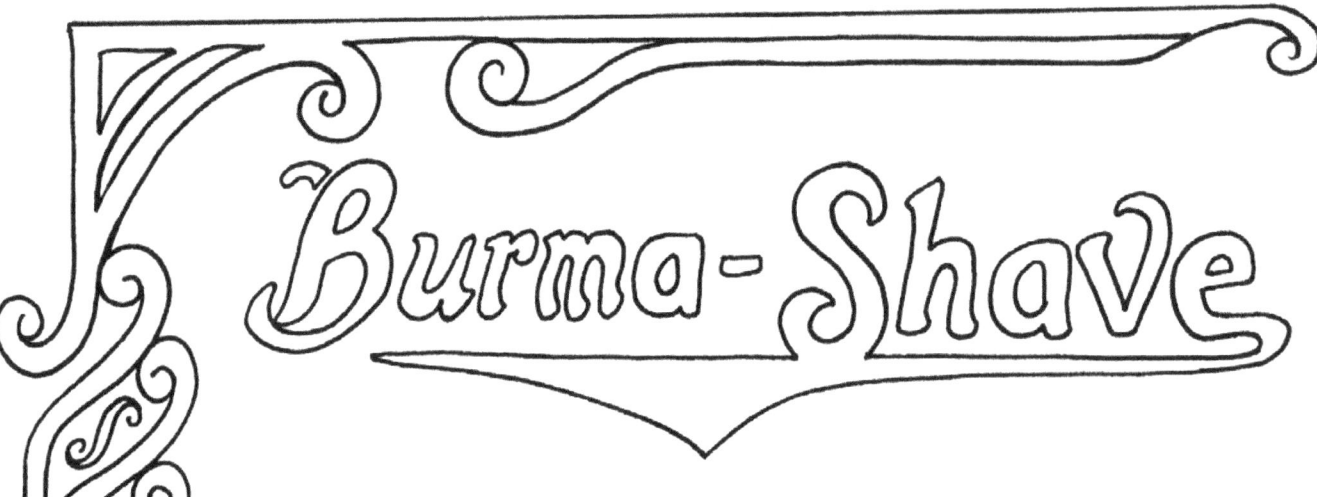

The Verse by the side of the Road

An American brand of brushless shaving cream was known for their humorous, rhyming poems on small roadside signs. Burma Shave was introduced in 1925 and once was the second highest selling brushless shaving cream until its decline in 1950's.

You will see many Burma Shave Verses along Route 66, write down the verses you have found here.

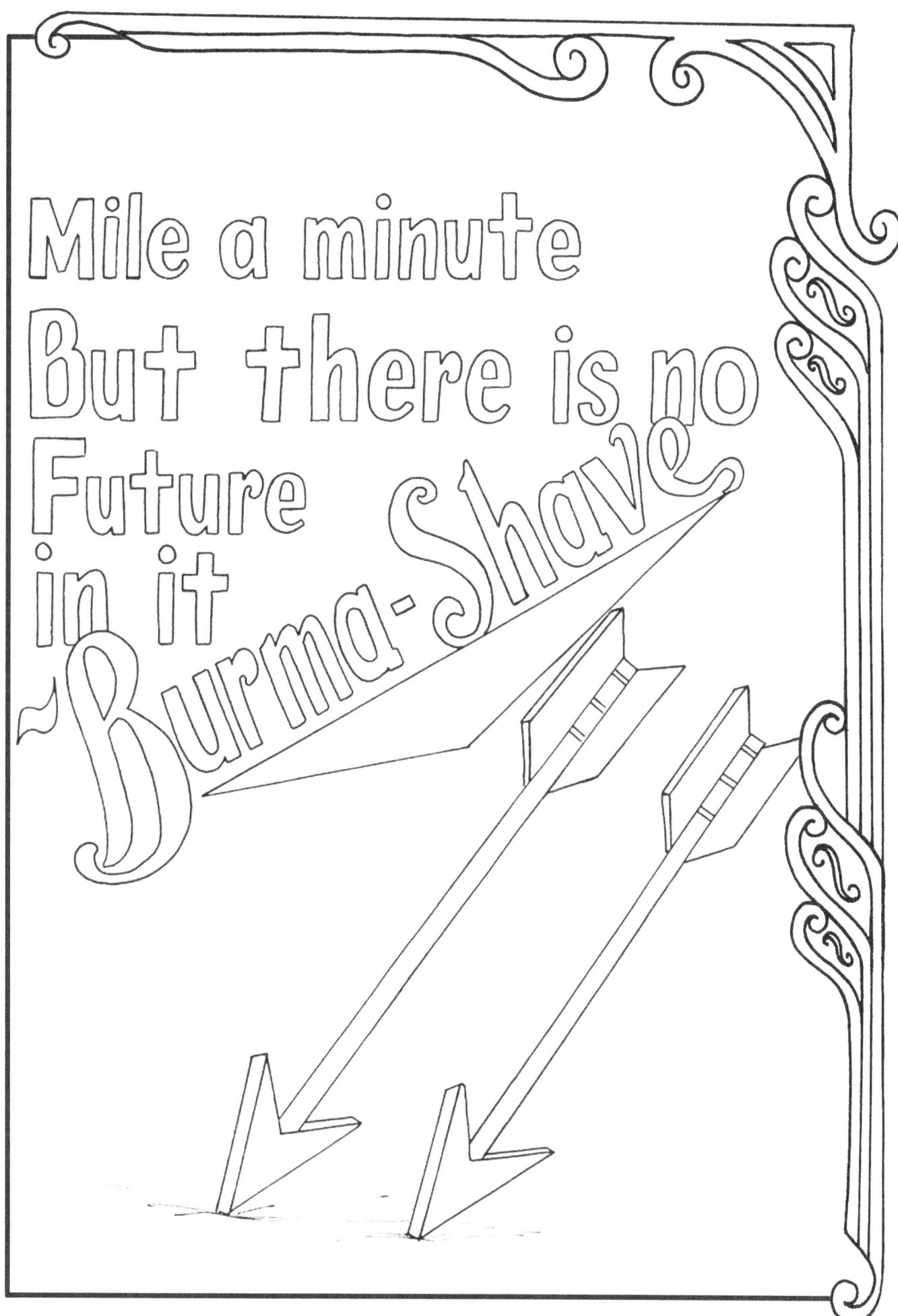

Bert's Dance Hall

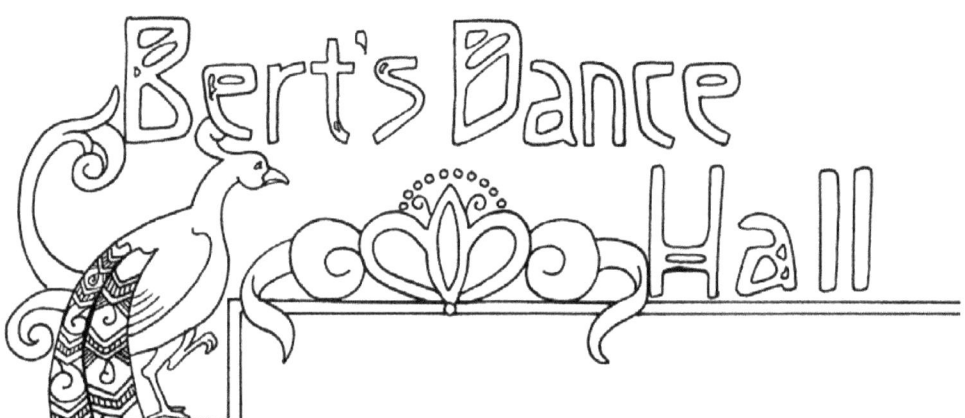

On a lonely stretch of Arizona's Route 66, between Seligman and Kingman, where the loudest sound is the wind or a lonesome train horn or the skitter-skatter of tumbleweed across the tarmac, stands a tiny bar where once Saturday nights echoed to the sound of fiddle and guitar and boots tapping on a wooden floor.

Now the music has fallen quiet, but the sign in Valentine still remains, attracting and perplexing passers-by as to what exactly was Bert's Country Dancing.

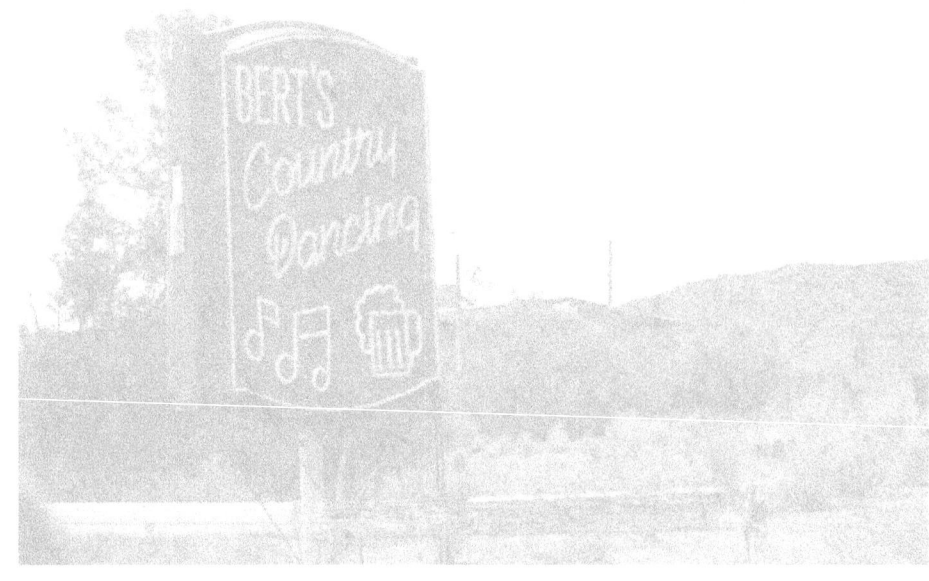

Use this space for photos, stickers, post cards.

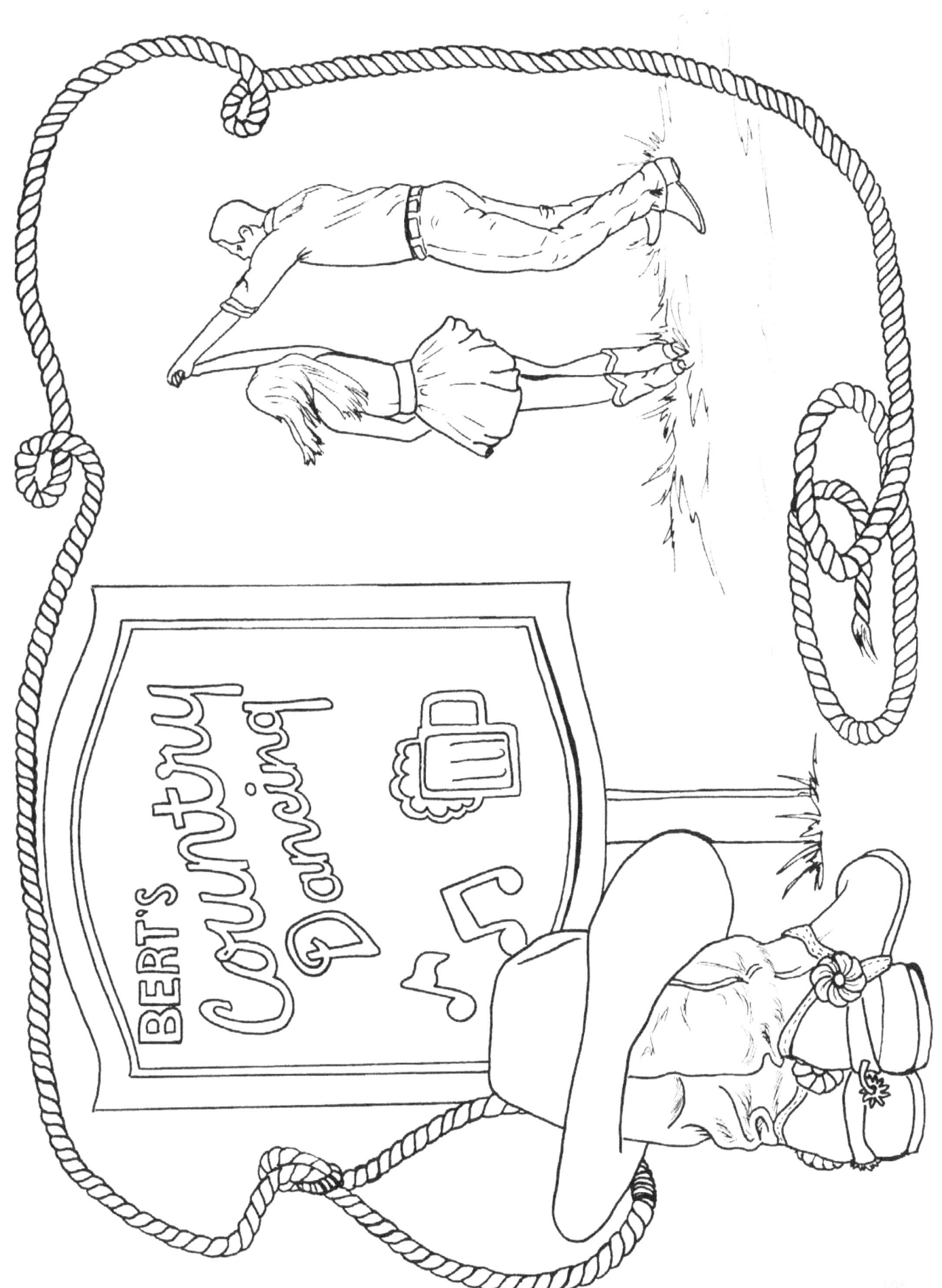

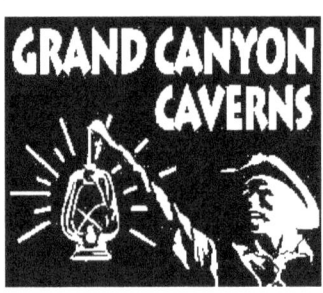

In late 1935, during the Great Depression, the Civilian Conservation Corps (C.C.C.) and the works Progress Administration(WPA), set up work camps to employ the many people out of work. The C.C.C. made a deal with Walter. If he would furnish all the materials, they would build a new entrance to the Caverns. When finished, this improved access included several components. The first 30 feet into the Caverns was a wooden staircase. Then came three ladders (15 feet each). The last 60 foot stretch was a beautiful swinging (suspension) bridge. This new entrance entailed 15 stories of walking in and 15 stories of walking out. After this phase of construction was completed, the price was increased to 50 cents a person. Now more than one person could enter the Caverns at a time! This was the only way in and out of the Caverns until 1962. Then, a new shaft was blasted 210 feet deep and a modern elevator was installed. At that time, the natural entrance was sealed off forever.

Today, the only way to enter the Caverns is with a guide and through the use of an elevator that takes you 210 feet below the earth's surface, a 21 story building!

In 1927, a young woodcutter, Walter Peck, was on his way to play poker with his friends. Before reaching the game, he stumbled and nearly fell into a rather large, funnel-shaped hole. Since he didn't have the proper equipment to explore the hole, he continued on to the poker game. Once there he started telling the boys about a new, big hole in the middle of his trail. The next morning Walter gathered some friends. With ropes and lanterns, they went to explore his new hole. A rope was tied around the waist of a local cowboy. He was lowered into the hole. By the time his feet touched the floor of the hole, 150 feet of rope had been let out. He found himself in a very large, dark cavern. Using the coal oil lantern, he began exploring. However, the only thing that excited him was the thought he had found a very rich vein of gold. As he'd cast the light from this lantern across the cavern it picked up some sparkles in the rock. He quickly gathered up a sack full of samples. He gave his signal, three tugs on the rope. Walter and the other men started pulling him back up out to the hole. Upon reaching the surface he excitedly showed the samples to Walter. Then he told his friends that , on a ledge at the 50 foot level, he'd seen the remains of two human skeletons and remnants of a horse saddle. By the time the newspapers had finished with the story, the bones had become the remains of a prehistoric caveman with no mention of the horse saddle. The story caused a great stir among people. Soon, scientists had come from the east to pick up and study the bones. While all of this was going on, Walter purchased the property and the Caverns in preparation for mining gold!

However, when the gemologist report came back, Walter was a mightily disappointed man. His cave full of gold turned out to be only lots of iron oxide or rust! Walter had spent his money on an empty, funnel-shaped hole and a rust factory. But, being a very enterprising young man, he soon came up with a brilliant idea. He would charge 25 cents to enter the Caverns and to see where the "caveman" had been found. He built a very primitive elevator. Visitors were tied to one end of a rope and lowered down by a hand-operated winch. These early tourists were expected to provide their own light source, usually a kerosene lantern. Upon reaching the floor of the Caverns, it would be unwise to untie the rope and stray away. For, if the light source were dropped or otherwise lost, the pioneering spelunkers would find themselves in absolute darkness.

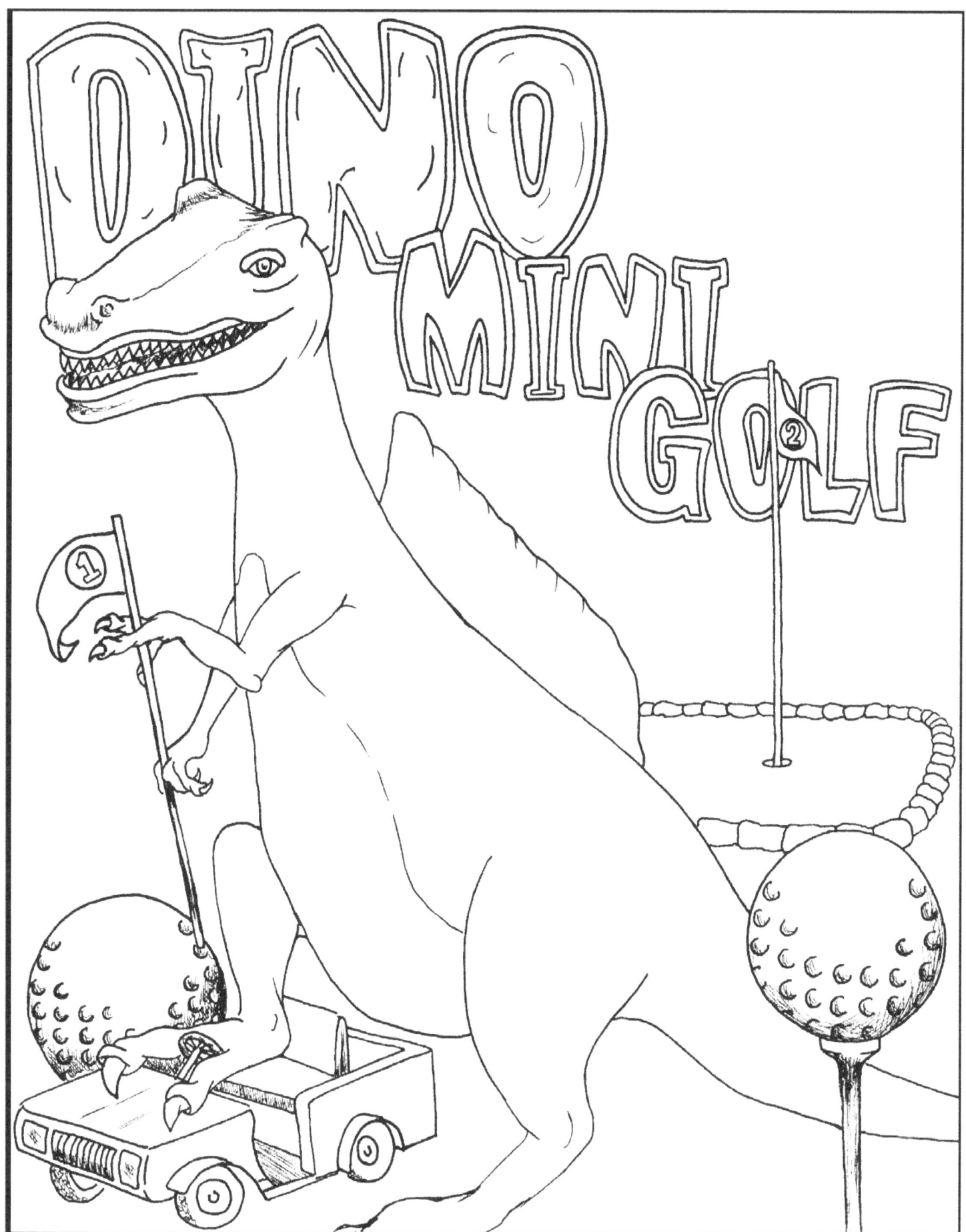

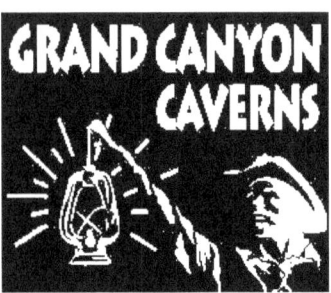

Imagine spending the night in the oldest, darkest, deepest, quietest, and largest suite room in the world. A cavern that took 65 million years to form, in a room that is 200 feet wide, 400 feet long with a 70 foot ceiling. The largest dry cavern in the United States, so dark that it is completely absent on any light, so quiet because it contains no life forms; nothing lives in the caverns, not a fly, not a mouse, a bat, bug or animal. Nothing. The only thing moving or breathing is you. The air is as dry and clean as one can get, coming in via 65 miles of limestone crevices from the Grand Canyon to the caverns. The limestone takes out all moisture and impurities… Please, re-read the above paragraph, slowly, and think about what each feature represents.

There is only one room available in the caverns that is completely furnished with all amenities one would need, 2 double beds, living room with a queen fold out sofa, (room sleeps up to 6), a library of old books and magazines such as a National Geographic collection dating back to 1917, dictionaries and other books dating back to the late 1800's. A working record player with records, table and chairs, bathroom, several lightening options for the over night stay in the caverns, and personal lightening. A comfortable "home for the night". Your check in time is normally with the last tour of the day (4 PM) and check out is shortly after the first tour begins. (10 am), but there is plenty of motel rooms above ground.

Contact
Motel: 928-422-3223
Caverns: 928-422-3223
Email: info@gccaverns.com

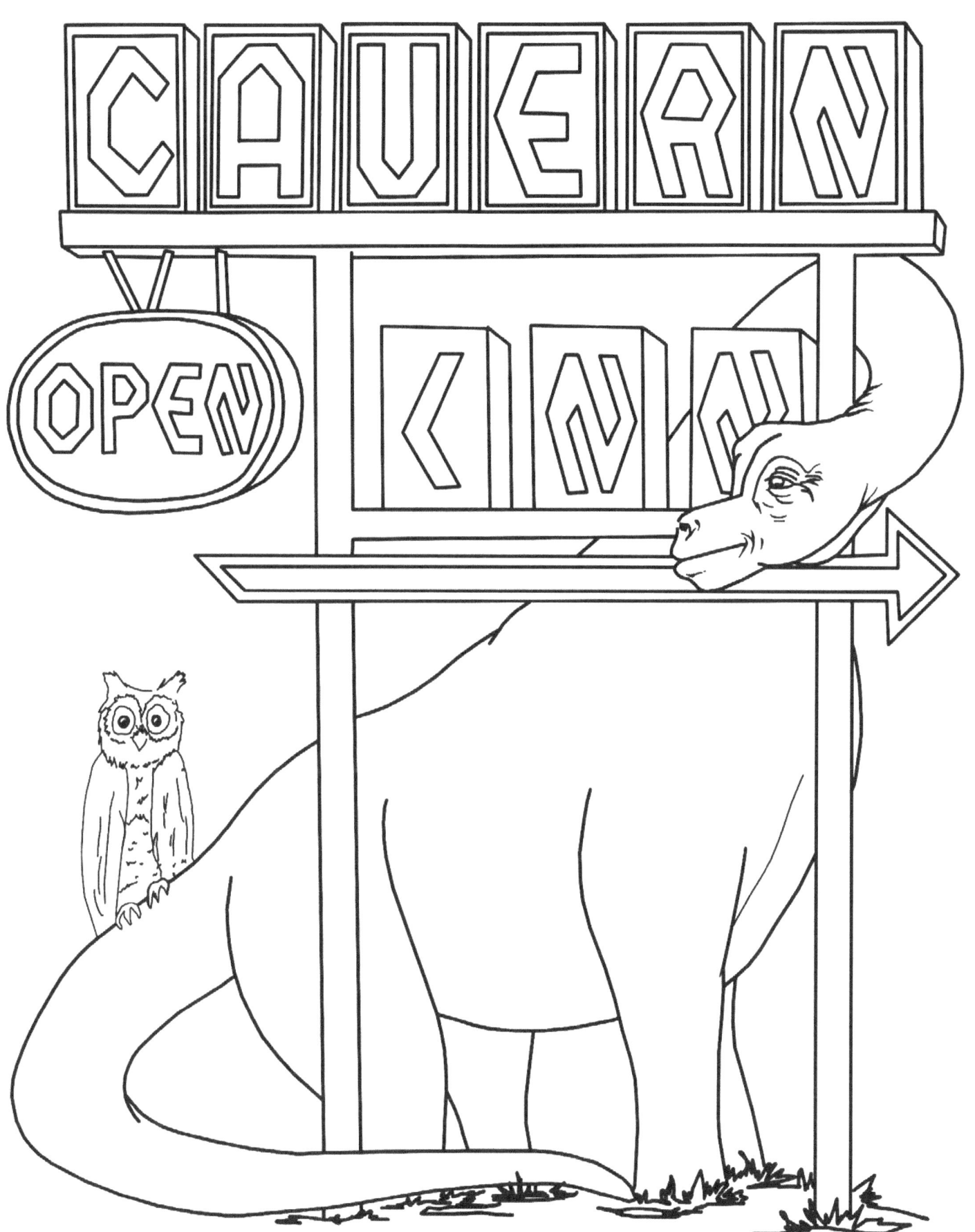

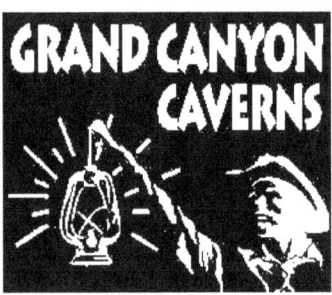

The Caverns claim to fame is not only the largest dry caverns in the United States it has the biggest coconut cream, to die for, pie. After your cave tour have dinner or lunch in the Grotto and don't forget to have some amazing PIE! you won't be disappointed!

Cavern Grotto underground dining area

The "Cavern Grotto", one of Arizona's newest dining experiences that takes you 21 stories beneath the Earth's surface. The Cavern Grotto, is one of the most amazing and memorable dining experiences one that you will never forget.
Reservations are a must: 928-422-3223 Ext 3

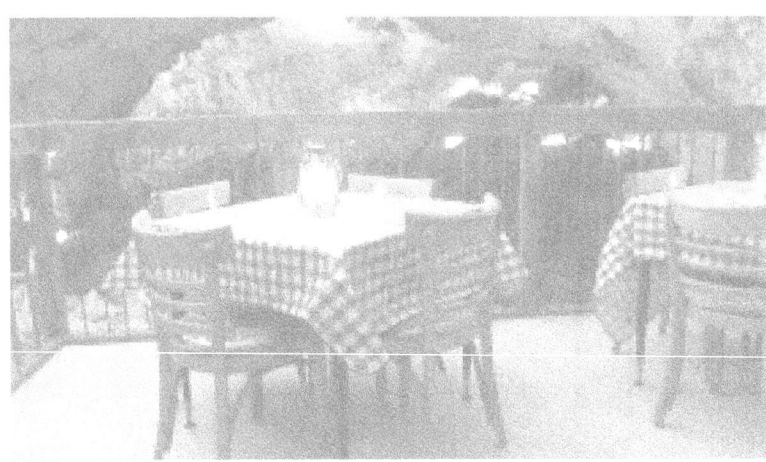

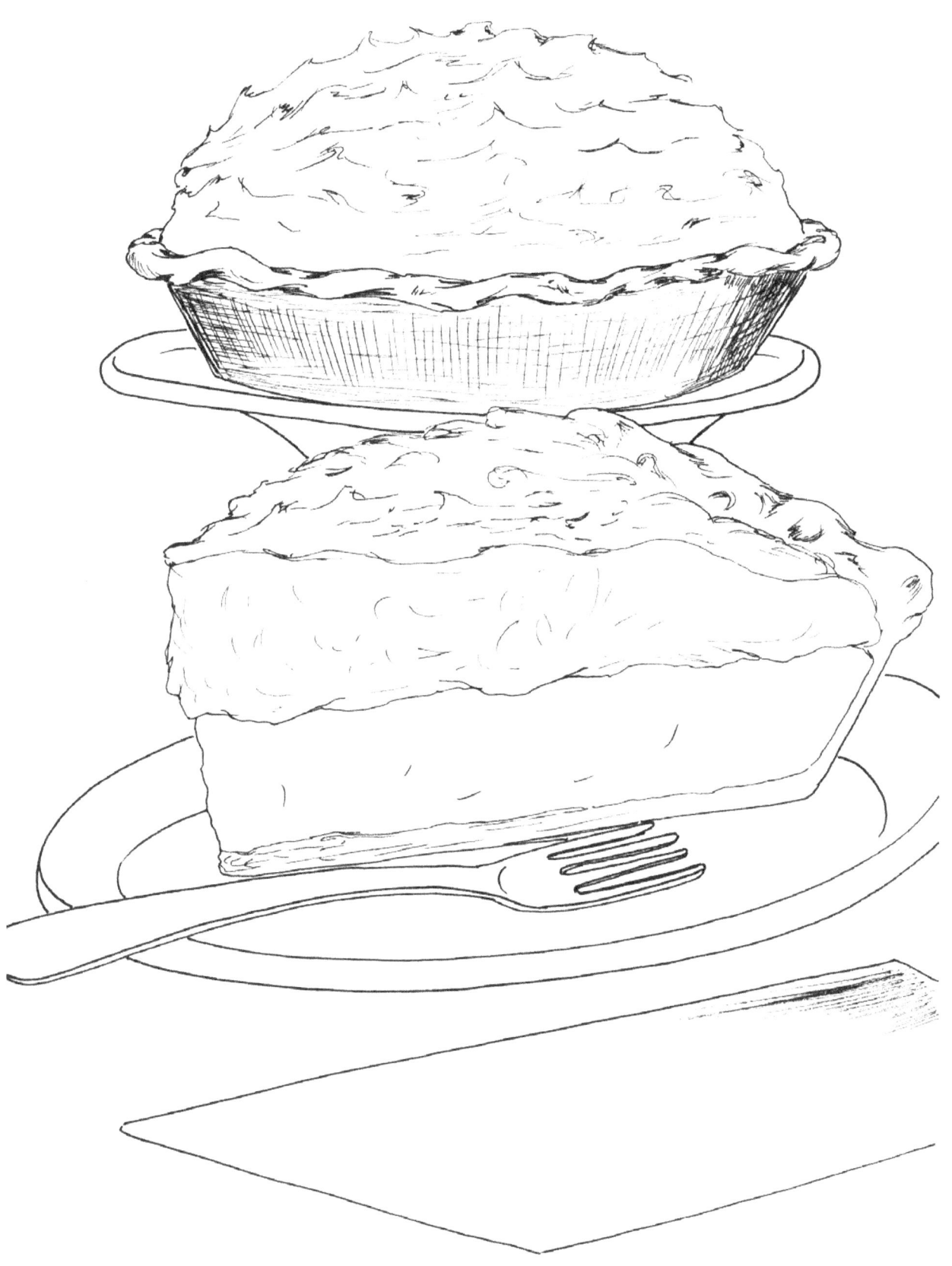

Peach Springs

The town derived its name from the Peach trees that the 18th Century Spanish missionaries from San Bernardino had planted. Later, the railroad set up a station and the post office shortly followed in 1887. The Trading Post opened in 1917 and in 1926, the National Old Trails became part of Route 66. Traffic boomed and so did the town.

John Osterman and his brother Oscar, both of Sweden, started a gas station in Peach Springs in the 1920's. John persuaded his brother to buy the gas station from him in 1925, just before Route 66 opened. With trade picking up, Oscar built a bigger garage with living quarters over the service bay. Next door to the newly built garage, Oscar built Peach Springs Auto Court, which is today the Hualapai Lodge.

After the decline in business upon I-40 opening, the town began to decline. The station hung on until about 20 years ago.   The town has experienced a re-growth after Route 66 was declared Historical in 1987.

With the setting that inspired the town of Radiator Springs in the Pixar film *Cars*, and many activities such as cave exploring, whitewater rafting and the famous Grand Canyon Skywalk, this little town should not be passed by.

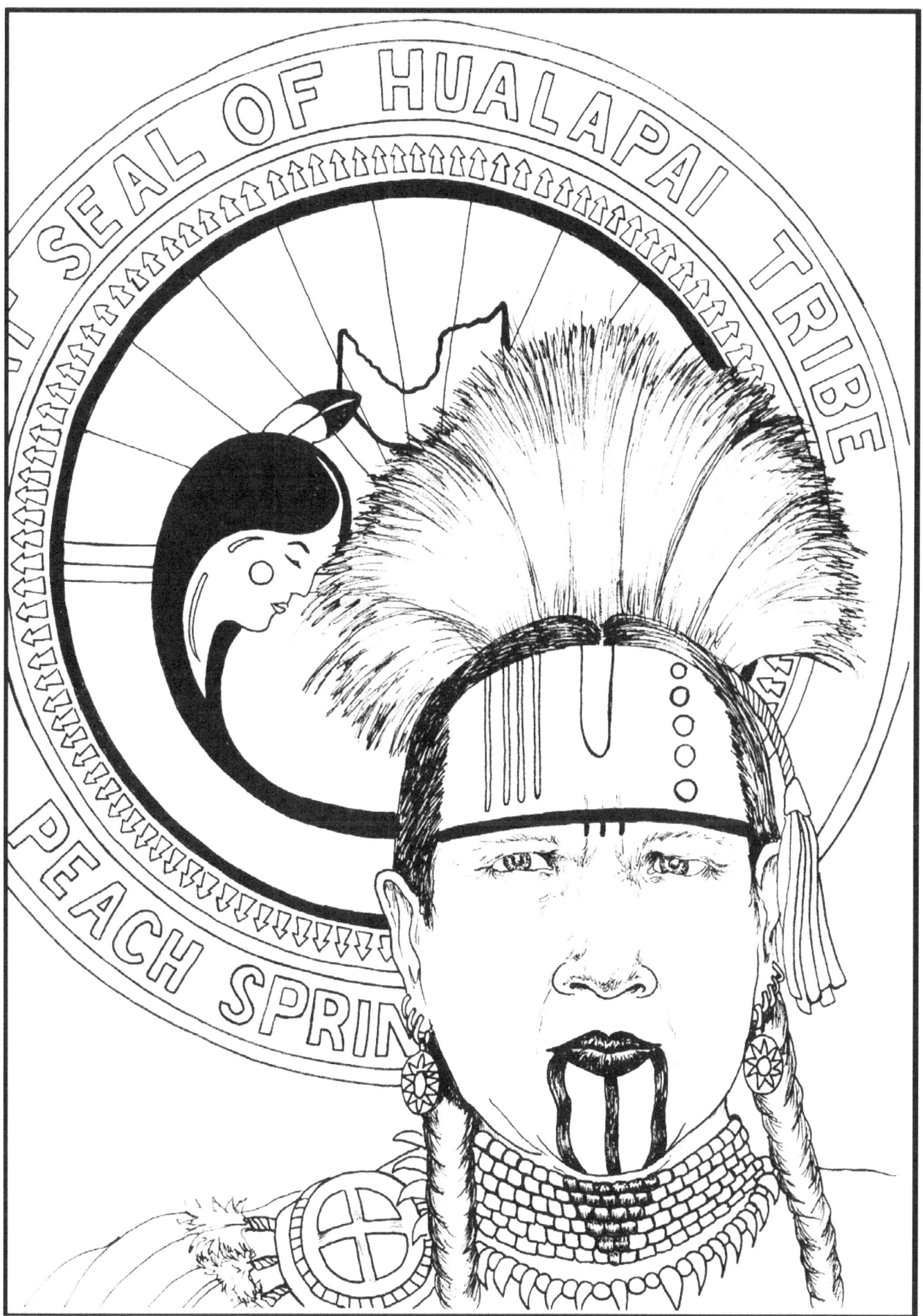

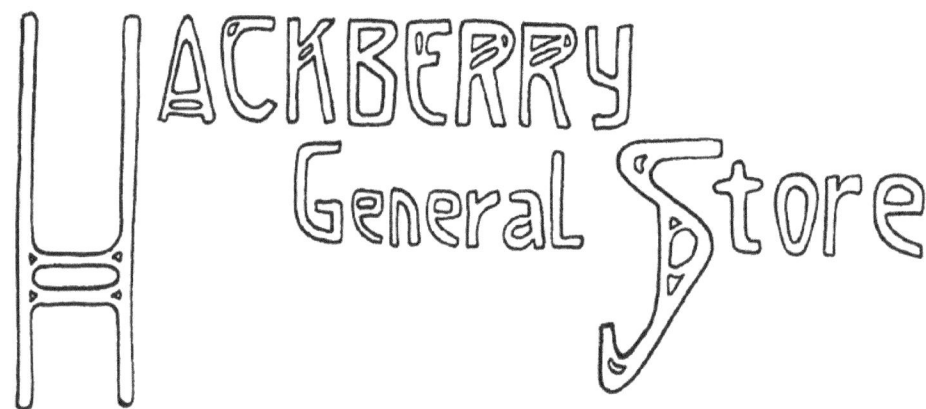

Originally a mining camp at the foot of the Peacock Mountains, Hackberry supported the twin trades of ranching and mining, bringing in the railroad in 1882. By the time the mine closed, some $3 million of gold and silver had been dug out.

The Hackberry General Store / service station was operated by John Grigg. He ran the Union 76 service station from the 1920's until his death in 1967. The grocery store known as Northside was established in 1934 and the store closed in 1978.

Almost every traveler on the section of Route 66 stops at the famous Hackberry Store, but few realize that there is more to Hackberry than a cold soda and some picturesque photo opportunities with old cars. Just to the south of general Store and Route 66, lies the remains of what was from 1874 until shortly after the Great War, a thriving town.

At a time when most schools were little more than wooden shacks or barns, the community of Hackberry had a rather grandiose Mission style stone building built in 1917. The school consisted of two tiny decorative towers and a Spanish style bell. The school had two classrooms, two bathrooms, a kitchen and living quarters for a teacher. The student body ranged from kindergarten age to the 8th grade. The school remained in session until 1994. The school is currently owned by the Grigg's family, with the hopes of one day refurbishing it.

The near demise of Hackberry was due to the closing of the mines and no off ramp from I-40. The town was literally forgotten almost becoming a ghost town.

Life began to return to the old mining town when a well know artist of Route 66, Bob Waldmire, saw the beauty in the rustic old store. He reopened it in 1992, turning it into a Route 66 Tourism Information and souvenir shop.

Bob and his 1972 Volkswagen Microbus was the inspiration for Fillmore in the Disney / Pixar movie *Cars*. Bob sold the business in 1998. The store remains open today as a must stop along Route 66 with its many photo ops and classic souvenirs.

(Snips of history about the school house were provided by Blue Miller "Never Quite Lost")

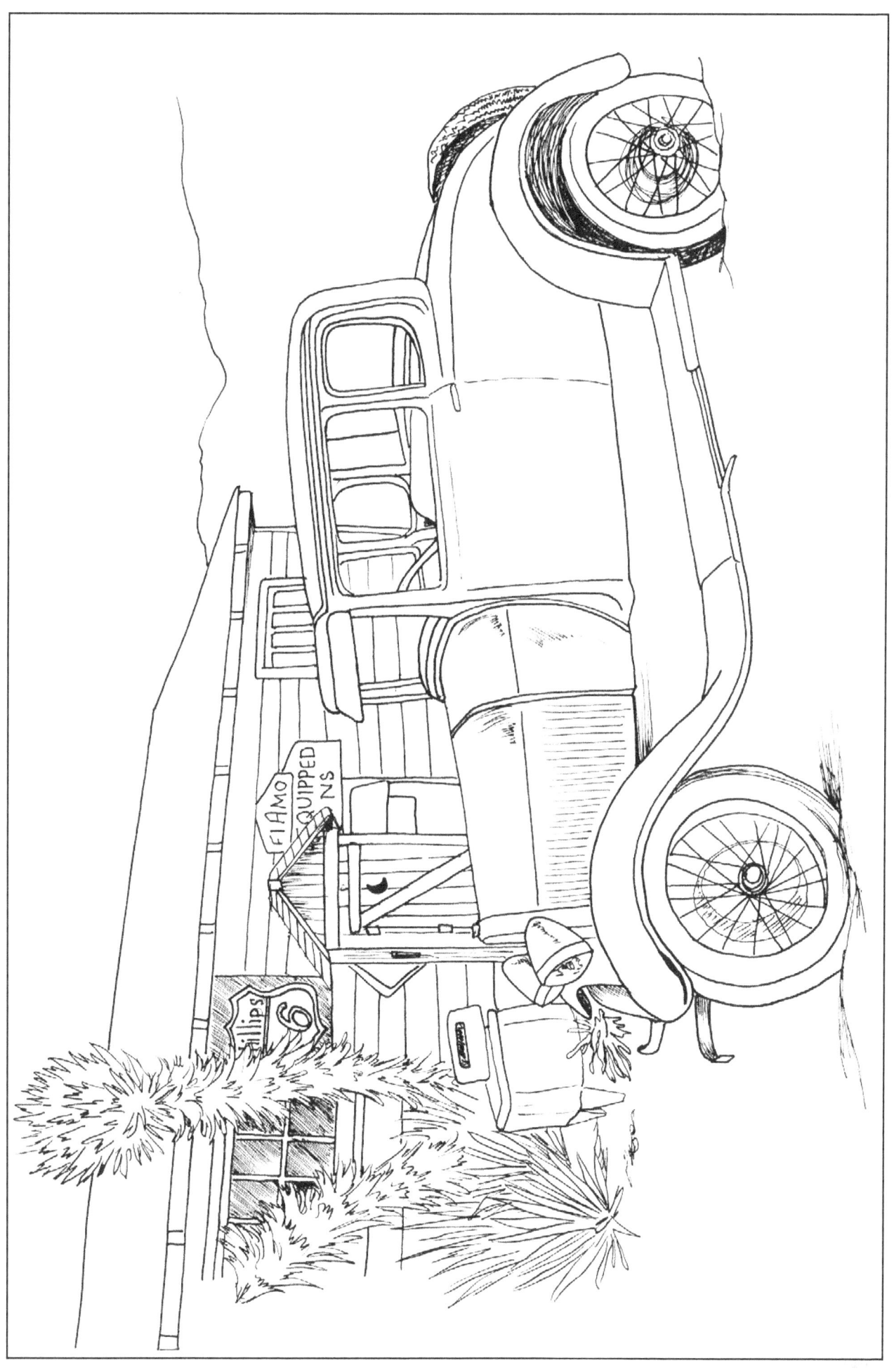

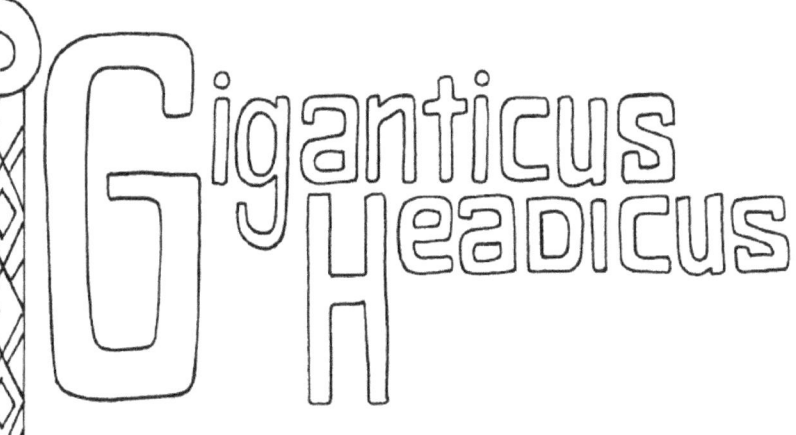

Walapai

The fourteen foot tall statue overlooks the beautiful views of the desert valley.

The creation of artist Gregg Arnold, inspired by Andy Warhol, the once Kozy Korner trailer park is now a Route 66 Antares Visitors Center. Antares offers coffee, gifts, souvenirs and t-shirts.

Adhere a selfie or a stamp from Giganticus Headicus

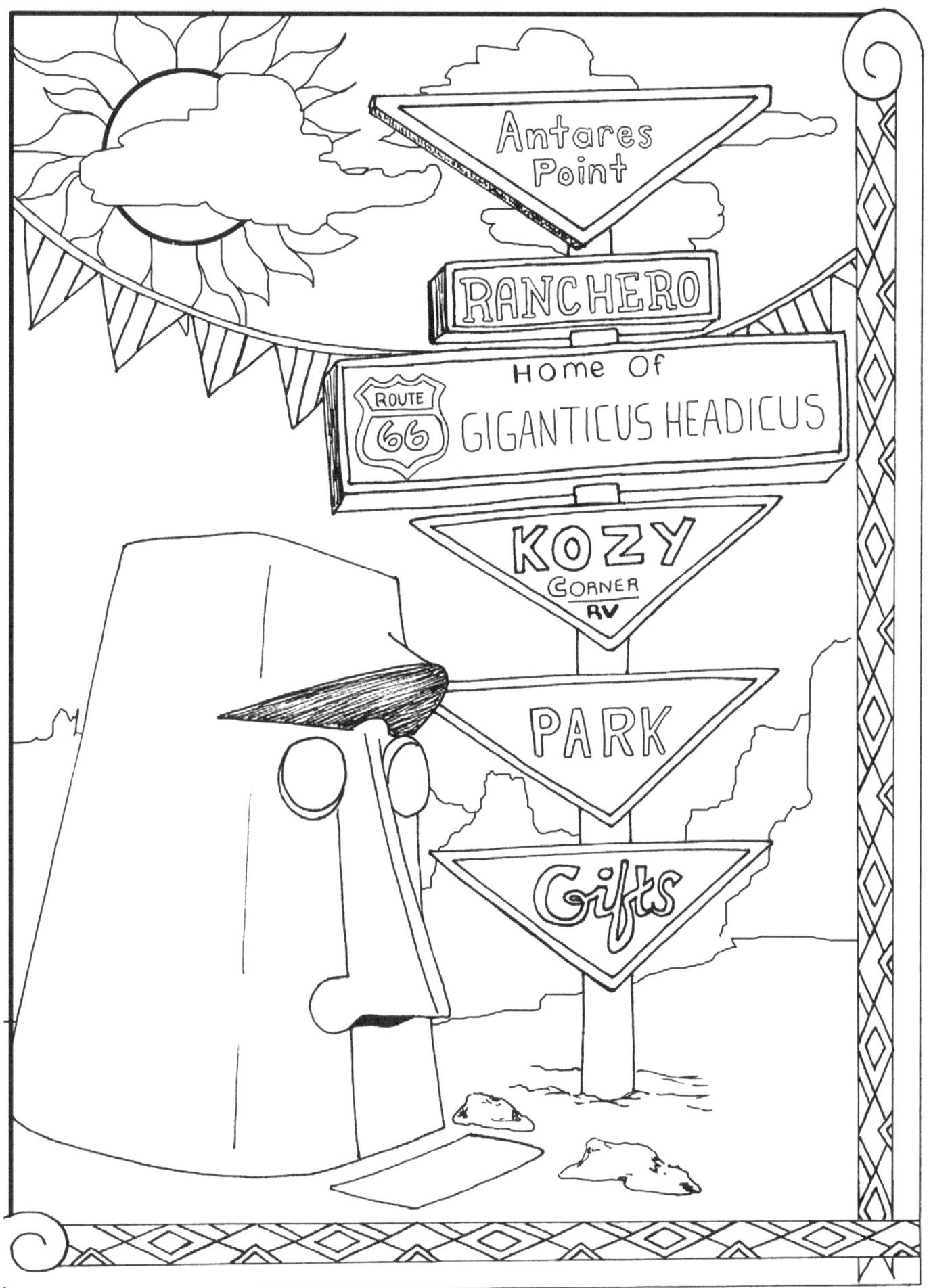

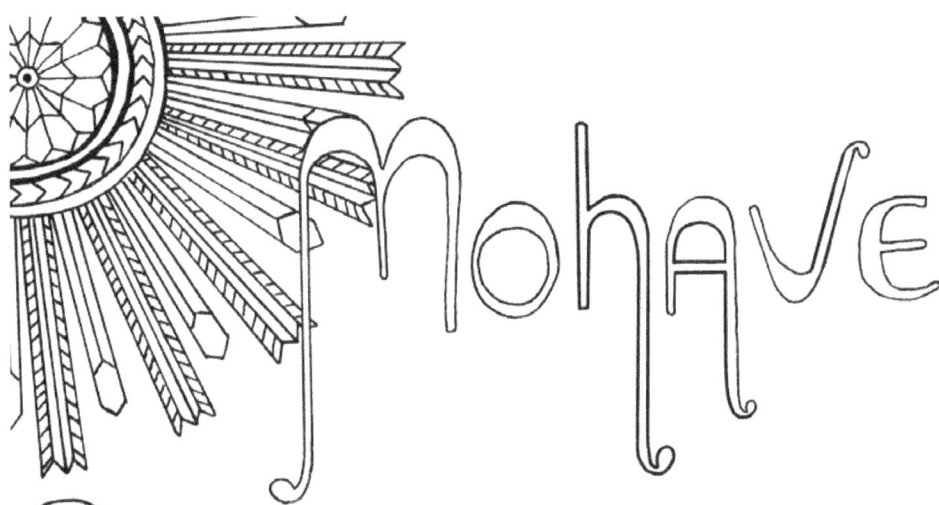

Mohave

Established in 1864 Mohave County is the fifth largest county in the United States and was one of the four original counties of Arizona.

The land of the Mojave stretched from the Black Canyon to the Picacho Mountains below today's Parker Dam, along the Colorado River.

The Mojave people were people of dreams and visions. They were once the largest concentration of people in the Southwest. The were people willing to protect their land and unafraid to venture far from it. The Mojaves were known as great traders with tribes as far as the Pacific Coast.

An important part of their beliefs was the art of tattooing. They would tattoo their faces with lines and dots in a fashionable practice.

They were hunters and farmers, growing vegetables and the woman made pottery from crushed sandstone decorated with geometrical designs.

A unusual burial tradition of the Mohave were to cremate their loved ones accompanied by their personal belongings, never to speak their name again.

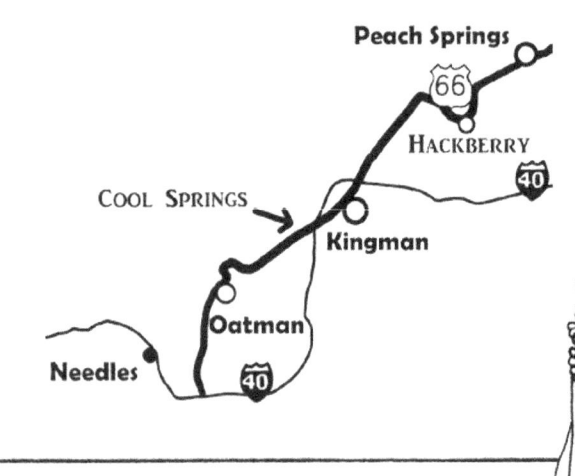

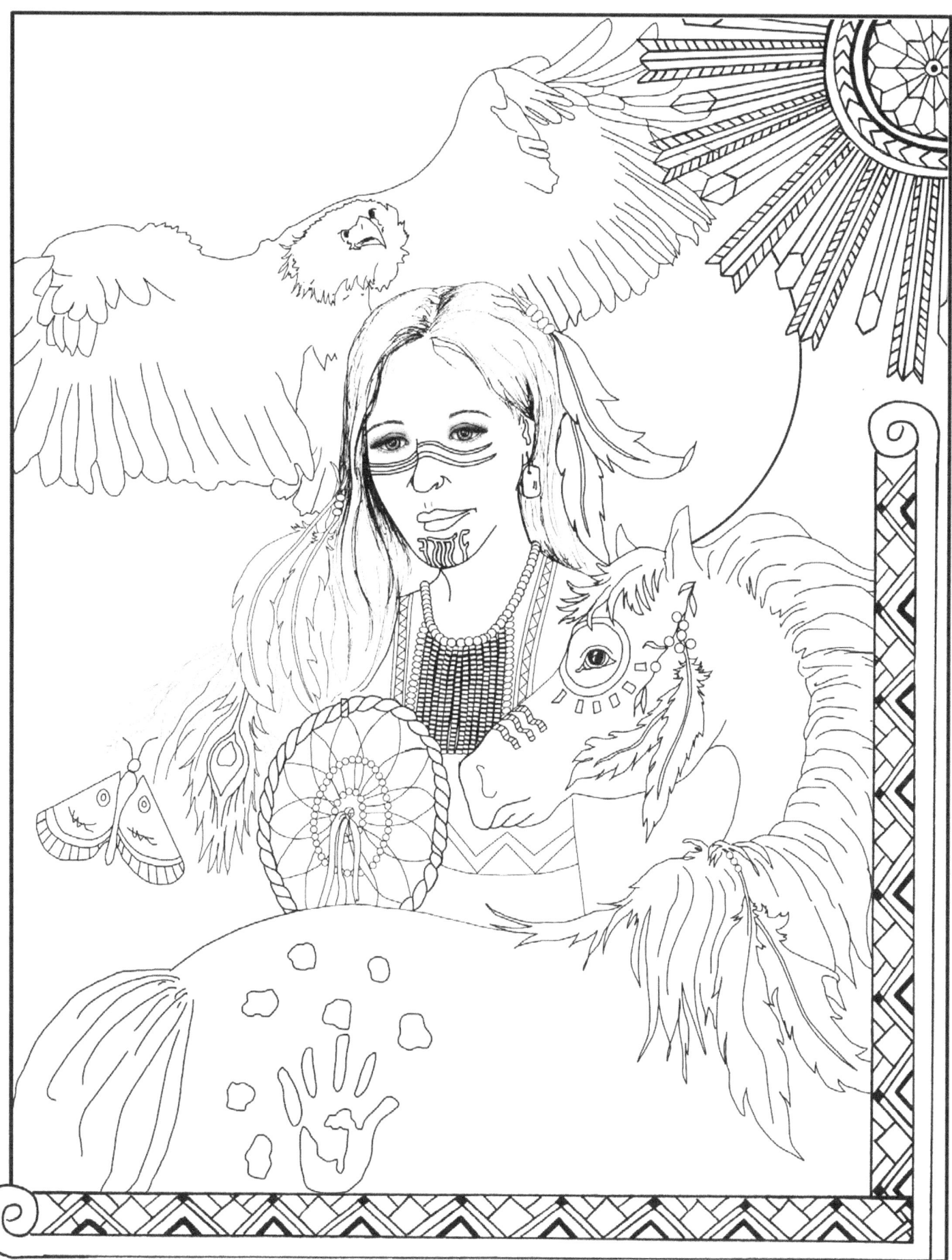

Kingman

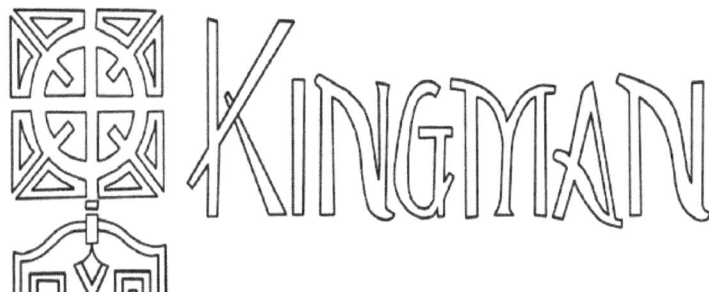

Located in a natural basin, surrounded by basaltic hills, the railroad town was established in 1880 when Lewis Kingman began surveying along the Atlantic and Pacific right of way between Needles and Albuquerque for the track of railroad to be laid. While the railroad was being constructed, establishments were built to accommodate the needs of the workers. The tracks were completed in 1883 and the town continued to grow, later becoming the county seat.

Stop into the Kingman Visitor Center, also known as the Powerhouse to get your book stamped and see an amazing display of the historic evolution of travel along the 35th parallel that became Highway 66.

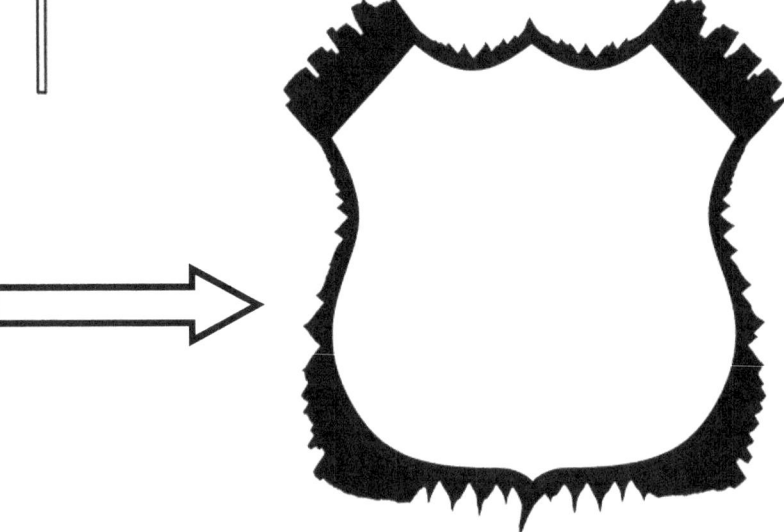

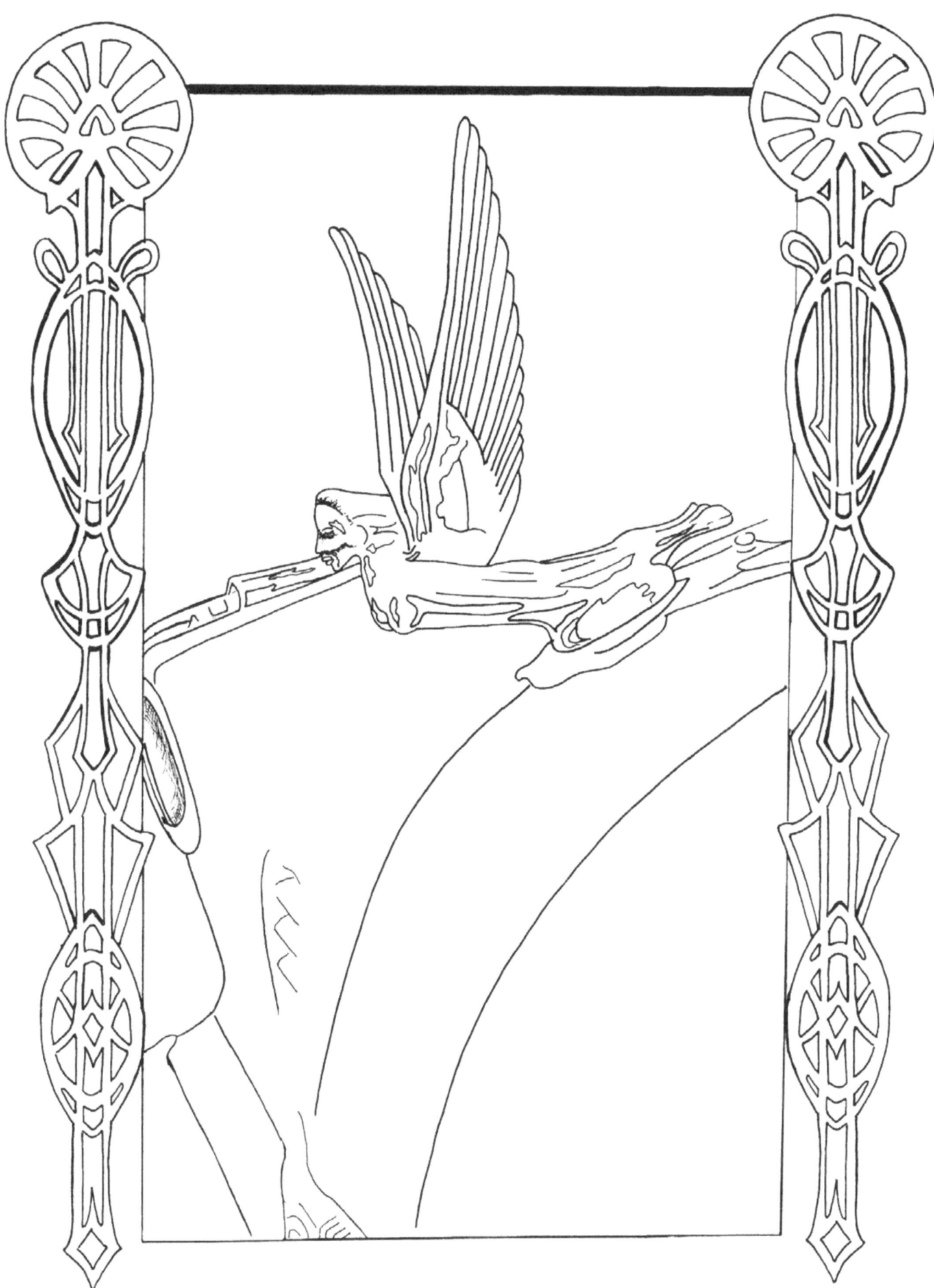

BEALE

Before Kingman was even a town, the Hubs House was created. In 1880, two sisters saw an opportunity for an income through providing an eatery for those working on the newly arrived railroad. They later added on rooms for rent. When one of the sisters married Harvey Hubbs, the establishment gained its name.

Harvey built a two-story, frame building with restrooms (a chamber pot in every room) in the rose garden right beside the Hubs House. Harvey called the new structure Hotel Beale after the Lt. Edward F. Beale, a man who is said to have been larger than life.

Lt. Beale was well known to many as the man who lead a brigade of camels through Arizona, carving away a path for wagons with settlers travelling to California.

The premier hotel was very successful for many decades with its grandeur, mahogany desk and stairway, the balcony overlooking the enormous lobby and atrium skylight overhead attracted visitors from all walks of life.

The hotel flourished, becoming the heart of Kingman and its activities. The hotel was remodeled in 1913 adding a sporting goods store and a soda fountain along with indoor bathrooms and electricity.

Tom sold the hotel in 1926, just at the beginning of the establishment of the Route 66 highway. Lulu Hall, the new owner, with great ambitions for the hotel, added three barbers, and additional shops. The newly added commercial activity and attracted travelers such as Charles Lindbergh, who stayed at the hotel while establishing a new air service.

After World War II, the hotel was remodeled again with more modern conveniences with the once over night rooms becoming apartments.

After falling on hard times, the hotel has closed. With many years of being vacant the building has become one of the most photographed landmarks in the city and is starving to be saved and restored to its former glory so that it can be enjoyed by generations to come.

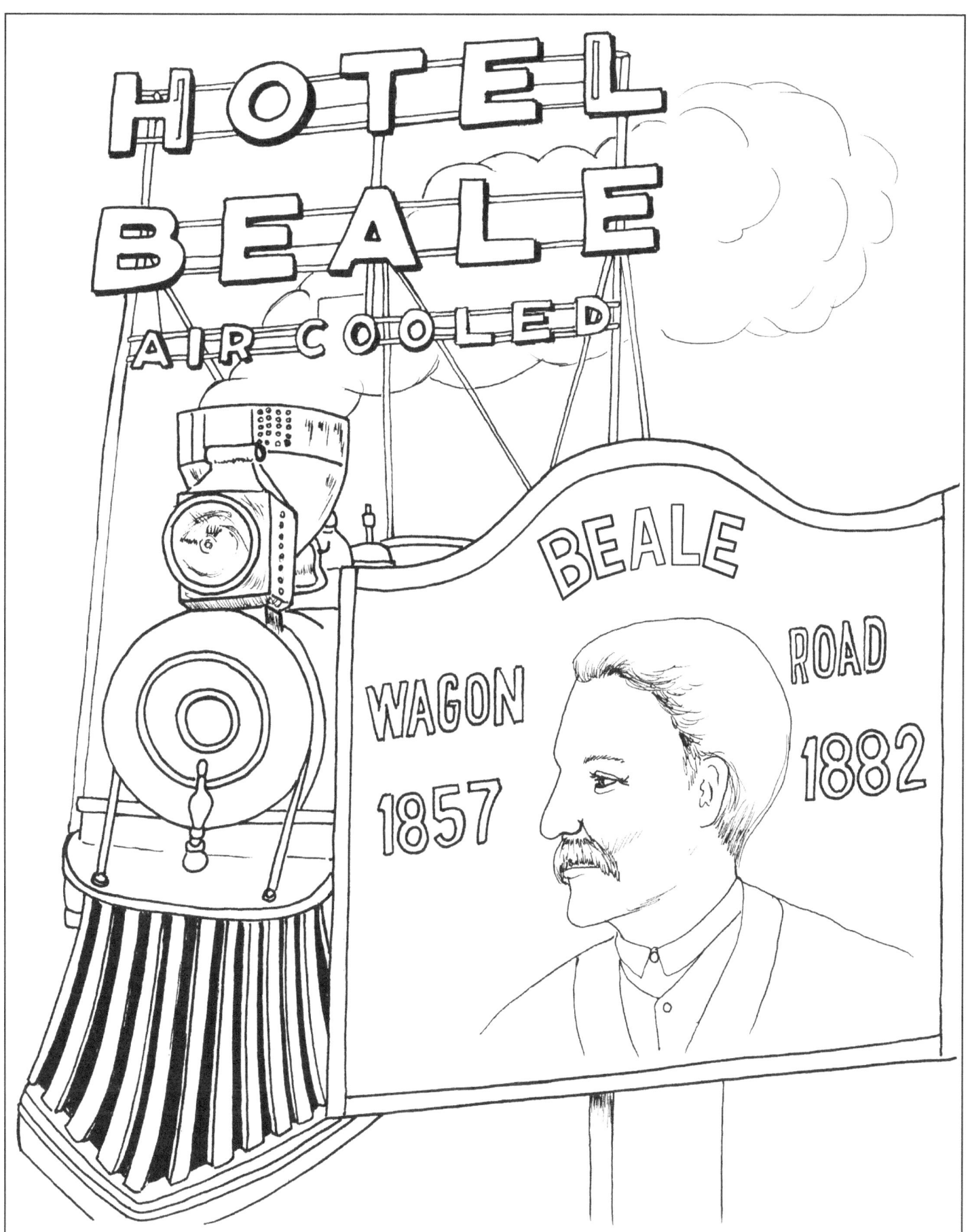

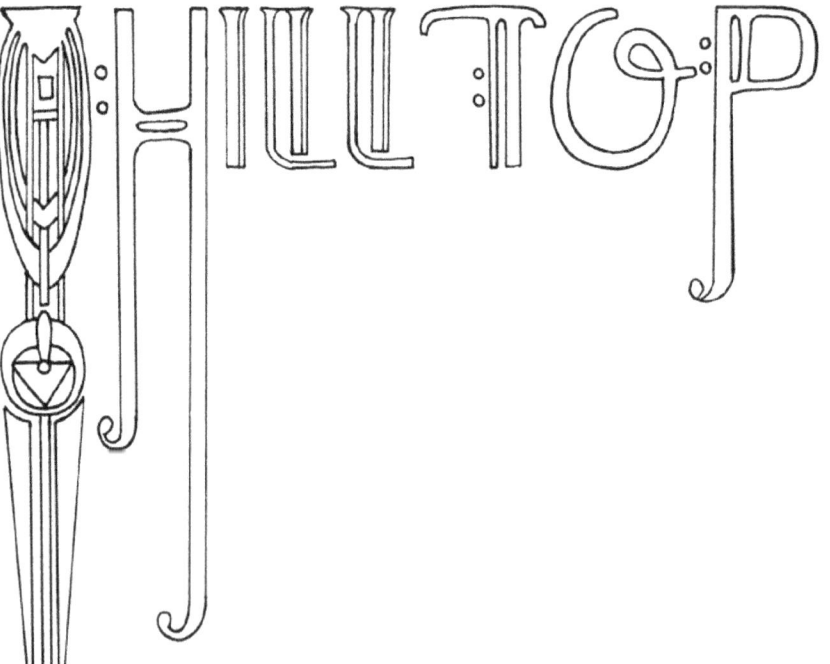

HILLTOP

Constructed in 1954 by John Mescheid, a land developer from Santa Monica, the twenty unit Hilltop Motel was constructed by local Kingman contractors. John wanted the look and feel of the new facility to be one of relaxation with no worries of tomorrow.

Today, the motel is still in operation with the goal in mind that even with the new modern conveniences, such as microwaves, refrigerators and TVs, the motel still wants to maintain the nostalgic charm and relaxed feeling of the 50's.

Use this space for photos, stickers, post cards.

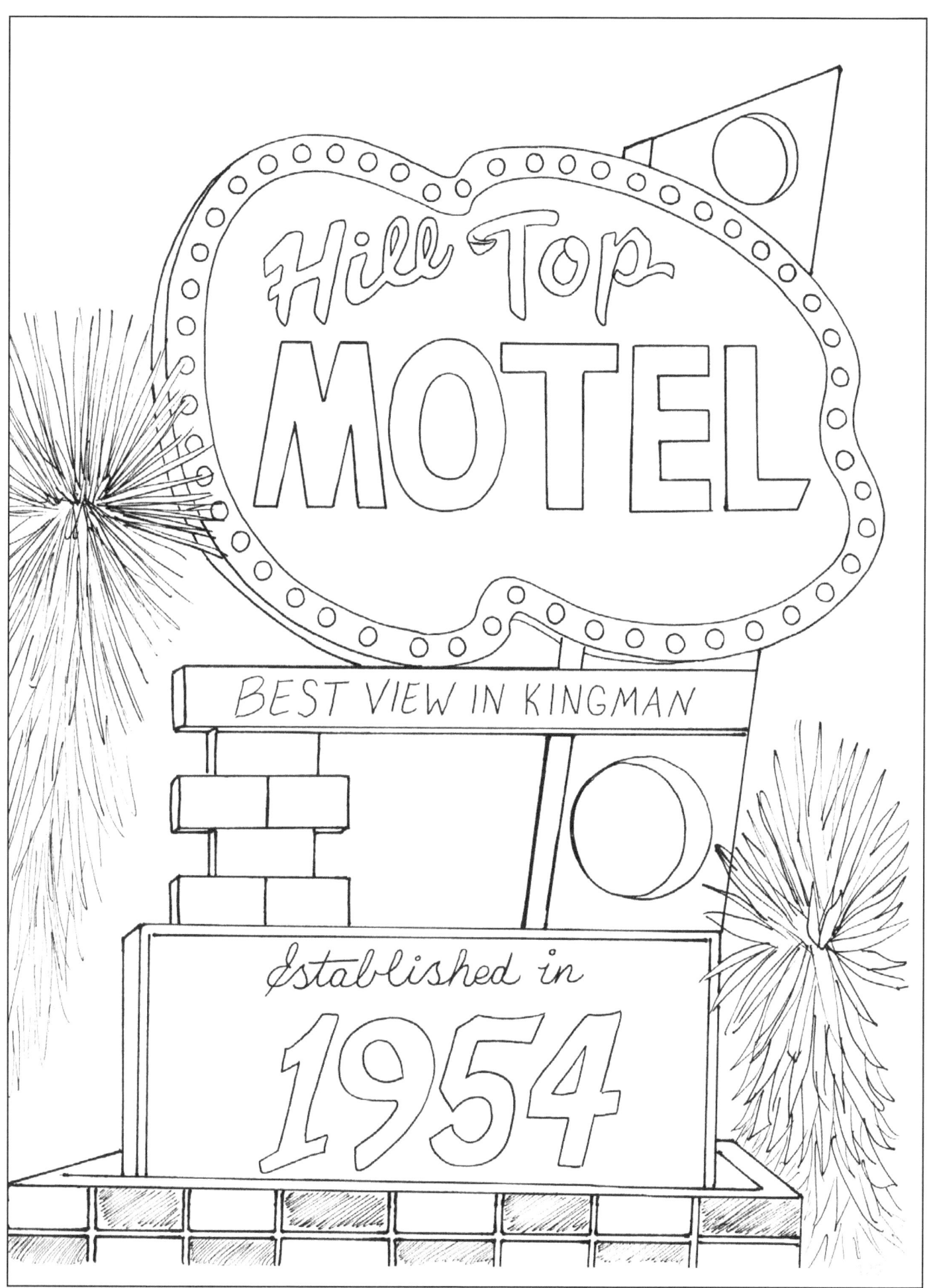

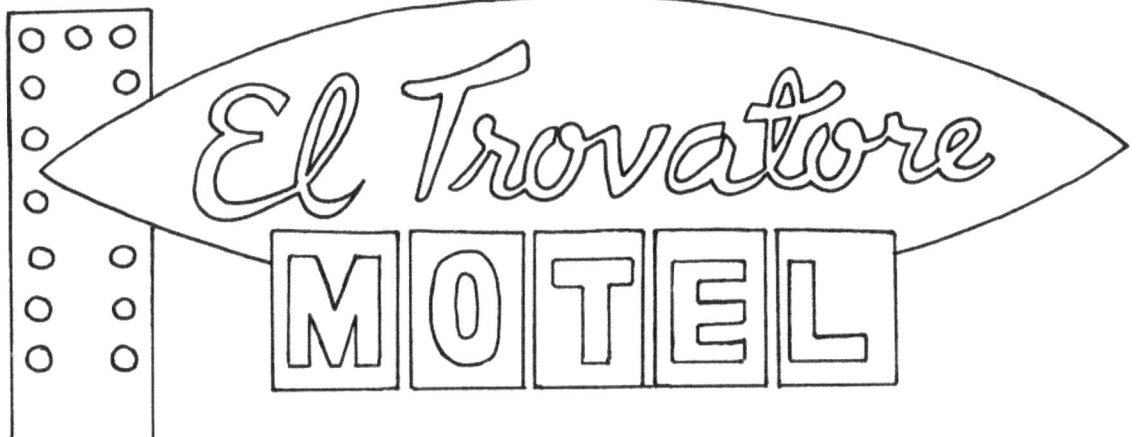

The El Trovatore Motel has themed rooms, celebrating American and Route 66 Icons. It is one of the few pre-World War II Kingman Arizona motels that are still standing. The motel started in 1937 as a service station, with the tourist court added later in 1939 and was first owned by John F. Miller.

This motel, with Hollywood themed rooms, is located on El Trovatore Hill, in Kingman with a location on a stony bluff that awards stunning vistas of the Hualapai Mountains and the awe inspiring landscapes that embrace it. The El Trovatore, recently refurbished, now has a map of route 66 mural that will soon join the list of the worlds largest roadside attractions.

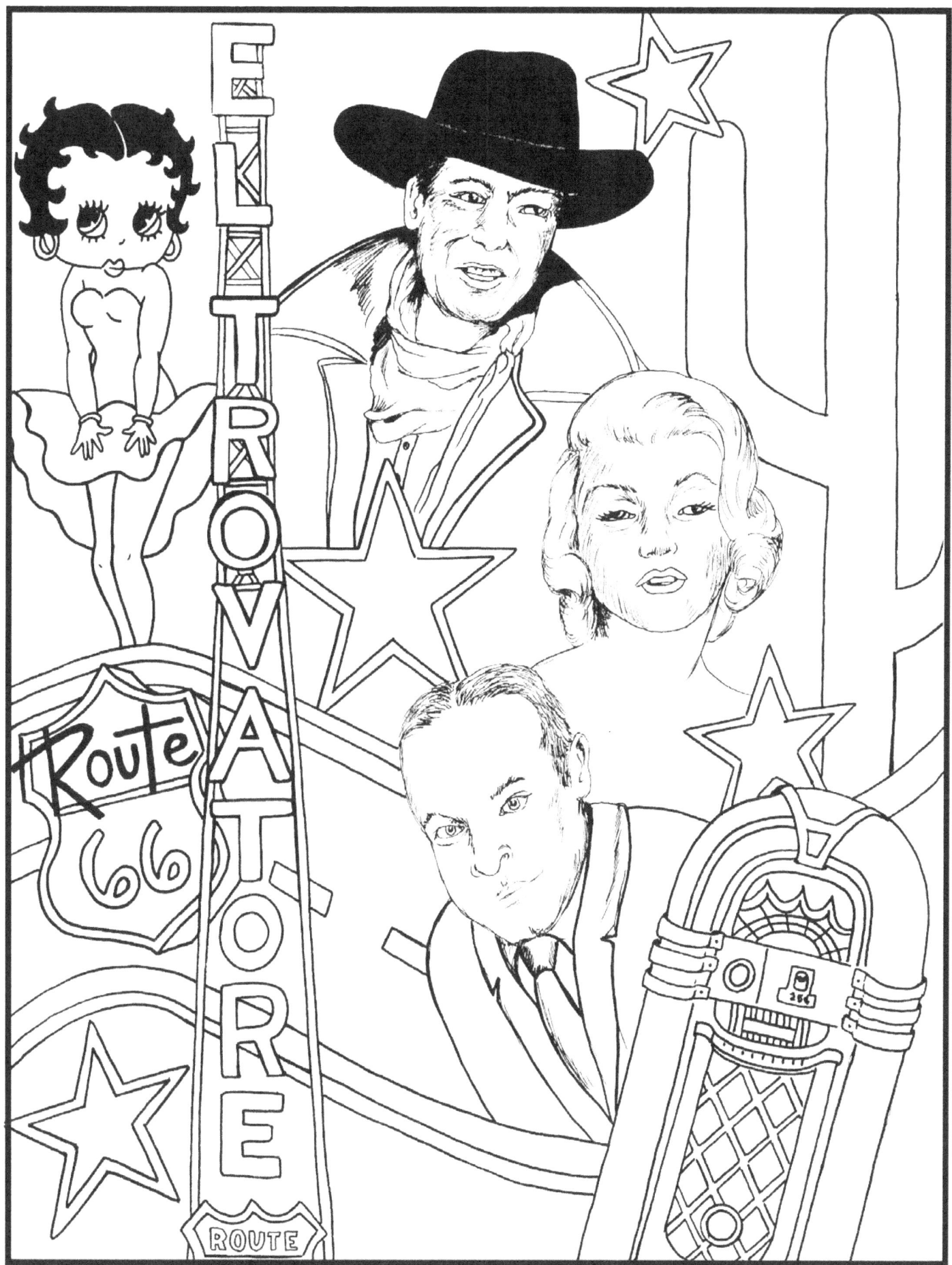

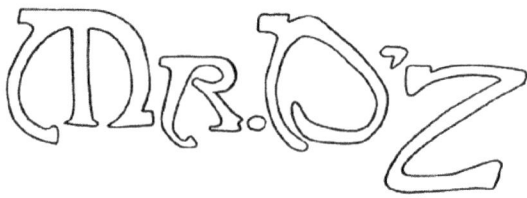

Mr. D'z

Mr. D's wasn't always a diner; it once was a small café and gas station in the 50's and 60's.

Mr. D'z Diner will serve you a root beer float or a burger & fries in their casual and relaxed environment: Vintage Americana diner flare in the modern world along Route 66.

Mr. D'z has been featured on Guy Fieri's TV show *Diners, Drive-In and Dives*.

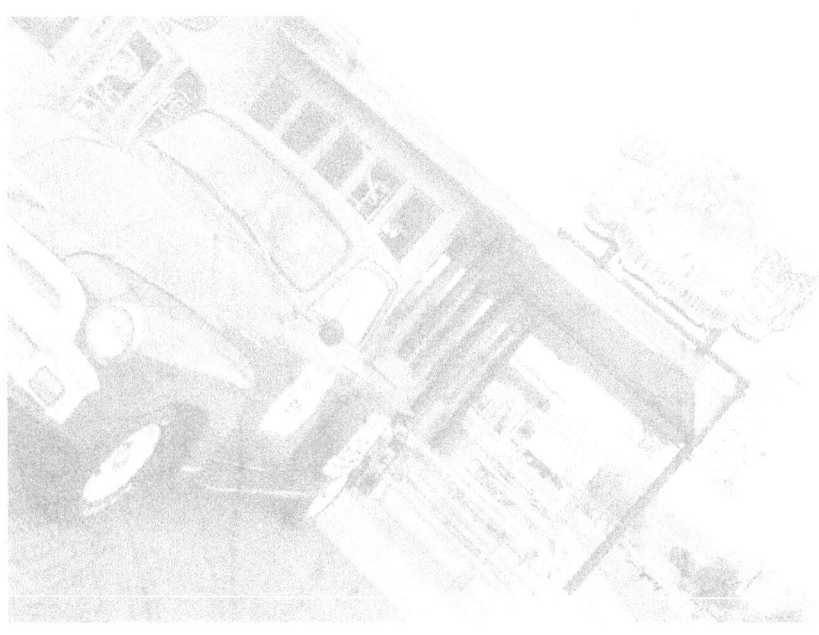

Use this space for photos, stickers, post cards.

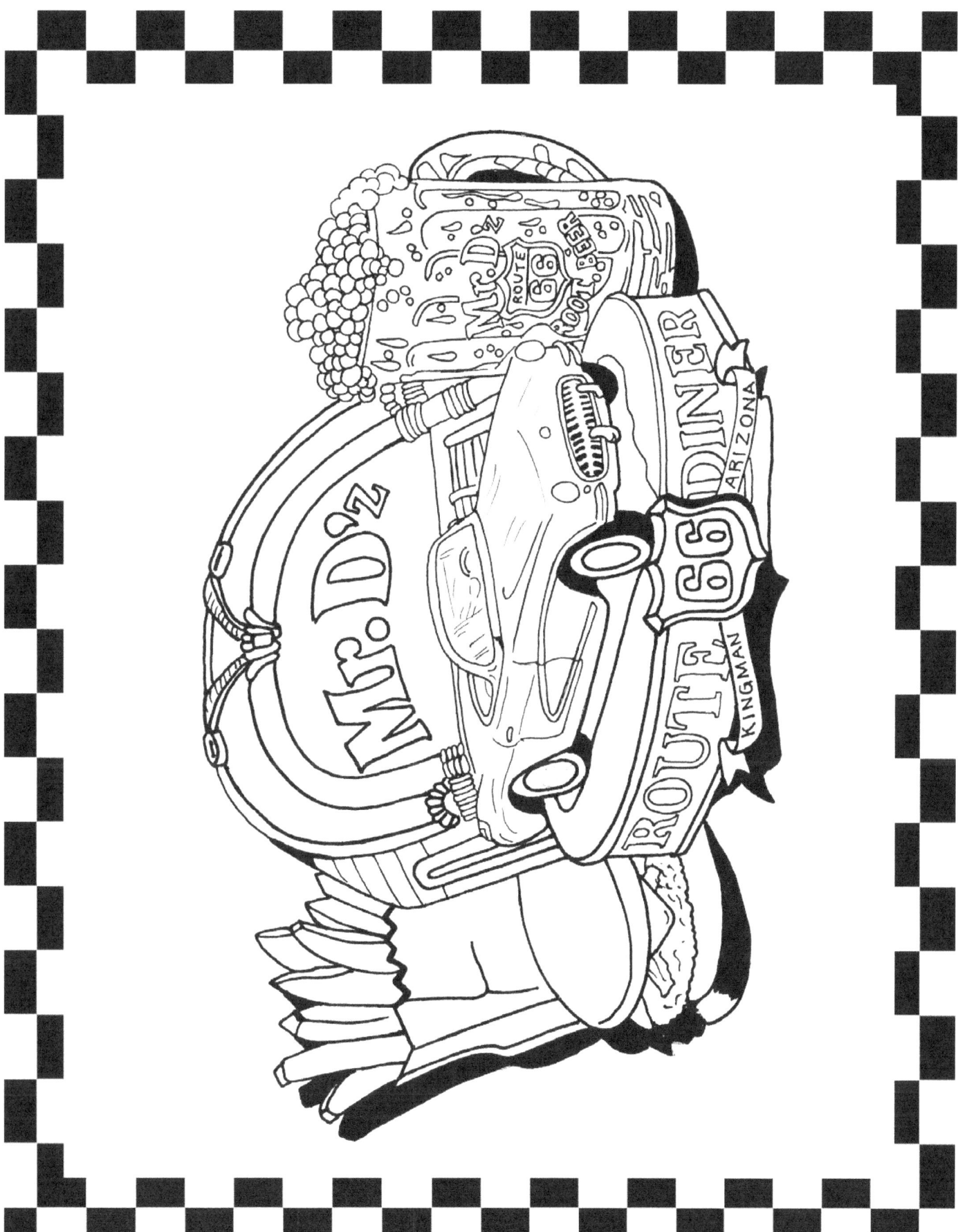

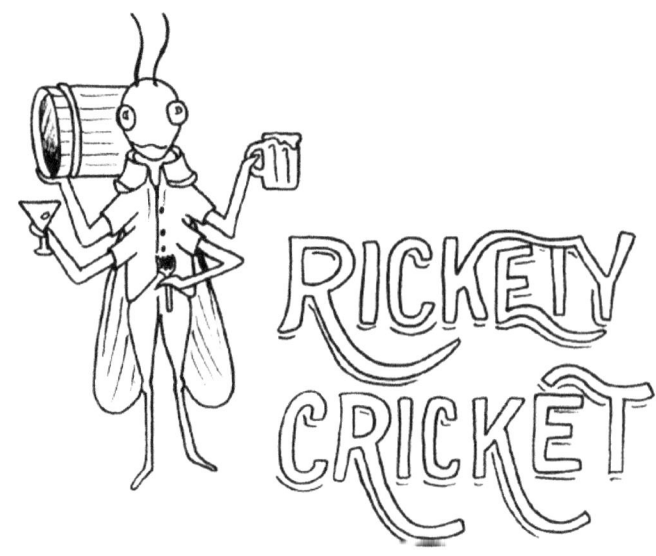

The Kingman Club dates back to 1944.
The new owners of the Kingman Club restored the neon sign, however the club is now known as the Rickety Cricket ~ The House of Hops, and has been in operation since 1963.

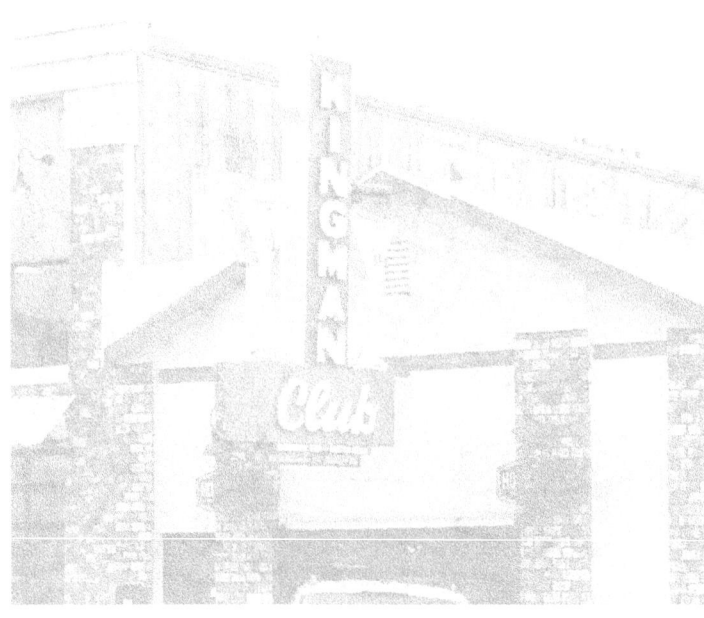

Use this space for photos, stickers, post cards.

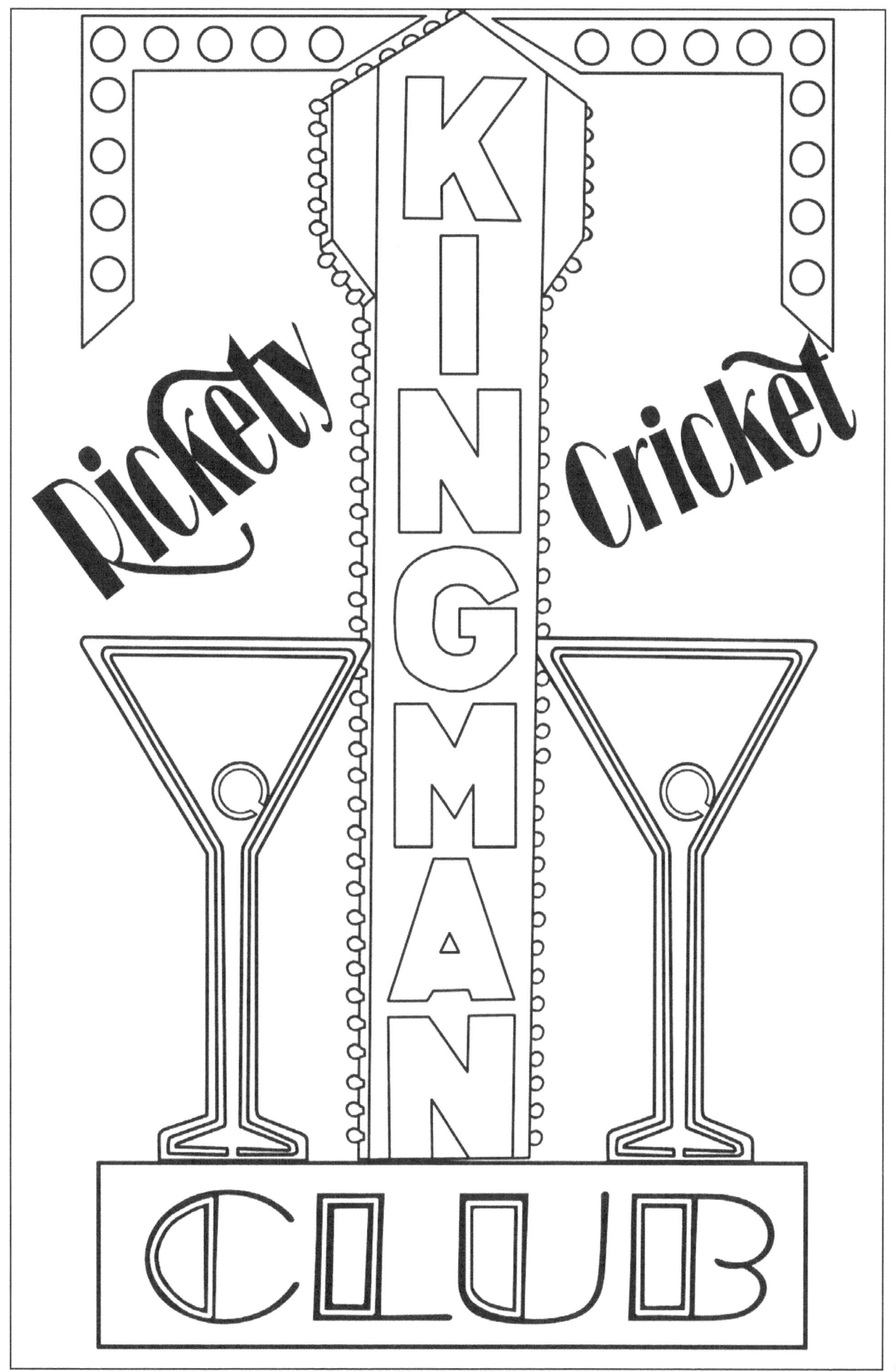

Roaming Wild

Oatman started life over 100 years ago as a mining tent camp, and quickly became a flourishing gold-mining center. In 1915, two miners struck a $10 million gold find, and within a year, the town's population grew to more than 3,500.

Oatman's "wild" burros are the descendants of burros brought here by the miners in the late 1800s; when the miners no longer needed them, they were turned loose.

Use this space for photos, stickers, post cards.

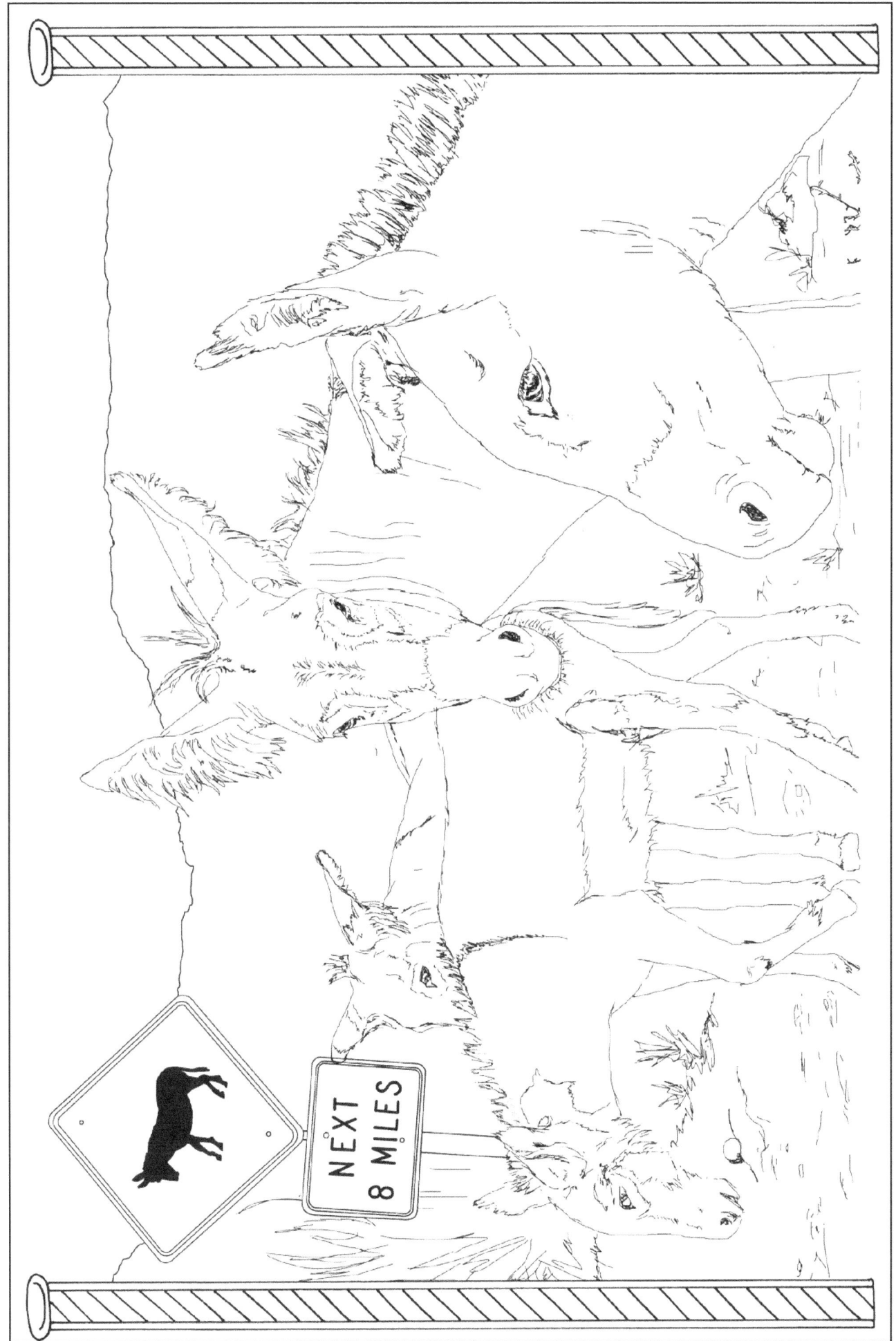

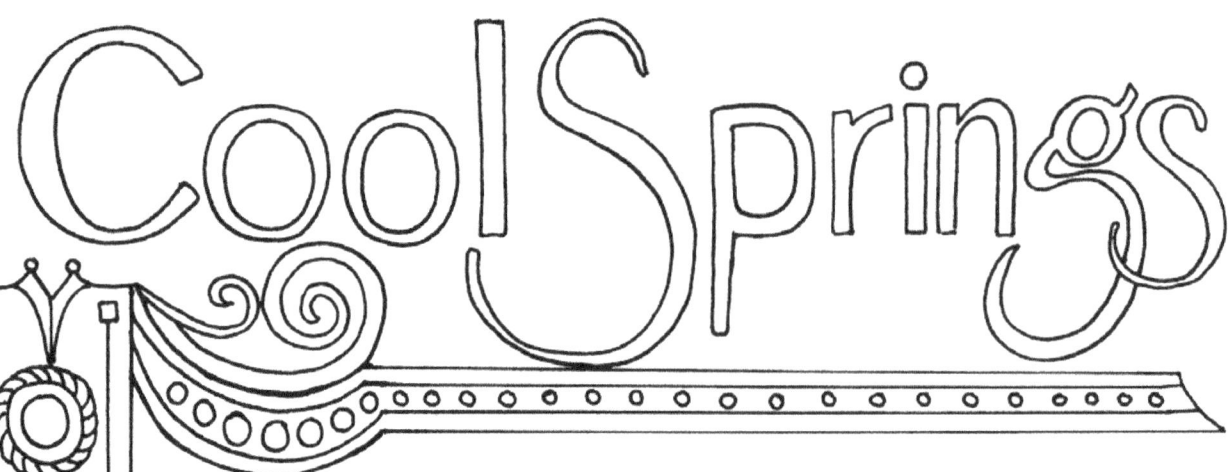

Cool Springs

From the very earliest days, Cool Springs camp and service station was an important stop for motorists traveling Arizona's Route 66. Cool Springs was built in the mid-1920s and has been connected with Route 66 from the very start. This route is the original Old Trails Highway that paralleled the Beale military road from 1857, and became Route 66 in 1926. Of all the stretches along Route 66, this was perhaps the most intimidating of all, with its steep grades, narrow road, and hairpin curves. Some travelers of old Route 66 would pay the locals to drive their car up the grade for them or even have their vehicle towed over the summit. In the mid-sixties, a fire burned Cool Springs to the ground. Nothing remained but fragments of the stone foundations and the original stone pillars. For the next quarter of a century, Cool Springs was just a forgotten memory, a crumbling stone relic along a forgotten road, home to lizards, tarantulas, and tumbleweeds. Then briefly in 1991, Cool Springs came to life again when Hollywood used it as a location for their movie "Universal Soldier". December 7th, 2004 was a banner day for Cool Springs. The power was hooked back up. As Ned puts it, "We had the power hooked up at Cool Springs last night. It marks the first time that the lights were on there since 1966."

After almost 40 years, Cool Springs is now open for business again. It is now presented as a welcomed stop for people to enjoy and cherish. It represents the end of the old era, and the beginning of the new appreciation for the days of the past. The construction will begin January 2005 on the building next to the station. This new building will resemble the old cafe, but the Leuchtner family is going to make it a museum. They decided not to do food service or gas distribution because of the many regulations, but they will offer soft drinks and snacks.

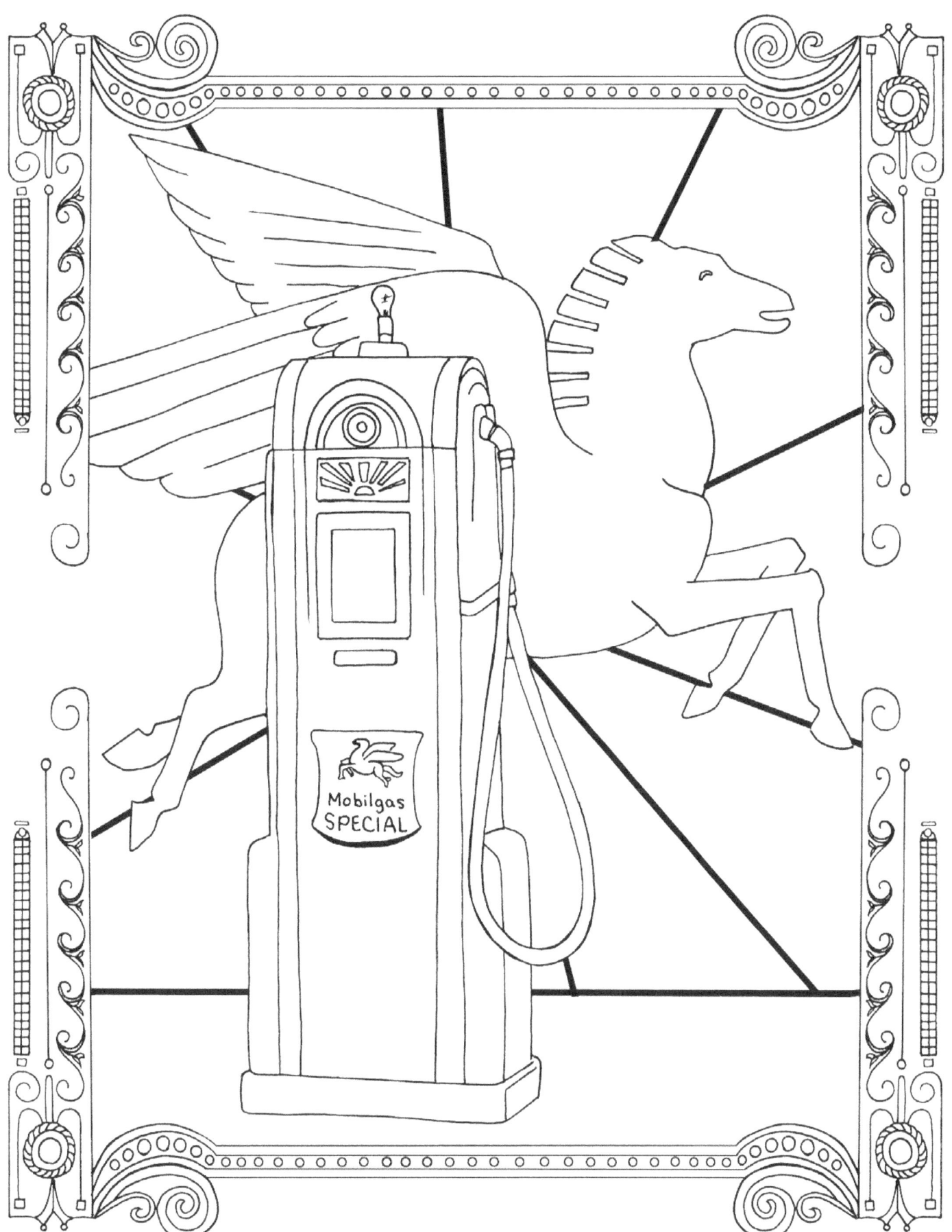

Sitgreave Pass

Sitgreave Pass is a gap in the Black Mountains of Mohave County where you can see Arizona, California, and Nevada. At the top of the pass, roadies can view the many crosses – memorials to deceased people whose cremains were scattered at the site.

Adhere your selfie here of the pass

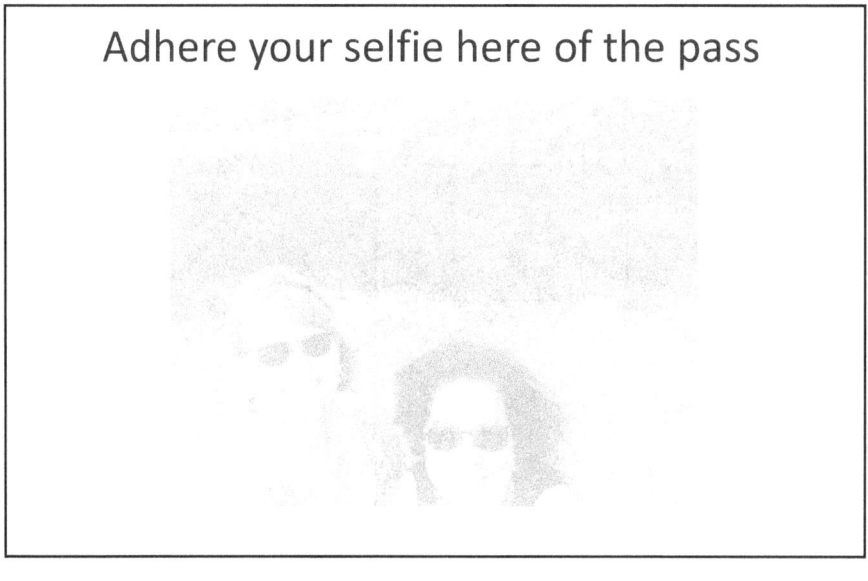

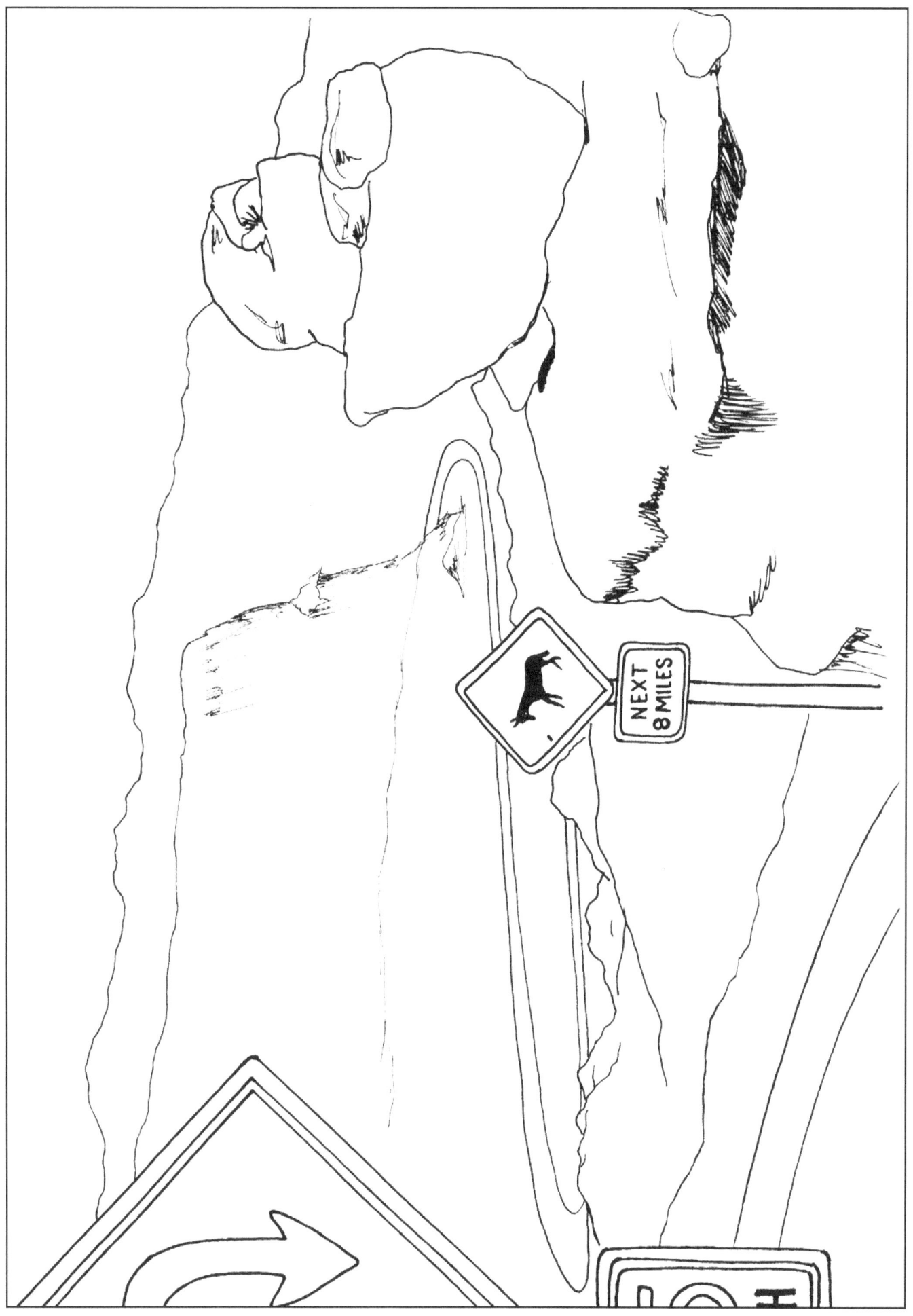

Olive Oatman

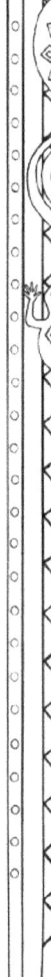

In the mid 1800's, many families ventured west, some to escape from slavery or the law others just wanting a chance at a new life. Knowing that it would be hard work and many dangers they still pressed on. Many families never made it to see the sandy shores of California due to sickness, the environmental conditions or meeting up with hostiles.

A group of 89 immigrants from Illinois wanted a taste of the new life and were willing to make the sacrifices to settle the new lands. Loading up their wagons with all of their belongings, their live stock and their children they headed west under the leadership of James C. Brewster. The year was 1850, the wagon train group were known as Brewsterites. Their journey began from Independence, Missouri with the goal of heading to the land that Mr. Brewster referred to as "intended place of gathering for Mormon's".

During those months of travel animosity developed, causing the group to split at Santa Fe. Amongst the group of immigrants that split off from the Brewsterites was the Oatman family of nine. Roys Oatman took over the group continuing their journey heading toward the southern route. The families reached Maricopa Wells where they discovered the road ahead was dangerous and hostile. All the families but the Oatman's decided to stay. Traveling alone, the Oatman's and their seven children, ranging from one to seventeen, met the Tolkepaya's tribe who were asking for tobacco and food. The Oatman family was unwilling to part with their dwindling supplies which resulted in the tribe attacking. The entire Oatman family were killed except the three oldest children. Lorenzo, the fifteen year old son was left for dead after being brutally clubbed and the two girls Olive, age 14 and Mary Ann, age 7 were taken.

Lorenzo survived the beating to only discovered his parents and siblings were slain. However there was no sign of Mary Ann and Olive. He walked to the nearest settlement where he was treated, later returning to the scene to bury his family.

The natives along with some of the families belongings and the girls travel over 60 miles to their village where the sisters became their slaves. A year after the girls obduction a group of Mohave Indians visited the village, saw the girls and traded two horses, vegetables, blankets and other trinkets. The Mohave took the girls to their village to what is now known as Needles. Here they were not slaves but were taken in by the tribal leader. As per their tribal customs, the girls were tattooed on their chins and arms to ensure that they would enter the land of the dead, and be recognized as Mohave's by their ancestors.

Approximately 1855 a drought devastated the region causing a food shortage, many natives parish from starvation including Olive's sister, Mary Ann. Three years later the commander at Fort Yuma heard the Mohave's had a white girl living with them, he requested her return. The commander traded blankets, a white horse and threats of destruction without the return of Olive. At the age of nineteen, Olive arrived at the Fort, where she discovered her brother Lorenzo was alive and had been looking for her and her sister the past five years.

Olive married and relocated to Sherman Texas where her and her cattleman husband, John B. Fairchild, adopted a girl they named Mamie. Olive died in 1903 of a heart attack at the age of 65. Olive's life was featured in a 1965 syndicated western series film, *Death Valley Days* in the episode "The Lawless Have Laws".

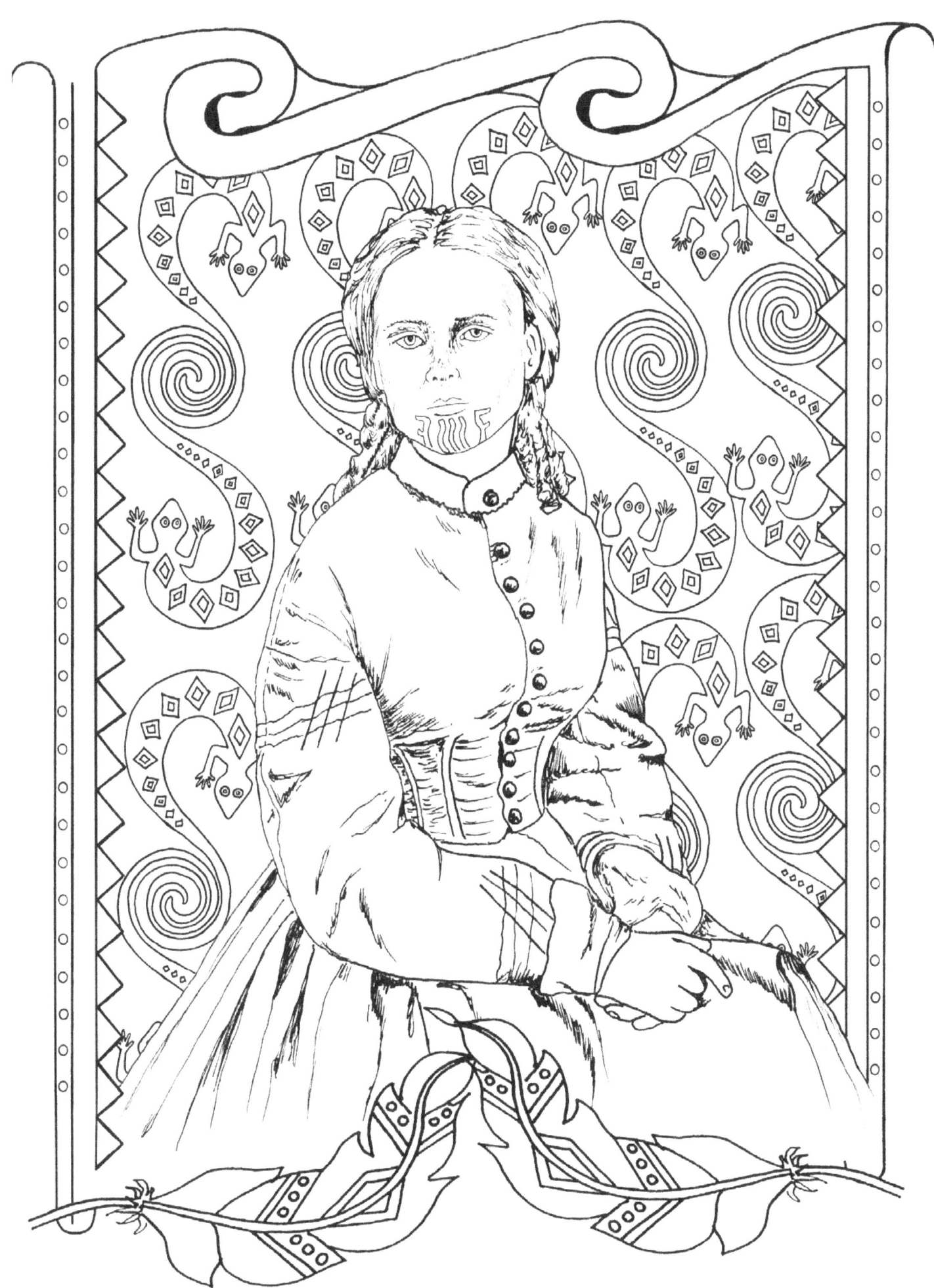

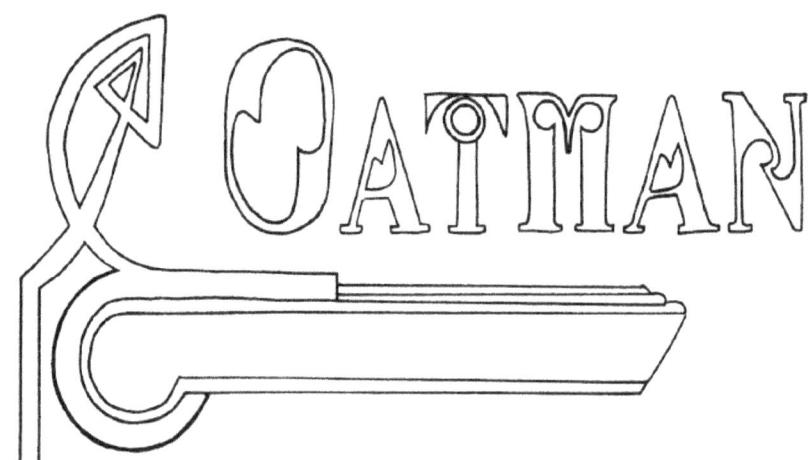

Oatman

A prospector, mountain man named Johnny Moss discovered gold in the Black Mountains in 1863. He staked his claim to the mine as well as several others. Naming one Moss, after himself, and one after Olive Oatman, whose story was widely known during that time.

After several years of mining, the gold ran out. The town created from the many miners began to die. Almost becoming a ghost town, Oatman was revived by another gold discovery in the 20th century by a man named Tom Reed. A body of ore in the nearby United Eastern Mining Company property was also discovered in 1915.

The boom of 1915-17 gave Oatman all the characters and characteristics of any gold rush boomtown. For a while, Oatman mines were the largest gold producers in the American West, however that too ran out. The town continued to breathe, even after the mines closings. With the town being bypassed with the new interstate I-40, extinction was looming in the air once again.

The little mining town managed to stay alive for the rebirth of the historical Route 66. Today Oatman provides many nostalgic shopping opportunities and daily entrainment of burros petting and gun fighting re-enactments entertain travelers from all over the world.

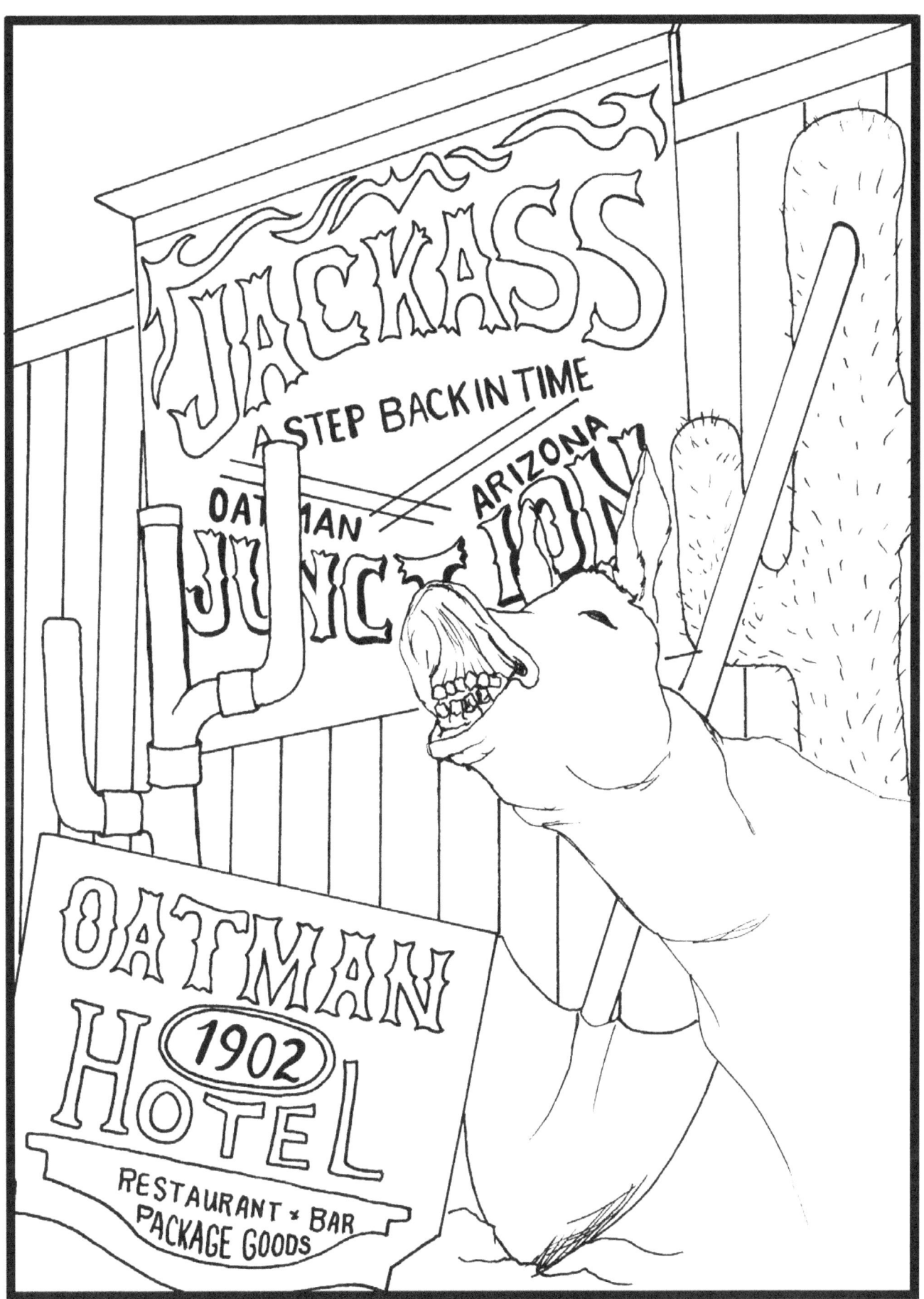

Arizona State animal

Ringtail Cat

Use this space for photos, stickers, post cards.

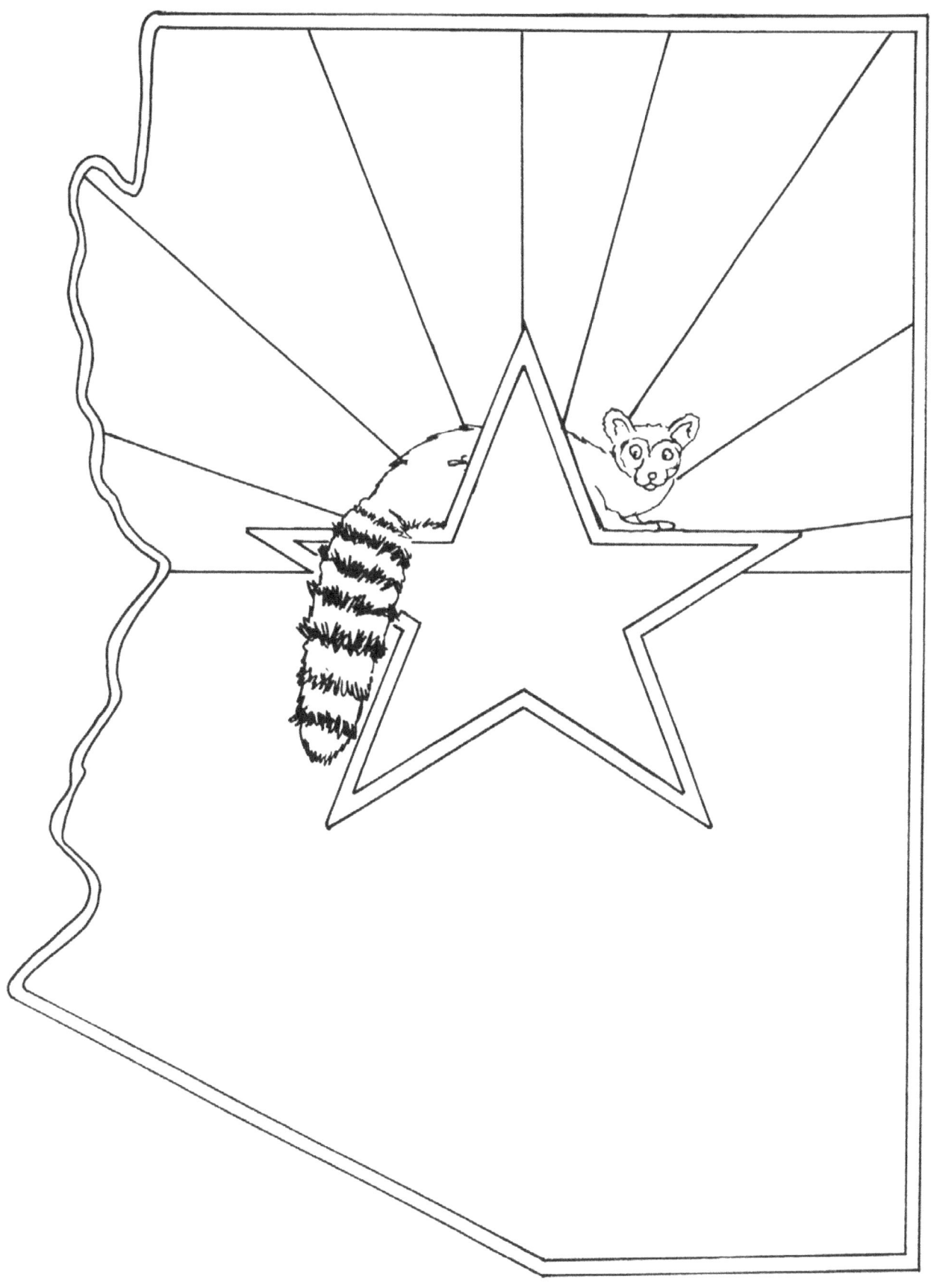

Use this space for photos, stickers, post cards.

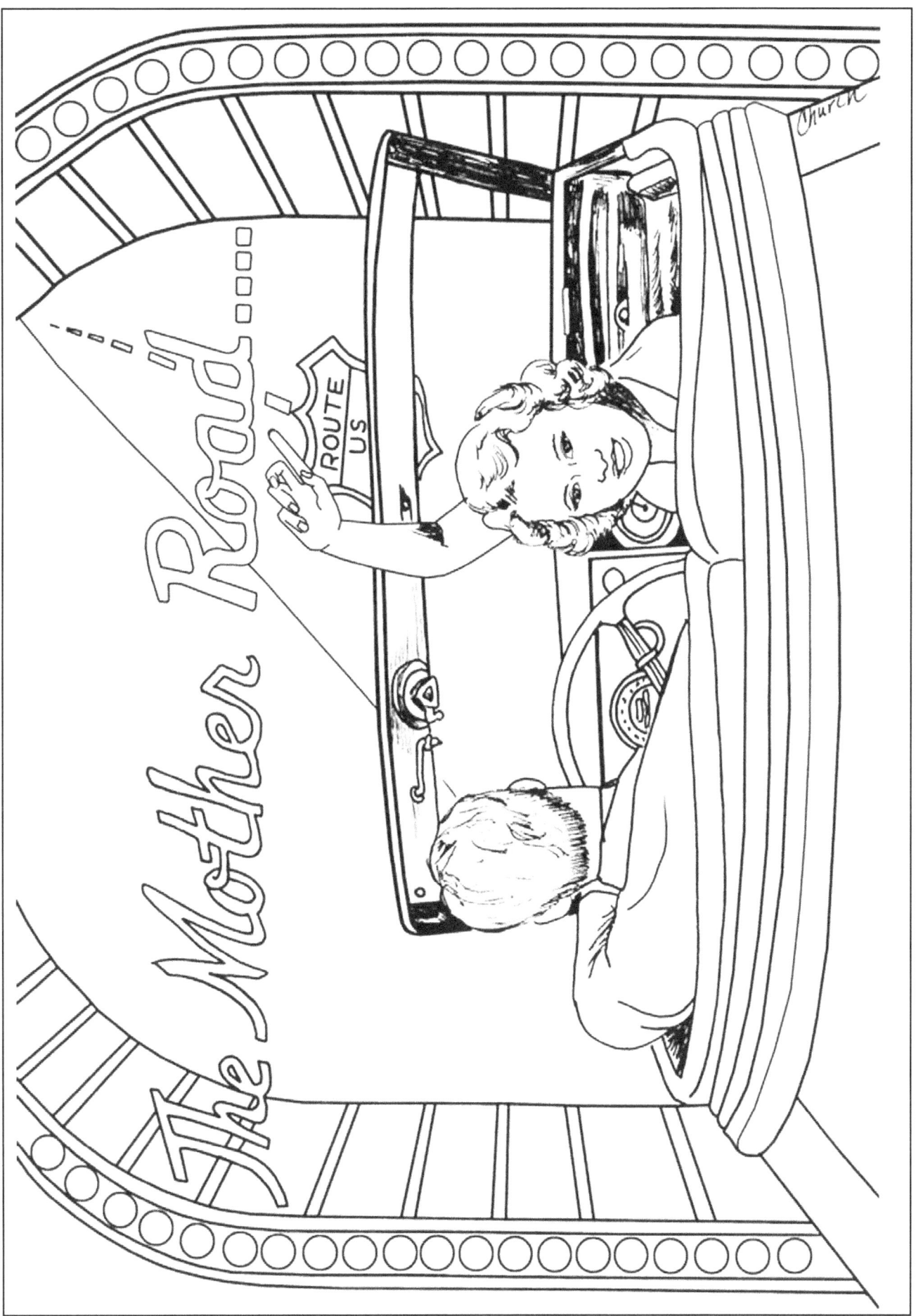

Resources:

Native Words Native Warriors. Smithsonian National Museum of the American Indian. http://www.nmai.si.edu/education/codetalkers/html/ Illinois Route 66 Association. http://www.il66assoc.org/
Arizona Route 66 Association., http://azrt66.com/
National Historical Route 66 Federation. http://national66.org/history-of-route66/
Crapanzano, C. (2010) A brief history of route 66. http://content.time.com/time/nation/article/0,8599,2000095,00.html
Weiser, Kathy. (2016) Legendary Route 66, Route 66 Information and history. http://www.legendsofamerica.com/66-info.html
Jensen, J. Road Trip USA. Cross country adventures on America's two-lane highways. https://roadtripusa.com/route-66/
The Mother Road, Route 66. http://www.route66world.com/66_history/ Will Rogers Biography, Bio. http://www.biography.com/people/will-rogers-40870
The People's Highway Route 66, American on the move. http://amhistory.si.edu/onthemove/exhibition/exhibition_10_3.htm "Life doesn't happen along the interstates. It's against the law." –William Least Heat Moon, Blue Highways
Warnick R. – Route 66 News, Sept. 2017
Hinckley J. ; James K. Backroads of Arizona, Your guide to Arizona's most scenic backroad adventures.
Sonderman J. Route 66 in Arizona

Traveling the Mother Road is an awesome vacation. To truly see and do everything there is to do, you need a lifetime. The road continues to evolve, some businesses go out but new ones come in. It is ever changing; each adventure will not be the same. The hospitality and friendships that you endure along the road are life changing and everlasting. Try as I might, I know that I did not get everything that there is to see and do along Route 66 and I am not so sure that it is possible to get it all in one book.

Hidden word key from page 51

```
G I G A N T I C U S H E A D I C U S J K L E D W A R
A P R O A D K I L L C A F E H C S A E J T D F S H D
C P R O N G H O R N F G H R J W E D M O H K V E Y E
Y N A M T A O R B C H C P E K W Y M R L R O P O P A
R P S C R H N S P T R A I N S I B N D I E R G F A C
U L H U H B U X L W W H X R O L Z X I P S R H L I H
S R F R C E R O N I M O R C P L Q O C I A E E A N S
A C O I R B N S C G R L G E E I N Z S U E H E G T P
V S R O H X U P V W V B Z U M A L K E Y R T R S E R
E P K S B C T R H A S R L R N M E T E O R O O T D I
R V R H P L H B L M H O B R O S J J A R C M D A D N
Y H X O S V N A V A J O H O P H G D E G I R A F E G
Y T O P O C K B C H L K R S L S T W R E T F V F S S
R L R L B H V W L L S C X H K R D E O A Y D A O E F
R A P S R C E K I P X Q L B I W E R E E W U R P R G
E P A H V B E D Q N R P S P H U A L A P A I T M T O
B O N R L X A E S H I E L I G M A N D R E P L U L E
K S G B H G L S C U P L X B E D K Z Q E T E E B Q W
C A E V L V E E S V T S O P G N I D A R T Z A Y U K
A D L E P R B R P C B C V W S P N S R E N I M L P O
H A D H C S L T X R H V A H S L G Z T E C J B H N L
Y E L L O W H O R S E R L C H K M K Y Z T W B B M P
C S G N I R P S L O O C M G A L A X Y D I N E R A Q
G R A N C C A N Y O N N K U H Y N T P R E J A C K R
```

www.ingramcontent.com/pod-product-compliance
Lightning Source LLC
Chambersburg PA
CBHW082332220526
45470CB00008B/2482